SEAN DOHERTY

GOLDEN DAZE

The best years of Australian surfing

SURFING
AUSTRALIA
Sharing the Stoke

hachette
AUSTRALIA

Contents

Introduction   iv

Isabel Letham • 1915   1

Snowy McAlister • 1928   5

Barry Bennett • 1960   11

Bob Evans • 1963   15

Peter Troy • 1963   21

Phyllis O'Donell • 1964   35

Midget Farrelly • 1964   41

Gail Couper • 1966   49

Bob McTavish • 1967   57

Claw Warbrick • 1967   67

Wayne Lynch • 1968   73

Albe Falzon • 1970   85

Peter Drouyn • 1970   91

Nat Young • 1970   99

Paul Neilsen • 1970   107

Mark Richards • 1971   111

Peter Townend • 1972   119

Michael Peterson • 1973   125

Ted Spencer • 1973   137

Stan Couper • 1973   143

Terry Fitzgerald • 1975   149

Ian Cairns • 1975   157

Rabbit Bartholomew • 1975   **167**

Mark Warren • 1976   **175**

Col Smith • 1977   **181**

Simon Anderson • 1977   **187**

Tom Carroll • 1978   **197**

Pam Burridge • 1979   **205**

Peter Crawford • 1981   **215**

Damien Hardman • 1982   **219**

Kong • 1982   **225**

Cheyne Horan • 1984   **235**

Mark Occhilupo • 1984   **241**

Wendy Botha • 1984   **249**

Barton Lynch • 1988   **255**

Wayne Deane • 1990   **265**

Layne Beachley • 1990   **273**

Pauline Menczer • 1993   **279**

Rod Brooks • 1995   **291**

Steph Gilmore • 2011   **295**

Joel Parkinson • 2012   **303**

Mick Fanning • 2015   **315**

Ross Clarke-Jones • 2016   **325**

Tyler Wright • 2016   **331**

Thanks   **342**

Photo Credits   **343**

Introduction

A phone call to Albe Falzon never fails to leave the spirits soaring.

On this particular morning, however, I'd caught him after a session at Crescent Head that had proved transcendental, even by Albe's standards. Paddled out at dawn. Water dropping from his fingers like molten gold. Head-high spinners the length of the point. His only company, 'the Mushrooms' – the group of old salts who surf Crescent every morning at first light. Surfing like a rocket into the setting moon, backlit by the rising sun, Albe, 75, threatened to break apart into his constituent physical and spiritual forms.

Albe first surfed Crescent back in the early '60s. He was part of the first convoys north out of Sydney, turning off the Pacific Highway with little more than a few whispers to go by, stumbling on pointbreaks like Crescent, posting up under the pandanus and just letting the days melt away in the sun. As a surfer who grew up on the North Coast 25 years after this gold rush, I suffer frequently from a form of generational envy. It's hard not to feel I completely missed the boat. The last time I was in Crescent I couldn't even find a car park on the point and parked two blocks back from the beach.

The morning I called him, Albe was having none of this. 'I just keep saying to people who go, "You should have been here five years ago or 10 or 20," I go, "Sorry, but for me it's just as good, if not better. Everything gets better if that's how you see life. It's a state of mind. I mean, the journey isn't the *journey*. It's the one inside. I think surfing makes you aware of that.'

Albe drives beside the Belmore River to get from his place down to Crescent. He's been doing the same drive for 50 years now, and once he gets on the straights and starts passing the dairy farms and honesty boxes, his van acts like a time machine. It blends those 50 years together and linear time is blown out of the exhaust. Albe drove this same road while filming *Morning of the Earth*. Time didn't matter then and it doesn't matter now. Trying to pin Albe down to talk about one particular year of his surfing life then proved challenging. But just as it was with the other surfers, the year itself was unimportant … it was their surfing, and where they were at in their surfing life that stayed with them.

Like Albe, all the crew you'll soon read about have left their fingerprints on Australian surfing in some significant way. A world title, a board design, a movie … even a single ridden wave. Interestingly, many of them talked about anything *but* what they're best known for. They drifted back to times in their surfing lives that sat fondly. Grommet years feature strongly. Fourteen-year-old Pam Burridge, 16-year-old Tom Carroll. Simpler surfing years. Just them and their board.

Two broad themes did emerge. In the first half of the book, it became clear just what a stuffy little planet Australian surfing was in the early days. If you put on a contest, everyone in Australia showed up like a family Christmas. Everyone knew everyone. Peter Troy sailed all the way around the world, then, six months later while being chased by a bunch of angry Hawaiians, he ran into the yard of a house on Oahu's North Shore and who opened the door to save him? Midget Farrelly!

The other theme is the idea that the coastline holds a mirror up to Australian society. Over a century, the big shifts in Australian life were all reflected in their own way on the coast, and surfing has left a deep cultural cachet on the Australian way of life.

When taking the book on I was warned by a surf historian friend, 'You'll be stuck in the last century, mate. It's like the twilight zone in there. Be careful, you won't get out. You won't *want* to get out!' Talking to these surfers about their surfing lives, a memory will upwell, a surf they had in another time. Their eyes will glaze over and suddenly they're back there. For my part I've emerged from the surf/time continuum with a deeper appreciation of the ridiculous good fortune I've had to be brought up on the Australian coast as a surfer … and how lucky I remain today.

For Albe, the golden days are still there every time he paddles out. 'I look at it and think, this is unbelievable. I've got to a point where I'm so grateful and appreciative for the opportunity to surf all my life, to be in good health, to have made the friends I've made on this incredible journey. To drive through the country and come out at Crescent Head and paddle out with a group of friends who smile and ask, "How you going?" You've got to be kidding, haven't you? Once you get down the path a bit you become more aware of it and your life expands accordingly. It feels sometimes like I'm just going to leave my body totally. I'm sure one day I will.'

Sean Doherty
Somewhere on the Australian coast

1915

Isabel Letham

In late 1908, over the course of three months, a pedestrian tunnel was blasted through the sandstone of Queenscliff headland on the northern beaches of Sydney. The tunnel was commissioned by Robert Lewers, the principal of a syndicate that owned 'Freshwater Estate' – a 50-acre block of real estate adjacent to Freshwater Beach, which had been subdivided a decade earlier but the blocks had stubbornly refused to sell. Lewers had also built a kiosk and beach sheds at Freshwater which, along with the tunnel, would encourage swimmers to make the trek north from Manly. If they bought a block of land and stayed, all the better.

Freshwater Beach was already a secret escape. Just a few years earlier swimming in the ocean on Manly Beach during daylight hours was banned, as was mixed swimming and, for women, swimming in anything shorter than neck-to-knee bathers. Manly had a rule for everything. Freshwater was free. Emerging from the tunnel into the white sunlight, Freshwater felt like a secret, untrammelled world. At Freshwater 'surf shooting' – bodysurfing – was popular. Mervyn Farley, whose parents owned the kiosk was the gun surf shooter, but there were a group of young girls who were equally keen. Mervyn's sister Peggy was one, as were Rachel and Lalla Lewers, Jessie and Agnes Sly, and a young girl from up the top of the hill named Isabel Letham.

The Lethams originally lived in Chatswood, but their holiday house in Foam Street, Freshwater, eventually became their permanent home in 1910. The pull of the coast was strong right around the country. The first decade of the new century saw Australians take to the beach in their thousands. With independence from England, an Australian identity formed around the sandy white strip of the coast. Isabel was a first-generation child of the beach. Along with surf shooting she also aquaplaned behind motorboats in the harbour off Forty Baskets Beach and was, in the vernacular of the time, a 'water nymph'. She also had an independent way about her. Isabel's mother, Jane, was politically active in the years when women in Australia had secured the vote and was part of the early Australian feminist movement. Isabel refused to adhere to the dress code on the beach. 'I never wore a neck-to-knee costume in my life and would never do so,' she'd later state. Instead, she chose to wear men's-style swimmers. Isabel embodied the changing times. She broke free from established expectations for women of the day – demure, refined – and instead got out into the sun and lived. Women were freer to swim, dance … or even surf.

Duke Kahanamoku arrived in Australia in late 1914 at the invitation of the Australian Swimming Association. The Hawaiian was the reigning Olympic 100-yard swimming champion, and in a swimming exhibition at Sydney's Domain pool the Duke broke his own hundred-yard world record. 'The swimming obsessed Aussies wanted to see the so-called "Kahanamoku Kick",' he'd later recall. 'And we were gratified over the royal treatment they gave us.' With his bronzed physique and eloquent baritone, the Duke indeed carried an aura of Polynesian royalty. While he was here as a swimmer, it would be his displays of the ancient Hawaiian art of surfing that would capture the public imagination. By this stage a handful of surfboards had already found their way to Australian shores from Hawaii. Manly's Tommy Walker had brought a Hawaiian board for $2 in Waikiki and brought it home to Manly aboard the *Poltolock* in 1909. Mastering it proved another matter altogether.

Enter the Duke. The Hawaiian spent Christmas 1914 at Boomerang camp, behind Freshwater Beach, and had set about making himself a surfboard, acquiring a slab of sugar pine from Hudson's timberyard – nine-foot by two-foot by three inches thick – and working on it with a planer. 'I was in Australia long enough to build a makeshift board out of sugar pine and with this hurriedly contrived board, I gave my first exhibition of surfing at Freshwater Beach on Sydney's northside,' he said.

The Duke arrived at the beach on the morning of Sunday 10 January in an open carriage alongside his board. The day was overcast but still 400 people had turned up to watch. The waves were chest-high with a light onshore breeze and, as the Duke walked to the waterline, he noticed the surfboat from Manly had rounded the headland. When told it was there to ferry him out the back he laughed. He put his board in the water and casually stroked out. 'I must have put on a show that more than trapped their fancy,' he'd recall, 'for the crowds on shore applauded me long and loud. There had been no way of knowing that they would go for it in the manner in which they did. I soared and glided, drifted and sideslipped with that blending of flying and sailing which only experienced surfers can know and fully appreciate.

The Aussies became instant converts.' The Duke rode toward shore with regal command, then rode backwards and pulled headstands to lair it up. The crowd went wild.

The *Sydney Morning Herald* reported the Duke's surf as 'wonderfully clever. He came out with his surfboard, plunged into the water, and continued to swim out until those watching from the beach wondered when he would stop. After covering nearly half a mile, Kahanamoku turned and prepared for a roller, which came along a moment after; he caught it, and as the wave carried him shorewards, he performed all kinds of acrobatic feats on the board, and finally dived into the water as the roller broke.'

Watching on from the beach was Isabel Letham. 'To see Duke stand and do all sorts of tricks on a wave, and then at the end to stand on his head – people couldn't believe their eyes.' She could believe it less when the Duke came onto the beach and asked for a female volunteer to surf tandem with him. Well known at Freshwater, Isabel was immediately 'volunteered' and soon found herself on the nose of Duke's board, out in the waves.

On their first wave Isabel locked herself to the board in terror. 'It was like looking over a cliff,' she'd recall. They caught three waves with Isabel too afraid to get to her feet. On the fourth, 'He took me by the scruff of the neck and yanked me to my feet. I said, "Oh no, no, no!" and he went, "Oh yes, yes, yes!" Then off we went down that wave.' Isabel would later equate the feeling of standing on the board to walking out on a plane wing, mid-air. They only caught four waves, but, 'from then I was hooked'. So was Australia.

The Duke and Isabel's surf left the Australian public fascinated. The magic of the Duke's surfing was one thing, but the tandem surf challenged social mores. Only a decade earlier men and women were banned from swimming together at all, and beyond that, the White Australia Policy was a decade old and in full swing. Isabel was 15, Duke 25. Suddenly here was a local teenage girl, skin-to-skin with this chiselled Hawaiian man, out in the ocean together, performing this exotic ritual. The fact that conservative Australia was not affronted by it, and was even celebrating it, was testament to both the admiration for Duke himself and a recognition of a Pan-Pacific simpatico. Australians proudly now saw themselves as saltwater people, just like the Hawaiians.

Three weeks later the Duke held another display, this time a few beaches north at Dee Why. This day the waves were bigger, the sky was again grey and the southern corner at Dee Why was full of seaweed. It was less than inviting. The pair reprised their tandem surf, Isabel this time having to swim out through the seaweed to meet the Duke. 'I wasn't afraid of the rollers, big and tough as they were, but I had visions of being pulled under by a monster!' Isabel possessed a morbid fear of sharks. 'Finally the Duke pulled me onto his board, which seemed to rise on a wave so high that the sheer fall into the trough was frightening. However, he rode it perfectly, and I jumped onto the beach with a sense of relief, but a feeling of exhilaration.'

The Duke would soon leave for home, but his surfboard – and surfing – stayed behind in Australia. Young Claude West was given the board, and he and Isabel continued to surf it at Freshwater despite the disapproval of Isabel's father, who considered the heavy board too dangerous. So disapproving was he that Isabel's friends in the Freshwater Surf Club would ring a bell if she was out surfing and they saw him walking down the hill. William Letham eventually not only gave up, but secured a slab of sugar pine and shaped Isabel her own board, which she'd surf with a friend, Isma Amor. Crude boards were soon hewn from lumps of wood and young men and women took to the waves, the ancient sport beginning again on a new shore.

Isabel's surfing exploits gained her local celebrity. She was dubbed the 'Freshwater Mermaid' and having left school the following year, at 16, took up swim coaching. She soon set her sights on America. On 1 October 1918 Isabel set sail on the SS *Niagara* – 'The Queen of the Pacific' – bound for New York via Honolulu. Her immediate plan was to work for the Red Cross knitting jumpers for American servicemen, but by the time she arrived the war was over. Her American ambitions lay beyond knitting. Her billing as 'the Diana of the Waves' preceded her and she took off to Hollywood. Mike Jay, a sports reporter at the *Honolulu Star Bulletin* Isabel had befriended in Honolulu, wrote her a letter on her departure for Los Angeles.

Glad to see you broke into the big papers. Had I thought of it I would have written to some of my friends on the New York papers and seen to it you were given a fireworks send-off to California. Now that you're a movie queen you'll be getting so many gush notes that you may not find the time to answer my epistles but don't forget to drop me a line now and then just for fun. Yours as ever, Mike Jay

1928

Snowy McAlister

If you'd looked hard enough you'd have spotted the snowy head of young Charles Justin McAlister, aged 11, in the crowd on Freshwater Beach the day the Duke had surfed. 'I was staggered,' he'd later recall. 'Everyone just clapped and clapped. Nobody had any idea how to ride those boards until the Duke turned up. And then he rode tandem with Isabel Letham, a great surfer at the time. What a finale.' The kid known as 'Snowy' would never run low on enthusiasm, and almost immediately began looking for his own surfboard, which in 1915 meant you had to improvise. He looked at his mother's ironing board and saw similarities in outline to the Duke's sugar pine slab. An hour later he was paddling it around South Steyne.

The McAlisters had moved to Manly from Broken Hill, a red dirt mining town in the state's far-west. They could have ended up in Bondi, but Snowy recalled how sandy and desolate Bondi seemed at the time. They chose the Norfolk Island pines of Manly instead and never left. For the rest of his considerable surfing life, Snowy McAlister would live no further than a hundred yards from Manly Beach. Young Snowy went to Harbord Public School before being shipped off to a string of Brothers schools in the suburbs. None of these saw much of him. 'One time it took the truant officer six weeks to get his hands on me!' Snow would boast. 'It was purely because of surfing that I had very little formal education.' His mother caught on soon enough. 'She eventually found out because I would come home sunburnt.'

Snowy's first surfboard (after the ironing board) was a heavy, 8'6" redwood slab. Agricultural in design and weighing as much as Snowy, it was typical of the boards being

ridden up and down Manly Beach in increasing numbers. 'I've often purchased a suitable length of dry selected redwood, carve the board out in the afternoon, varnish it that night, and surf with it the next day,' said Snowy.

Shaping them was one thing, surfing them another. 'We were getting murdered in those early days. The boards had no fin. We were going straight down the wave and not surfing on the corners as the Duke had done in his display. Then I thought he was just riding crooked. We had not learned the lesson from Duke's display of angling across the wave. He actually rode *away* from the white water on the green edge of the wave. This movement was lost on us; we continued taking every wave straight on. Eventually we learned the secret. We would select the edge and slide down the green face of the wave on an angle. Mind you, we had no fin at that stage to guide us and a slippery 60-pound board at speed was hard to control. We had to resort to half-kneeling or cupping the water with your hand to correct your angle position and trailing a leg over the stern to act as a tiller.

'The harsh Australian east coast shorebreak of our beaches made the surfer very cautious in his selection of waves,' recalled Snow. 'Many accidents were reported and in those days the saying was, "If you live long enough you become a boardrider."' The fact that most boardriders on Manly Beach were also members of Manly Surf Club put them on a collision course with the surf club brass, many of whom saw surfboards as an 'auxiliary nuisance'. A memo put out by Manly Surf Club on 2 April 1928 read, 'Members are notified again that surfboard shooting must not be carried on among the bathers and that the recent dangerous practice of diving from the back of the board and leaving it uncontrolled in the surf, must cease. The Manly Council has threatened to take action if these instructions are not carried out by the club members.' They weren't finished, the memo also included a reminder that no motorbikes or bicycles were allowed on club premises. Nor dogs. 'Further breach of this will be brought under the notice of the Manly Municipal Council.'

The surfboards did, in time, prove their worth in saving people as much as running them over. Claude West, the young lad who'd received the Duke's board back in 1915 had become not only Manly's champion boardrider, but the Australian champ. On a big day at Manly Beach four swimmers had been swept out to sea, and with the beltman and the surfboat unable to make it through the waves, Claude West paddled out on his board and one by one brought them back to shore. He had three of them safely on the beach and was on his way to pick up the fourth when the surfboat, which had given it another crack, ran him over. Claude was knocked unconscious and had to be rescued himself.

Claude West had been Australia's first surfboard champion in 1920, and held the title for the next four years. The surfboard riding championships were run as part of the surf club carnival, billed dismissively as 'surfboard displays' and held after the serious stuff was finished. As the range of the surf clubs at that point barely extended beyond Sydney, the New South Wales Titles were in essence national titles. At the 1925 titles on Manly Beach, Snowy McAlister was crowned national surfboard riding champion. He'd defend his title in 1926 and again in 1927.

Other surfboard contests sprang up in the meantime, and it was in Newcastle where Snowy rode the wave that would etch him into surf folklore. Built low to the ground, the headstand was Snow's signature move. With a six-foot swell running and a wild backwash, the shorebreak at the Newcastle contest in 1928 was not conducive to headstands. As Snow hurtled toward it, upside down and facing out to sea, our plucky hero appeared doomed. What happened next would be retold for decades, mostly by Snow himself. He beached the headstand. 'I was still standing on my head when the wave ran out and the judge ran down and tapped me and said, "Snow, you've won mate."'

By the time he'd won his third Australian title, Snowy was a well-known name in Manly and beyond. When the Duke and Duchess of York visited Manly for an exhibition surf carnival held in their honour, Snowy had represented Manly Surf Club in the surfboard display. A friendly little terrier of a man, he moved easily between the new tribes of surfers springing up all around the Australian coast. He also possessed a larrikin streak. While he had a deep respect for Australia's young surfing history, Snow identified most closely with William Gocher, the local newspaper editor who in 1903 defied arrest by swimming on Manly Beach during daylight hours. Gocher's act of civil disobedience saw the absurd law lifted soon afterwards. Gocher died in 1921 and Snow pushed for him to be posthumously honoured. Snow wasn't big on rules, and was never happier than when surfing split from the surf clubs after World War II.

In June 1928, Snow – along with Manly clubmate Tommy Farrell – was invited by close friend Andrew 'Boy' Charlton to attend the Amsterdam Olympics, where Boy was competing as a swimmer. They sailed on a tourist class passage aboard the liner *Jervis Bay*, but a delay caused by a stowaway saw them miss the blue ribbon 1600 yards (1500 metres) race, which Charlton won. Charlton's biography charts their eventual arrival. 'Having gone 48 hours without sleep they arrived at the pool while Charlton's 440 yards (400 metres) heat was being swum. McAlister, a champion boardrider, talked his way onto the starting boards and saw the rest of the races from a prime position.' Charlton took silver in the 440 yards, then introduced Snow to some famous friends. 'Boy introduced me first to Tarzan – Johnny Weissmuller – who was swimming that day in a relay with Buster

Crabbe. Buster was a great waterman and could sprint-swim like a fish.'

With a sense of civic duty, Snow took it upon himself while in Europe to teach the English how to surf. 'I went across to show that the Australians could surf and were not cannibals.' His efforts were recorded in the 12 September 1928 edition of the *Daily Mail*.

'An effort is to be made to popularise surfboard riding, described as the most thrilling sport in the world, at English seaside resorts. Mr Justin C. McAlister, an electrical engineer of Sydney, New South Wales, is the amateur surf riding champion of Australia who has just arrived in England after attending the Olympic games in Amsterdam.'

Snowy explained the concept of surfing to the English press. *'The secret consists of keeping your balance. If you are experienced you find the right balancing point, and it is possible to stand on your head.'*

Returning by ship from England, Snow and his fellow passengers were told off the coast of Africa that a lad on board had contracted smallpox and they'd be quarantined once they got back to Australia. Snow remembered a group of World War I soldiers quarantined on North Head upon returning home, simply getting up the next morning and marching off in formation down Darley Street, Manly. Snow would be quarantined at Point Nepean in Port Phillip Bay for a week. Point Nepean, it turns out, was a short walk to the beach. 'I had been abroad for nine months and as a Manly lifesaver I was very anxious to get back into the surf,' Snow recalled. 'There was a beach nearby. So daily after breakfast I tucked my costume inside my shirt, followed a goat track through the dunes outside the quarantine station, and bathed with the locals and holiday makers.' While his fellow passengers were subjected to formalin baths and stripping to have their clothes fumigated, Snow was living it up. 'What a joy it was to have a whole week of surfing!'

1960

Barry Bennett

On the evening of 24 November 1958, twenty-seven-year-old Barry Bennett sat down at the dining-room table in the family home in Harbord and wrote a letter to Greg Noll in California.

Dear Mr Noll,

As a surfboard manufacturer in Sydney, I am writing to you in the hope that you may be able to provide me information on any of the latest ideas in the States on balsa surfboards.

In Sydney at present with the balsa boards produced here only two years old, I feel that we are way behind in ideas and shapes. I am making a great many "pig" boards now, I don't know what you call them over there, but they are wide at the tail with a lift up and come to a point with the front being narrow and bullet shaped. They also have a much larger fin than the Malibu type board.

I received your name and address from Dave Webster, who wrote the article on the boards in the *Saturday Evening Post*. The article caused quite a bit of interest among the boardriders here. The balsa we receive out here does not seem to be the same quality as your boards are made of, a lot of core and knots, but I believe there are different grades of balsa.

The surfing season here is in full swing now and I am receiving orders at the rate of two a day. It seems that every second person at the beach will have a balsa board the way they are selling. The cost of them here is £27 (Aust approx. 54 dollars, how does this compare with the price of your boards?)

If it is not asking too much, could you write to me and send any plans, scale drawings or any other literature or articles on boards, surfing or the surfboard rallies which are held regularly in Hawaii, California or South America. I would be happy to return any information which you may wish to obtain from me which may help you in your business.

Thanking you and hoping for a reply in the near future. Wishing you a Merry Xmas and a Happy New Year,

Yours faithfully,
Barry Bennett

Surfing in Australia was booming, and the handful of Australian surfboard manufacturers couldn't keep up with demand. But they were not only struggling to find supplies of usable balsa wood, which had to be imported from South America, they were also running short on ideas about what to do with it. Barry could see the opportunity but was at an impasse. The Pacific Ocean was exceedingly wide in those days, and news of surfboard development in California travelled slowly, if at all. Barry swallowed his professional pride and posted the letter the following day. He'd never met Noll.

Greg Noll had started the boom. He'd been part of the US surfing team that had flown to Australia as part of the 1956 Melbourne Olympics. They appeared to have arrived from both California and from some point in the future. The Americans' nine-foot balsa wood 'Malibu' boards were almost half the size of the clunky plywood 'toothpicks' being ridden by the Australians. The Australians were simply passengers on their boards. The Americans surfed theirs and the huge crowds in Torquay, Avalon and beyond were mesmerised. The Americans turned up relaxed and ready for a good time. These guys were having a hoot. The Malibu boards broke surfing in Australia free … free to express itself, free to explore the coast and free from a sense of duty to the surf lifesaving clubs. It was Australian surfing's BC/AD moment.

Once the Americans left, Barry was one of the first to build a Malibu board. One of a small club of board builders, he got his hands on as much balsa as he could and started producing surfboards under the house in Harbord. He worked a day job as an electrician for Mackellar County Council, but at the end of each day he returned home and immediately got to work in the garage. He'd pick up orders on the beach or at the Harbord Hotel, 'The Office'. But two years after the Americans left progress had stalled.

Noll never replied to the letter, but Barry eventually found his answer in America anyway. He'd solve his balsa problem by doing away with it altogether. In 1960, *Surfer* magazine had been founded in the States and Barry had negotiated the licence to distribute it here in Australia. It was in the pages of the American magazines where he saw that balsa was being replaced by a new material simply called 'foam'.

'We knew about [foam boards] mainly from the magazines,' Barry told *Surfing Places, Surfboard Makers*. 'You learnt as much from reading that as from talking to anybody.' Polyurethane foam had been developed by the Germans during the war. It was light, strong and rigid. The foam could be shaped and sanded. It also bonded with polyester resin, which could be used to form a hard shell around the board. The problem was you had to mix the stuff up yourself. Barry loved a challenge. He had a surfing mate working as a Qantas engineer in America, who 'fossicked around and got some information from a few people, and we started playing around with making the foam here'.

However, making foam was dangerous. To create it required a volatile cocktail of liquid petrochemicals, catalysts and blowing agents, mixed in specific ratios in specific orders and poured into a mould, where the foam would expand and set solid. The use of polyurethane was relatively new, and the surfboard guys had to learn on the fly. When they got it right they produced a polyurethane 'blank' that could be shaped down into a surfboard. When they got it wrong, they ran.

'Really the raw materials were the things that you couldn't control,' Barry recalled. 'There was one company here, AC Hatricks, that supplied the chemicals, but everything was as hit-and-miss for them as it was for us. What they sold us, everybody had a lot of problems with the ratios, the A and B components, the catalyst, and they used to blow up! We used a Freon refrigeration gas, that was a blowing agent to expand the foam. Well, on a hot day you're trying to mix things together and it was all just a bit of this and a bit of that, trying to make it work.'

The hit-and-miss would see Barry blow a hole in his garage wall at Harbord, straight through into the lounge room. Beyond the volatility of the chemicals, they were also toxic. Barry said in the film *Men of Wood and Foam*, 'The doctor said you've got to get out of the house 'cause it wasn't doing the baby, Greg, any good to be there with dust and resin fumes and Christ knows what and that's when we built the factory in 1960.'

The land west of Curl Curl Beach had originally been a market garden, but had been pegged out as a new industrial estate. Barry built a factory at 188 Harbord Road,

Brookvale, and the other board manufacturers all soon gravitated to the area. In time, Barry Bennett, Gordon Woods, Bill Wallace, Scott Dillon, Denny Keogh, and Greg McDonagh would be known as 'The Brookvale Six' and acknowledged as the founding fathers of the surfboard industry in Australia. But in 1960 they were flying by the seat of their boardshorts, not only trying to master new materials but keeping up with demand.

A confluence of surf music, surf cars and surfboards saw the beach scene explode across the country. 'I know everybody was making boards as quick as they could and selling them,' Barry said in the documentary *Bombora*. 'There was a waiting list of six weeks, so we were doing 60 boards a week in 1963. Come October, we couldn't take any more orders before Christmas. That's how good it was.' Barry knew surfboards and he knew business. Having come out of a surf club background he was hard working, no bullshit, and with a mercantile streak. Other parts of the surfboard industry however reflected the surf culture itself in a laidback, three-surfs-a-day kind of way. 'It wasn't a great industry,' recalls Barry. 'Most of them didn't have any idea of how to run a business or they were always in trouble with tax or they couldn't pay their bills. They thought every dollar they got in the front door was profit and they spent it like it was.' Barry meanwhile ran a tight ship, and would soon manufacture blanks for shapers right around the country. Bennett's would in time become the backbone of the surfboard industry in Australia.

For now it was all blue sky for Barry. Boards were flying out the door, money was flying in, and although he recalls a slight dip in sales around the time of Beatlemania, it was more than offset by Midget winning the World Title at Manly.

1963

Bob Evans

Twenty-five years from now when a surfer powers across the wall at one of the new thriving resort communities on the north coast, probably his last thought will be for the person who opened up this new area to surfers. You might say is it really important? *Surfing World* knows it is and we aim to put it on record now that we have pioneers in our midst. Easter of this year saw the greatest exodus of surfboard men ever to leave Sydney in search of surf. Frustrated by crowded beaches, overcrowded waters, no parking places and other controls, the enthusiastic 'surfie' is seeking newer and more secluded pastures and finding with relief that they exist in great numbers on the beaches of the north and south coast of NSW. Your editor was typical of these explorers, and this story describes how we travelled and where, what we found and who made the scene ... Bob Evans, 'Discovery in the North', *SW, December 1962*.

Bob Evans had been tipped off to the waves of Angourie Point by his brother, Dick, who saw it more as a good fishing spot than a surf break. Bob's exposé of Angourie in the pages of his magazine and his movie, *The Young Wave Hunters*, was emblematic of the scene. Escapism was a central theme running through *Surfing World* – stories of Peter Troy's global odyssey and road trips to Bells, Byron and Crescent Head ... all fuelled by Ampol petroleum, who advertised prominently in the magazine's pages. Just as Angourie was an El Dorado waiting for surfers (and developers), surfing in Australia itself was an El Dorado. Evans could see surfing about to boom ... but to do so it needed someone to run it, and a big idea to orbit around.

I honestly can't see any real obstacle in staging the 1964 World Board Riding Championships in Australia. Can you imagine what a tremendous boost this would be to boardriding in Australia? I have seen two world titles in Hawaii and I am convinced that with perhaps commercial support we could eclipse anything the Americans have done over the past two years. It would not be fair for me to knock the Hawaiian presentation of the titles, as a guest of this wonderful place I have been treated in a typically Royal Hawaiian manner. But I am certain we could present a world championship that would be second to none. Many of the American and Hawaiian entrants in this year's world championship have expressed a keen and genuine interest in tasting the Australian surf. It's just a thought at the moment but I have no doubt about its ultimate success. Bob Evans, 'Title Contest For Australia?' *SW, February 1963.*

It was more than just a thought; Bob Evans was already working on it. Bob got back from Midget Farrelly's Makaha win in early 1963 and hit the ground running. It was a big job, but as the old saying goes, if you want something done, give it to a busy man. In 1963 it was probably easier to catalogue the things Bob Evans *wasn't* involved with in surfing. The mercurial and mercantile Evans was an entrepreneur, publisher, writer, filmmaker, editor, surf reporter, columnist, impresario, promoter, wheeler, dealer, former lingerie salesman and sunset connoisseur. Surfing sat at the middle of all of this, and Bob's specialised skill, honed sharp in '63, was building bridges between the surfing world and the business world.

Evans had the stars aligned. Through his magazine, movies and his contacts in the Sydney media and business world he'd been able to turn Midget into Australia's first bona fide surf star. Bob, however, was personally closer to Nat Young. 'Bob Evans was my mentor,' recalls Nat, who was 15 at the time. 'He was my dad in more ways than my biological father. He taught me never to talk business at lunch, that was bad manners. Always put your best foot forward, always go and buy a new tie and a shirt if there was a really important deal on the table.'

It was an era when the idea of making money from surfing – making surfing your job – was as unthinkable as it was cool. Bob made both a reality. 'At a time when I was learning about how to make a career in surfing,' recalls Nat, 'making some money in surfing, if it wasn't for Bob's understanding of and influence in the commercial world of surfing I'd never have done any good. I had a shaping apprenticeship with Gordon

Woods, but Bob negotiated on my behalf for Gordon to pay me to ride waves. I was told I was going to be paid 50 pounds a week or something, and that was my fee to go out and surf. I suppose at that point I was the only person in Australia who was paid to surf.

Naturally, I just thought it was amazing, and after I was given that freedom I could just go. It changed my perspective and allowed my surfing to take a quantum leap.'

Evans was a good surfer in his younger days at Manly, but he'd had a bowel cancer removed in his early 20s and wore a colostomy bag. By age 35 he was rarely seen surfing. Bob lived up the hill at Elanora with his wife and three kids, but in 1963 Bob didn't have a lot of spare time for anything else but his grand vision – the 1964 World Contest being held on Australian sand. His earlier grand vision – the South Pacific Surfriders Club – a social and competitive club modelled on the Outrigger in Waikiki finally, after years of struggling financially, had gone under on 6 May that year. What drove Evans's endeavours is hard to single out. It seemed neither ego nor monument building but more a combination of cultural and commercial motives. Maybe it was more the momentary frisson of a deal being closed, hands shaken, and a celebratory cocktail quaffed.

Australian surfing at this point was a handful of ragtag boardriding clubs and a rabble of kids on beaches around the country. Surfing didn't lend itself well to central administration, having broken away from the regimented Surf Lifesaving movement and run in the opposite direction. But while Evans' dream of Australia hosting the first World Contest was a primary driver to create a central body run by surfers, so was the threat of the clubbies hijacking the idea and doing it themselves.

It started with 'The Australian Surfing Movement' holding an 'Interstate Surf Meet' on 4–5 May that year under the slogan, 'It's on at Avalon!' It welcomed all comers, all craft, no entry fee. The Movement now needed to coalesce and centralise which, nudged along in the *Telegraph* by Bob Evans, it soon did. The Australian Surfing Association (ASA) formed on 27 August 1963 at a meeting at Mike Alexander's parents' house in Collaroy. Midget Farrelly was elected its first president, while Bob Evans was one of several vice-presidents. Evans remained arm's length from the organisation, as his tightly knit and co-dependent set of business interests presented a conflict. Evans postured as both the front man and the shadow man of the World Contest. He made the phone calls to surfing bodies overseas and cut the sponsorship deals straight out of his black book.

The ASA held the first 'Australian Invitational' at Bondi on 22 November 1963. It was a scratched-together Australian Titles that legitimised Australia's claim to host the World Contest the following year. It also doubled as a dry run. As the second day began at Bondi the news filtered through that John F Kennedy had been shot in Dallas, but the beach fizzed regardless. Plenty of waves, 30,000 people on the beach, a stomp on the sand and even Duke Kahanamoku on hand to present the trophies. At the end of the day Bob announced officially the World Contest would be held at Manly in May the following year.

1963

Peter Troy

Before he walked up the gangway of the ocean liner *Castel Felice* ('Happy Castle') about to embark on an open-ticketed odyssey to the surfing New World, Peter Troy had already blazed trails. During the 1956 Melbourne Olympics, Troy's hometown of Torquay had hosted an international surf lifesaving carnival in front of an estimated crowd of 50,000 people. Troy, just 17 and the local champion, paddled out at Torquay Beach on a traditional, hollow 16-foot surfboard. The American team included big-wave legend Greg Noll and famed lifeguard Tommy Zahn, who was so zealously committed to surfing and clean living that he'd dumped Marilyn Monroe because she smoked. But it wasn't the star power of the American team that had young Troy spellbound, it was their surfboards. They rode nine-foot balsa and fibreglass Malibu boards. Zahn let Troy catch some waves on his board and his young mind was blown. The boards turned. Troy later likened it to playing an electric guitar for the first time.

Troy had also been one of the original surfers who'd set out from Torquay across neighbouring farmland to the crumbling right-hand 'slides' of Bells Beach. Leaving the regimented surf club behind, the surfers of Torquay congregated out at Bells on their new Malibu boards. Troy was the best surfer in Victoria at that point and the leader of the Bells movement. He threw in his job as an accountant in Melbourne and became a surf movie impresario. He screened Bud Browne movies at the Dendy in Brighton, Troy, resplendent in a white suit, greeting punters. It was a good business and Troy squirrelled away his money. He had a plan.

Troy's story was emblematic of young Australian surfers at this time. The post-war conservatism was lifting, and the cultural backwater of Australia was being infused with exotic ideas from the four corners. Troy flicked through the pages of America's *Surfer* magazine and his mind wandered. However, it all went back to that November day in 1956. 'When I met those Americans,' he recalled years later, 'these guys who spoke English with a different accent, I think that was when the wanderlust seed got planted.'

Troy's plan in 1963 was to sail to Europe, compete in the first European surfing championships in France and earn himself an invite to Hawaii's fabled Makaha event in February 1964. His plan was to join the dots but exactly how he was going to pull it off, he had no idea. But he was leaving Torquay, on that matter he was adamant. As Bells surfer Brian Trist remembers, 'One day he was sitting out the back at Bells, then he just disappeared.' Peter Troy would be gone for three years. He was 24.

Troy boarded the *Castel Felice* with his parents Col and Mardi seeing him off from the dock. The ship, which had arrived in Australia full of '10 Pound Poms' was headed back to Southampton with a reciprocal exchange – young cultural refugees from Australia. London was just starting to swing, but Troy wasn't heading to London. London didn't have surf. Troy was going much further.

Soon after the ship left Melbourne Peter Troy's first letter home arrived. 'Dear Mum and Dad, well this is it! How do you both feel?' His filial devotion was strong, and his letters home to his parents over the next three years from all over the globe would document his extraordinary travels. The handwritten letters (excerpts from which appear in these pages) would not only paint a picture of a nascent surfing world, but of the world itself. The accountant in Troy would itemise the cost of every transaction (he was notoriously tight and prided himself on being able to live on a pound a day), while Troy the travelling romantic would document the human condition wherever he found it, from English dandies to Amazonian tribesmen. And if these people seemed strange and wonderful to Peter Troy from Torquay, you can only imagine how the tall, blond Westerner with the unplaceable accent and the strange craft under his arm might have appeared to them. If Peter wasn't the first Australian many of them had seen, he was certainly the first surfer.

Before taking to the open sea, the *Castel Felice* sailed up Australia's Eastern Seaboard and berthed in Sydney for the day. Peter headed over to Manly for a final surf and to say goodbye to friends. While the world in 1963 was big, the surfing world was stuffy. Everyone knew everyone. During his travels, one of Peter's regular correspondents would be Snowy McAlister. Troy had also done a deal to post stories of his travels to Bob Evans at *Surfing World* magazine. Peter spent the day on the northern beaches surfing and organising a rendezvous in Hawaii early the following year with several surfing friends, who at the end of the day headed back with him to Circular Quay to say bon voyage.

16 May 1963

Next step took me to Denny Keogh's board shop. No Keogh, but 'Midget' Farrelly was there shaping away on a board. When Denny arrived, I borrowed a board from the factory and we spent the afternoon travelling up the north side from Manly to Palm Beach and eventually surfed at Long Reef. 4 to 6 foot, smooth and good surf – I was quite happy with my riding. We cleaned up generally and went to meet 'Snow' McAlister and found that everything had been organised for a farewell send off. By the way, Bill Davis and Gaylord Wilcox never made it to Queensland so they were also present. Send off committee: Snow McAlister, Graeme Treloar, 'Wheels' Williams, Mick Hall, Denny Keogh, Midget Farrelly, John Witzig (Paul's younger brother) and two young femlins – they are girl gremlins. Also a Californian by the name of Joe who will be back home when we pass through America. Quite a cabin party you could imagine.

After six weeks at sea, sailing through the Malacca Strait, across the Indian Ocean, through the Suez Canal and across the Mediterranean, the *Castel Felice* docked in Southampton. Troy immediately split for the Channel Islands to find work as a surf guide, en route to France. His first letter home from Jersey hinted that his humble travels would have an uncanny, Forrest Gump-like way of intersecting with seminal moments not only in surfing, but in modern history.

1 July 1963, Jersey

Arrived at St Helier (capital of Jersey) – population of Jersey is 65,000 and the island is only 350 foot high at the highest point, 7 miles wide and 12 long. 40,000 in St Helier but altogether at first sight a great place and is the playground for the English people who can afford the cost of the large, expensive hotels that front the shoreline at every opportunity. I immediately found an address at Duhamel Street where all the Jersey beach guards lived. Oh! What a hovel – 13 of them in three rooms (four in one 6' x 10'). I left my cases and board here and went to a hotel with them where I met the others who were living in a house out of the city; Bob Armstrong, who is a friend of Bob Evans, Des Couch, who I had met in 1956, and a fellow from Lorne SLSC, Roger Kennedy.

I have had some waves at the only surf beach in Jersey at a place called St Owens – about 8 to 10 foot with a corner; in this case mainly left slides but extremely hard to negotiate the various breaks over the sandbars to get out the back. I am not particularly used to the Anglesea type of surf, as this place reminds me of, and to any of the boys asking about the conditions here, this would most likely give them the best impression.

Have had the best surf at Jersey for a year – been running for almost one week and the wind for the whole of that time has been directly offshore – a breeze until midafternoon and then freshening towards the evening. I am presently trying to collect a few photos and write up an article to send home to Bob Evans as I feel the area warrants it. Not spending too much money, and at present averaging £1 per day since leaving Australia. From now on, I think I shall not try to prophesise what and when I will be doing certain things as events invariably do not materialise that way – I am glad that I have not got a set programme because it must be forever very frustrating to have to move on.

I went to a party here the other night and left at 5am. The personalities are rather strange – all chorus girl dancers, male models, showbusiness people, rock and roll singers (a group called The Beatles were there and this group currently have the top-selling disc in the UK). Boy! Are these types way out and certainly are queer. I was introduced to one fellow who, I was previously told of, was a homosexual and received money from other males, and then with this money bought expensive clothes and a car and then took out these rather attractive girls merely as a handsome male companion. This, mind you, was his job. First time I have encountered this type of activity and was he strange.

I have had seven orders (four certain and three temporary) for Keyo boards here and today I am giving my first lesson at 10/- an hour as a surfboard riding coach – yesterday a man about 28 years came up to me on the beach and inquired if I knew a Peter Troy. I told him who I was and he said he had heard that I was giving professional lessons at 10/- an hour (quick on the uptake with YES).

I have no other news and after 3½ weeks in the one place, events tend to become repetitive so news hard to scrape together. I have enclosed a cutting of my first rescue – very close to a drowning and the closest I have had – definitely down for good and the next day when he was feeling better hardly a word of thanks even – amazing the way people take this service as a matter of course sometimes.

28 August, Biarritz

To put the record straight my first surf in France was 6 foot peak surf, offshore wind with a continuous left slide towards a breakwater, where within 15 yards the wave completely dies out due to the very strong run out. Boy, this was a great surf (for the information of the surf boys the place strongly resembles Southside at Bells with the rock reef being the stone pier and the lefts being comparable but the ride three times the length at Le Barre). It then happened that the organisers of the contest decided to hold the surfing championships on the same afternoon instead of Sunday (only 5 hours after I had arrived on the scene and after one surf of the area – also no sleep from Wednesday). There were some very good surfers here and I didn't fancy my chances very much, but I seemed to have gained a reputation from my morning surfing (also the name Troy – Captain Troy is a favourite in France with children and naturally the gremmies also). The stage was set – Fox Movietone cameras in attendance, people, spectators, fishermen, etc. crowded on the pier and families, girls, and others on the beach. Bill Davis did not get back here and at present have lost him, but Gaylord Wilcox was here after having been via Singapore, South Africa, Italy and Spain. The surf was 8 foot for the contest and great conditions. European Surfing Champion – P. Troy.

I will now mention the last things of interest concerning Biarritz – the day before I left, Sunday, was the presentation day and I received a new shiny cup from the mayor of Biarritz; there was wine and food and general festivity. And I've been offered a free haircut in the most exclusive 'coiffure' in Biarritz (only because it is owned by one of the surfers, Plumcoq). Don't think at this stage I can write another page so will say goodbye for now. Haven't heard how Geelong is faring!

Troy travelled solo for much of his time abroad, but would attract an ensemble cast of fellow travellers – surfers, bon vivants, vagabonds – who he'd befriend and who would join him in cameo roles on the road. Most notable of these in '63 was Rennie Ellis, a young Melbourne photographer and Peter's old surfing mate from Torquay. Ellis, like Troy, was escaping the cultural yoke of early '60s Australia. He'd already

MENT

Student.

, Vic. Australia

ovember 1938

ht Brown

nil

Le titulaire est accompagné de
ses
ENFANTS

e of birth   Sex
de naissance   Sexe

Signature of Bearer
Signature du Titulaire

SURFING-CLUB de la CHAMBRE D'AMOUR
PISCINE DE LA CHAMBRE D'AMOUR
ANGLET (B.-P.) France

MEMBRE D'HONNEUR

M PETER TROY.

Adresse TORQUAY, VICTORIA,
AUSTRALIA
                    Le Président
                    juel de gosny

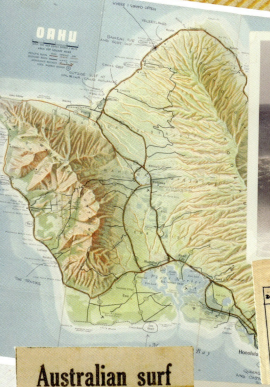

OAHU

yacht "Bettina" - voyage Tenerife, Canary Is. to Antigua, Leeward Is.
Departure 9th Nov 63.

100

DAY	ACTUAL NUMBER OF MILES	WATCH ESTIMATE	COMMENTS ON DAY'S SAILING.
1	50	46	on leaving Santa Cruz, Tenerife set main and ripped it on topping lift cleat. - beating, before changing course Desire to travel approx 1000 m. SW
2	16	16	due W. for Antigua, becalmed 13 hrs. scraped hull of barnacles since port, - tacking and astern breeze for first time
3	42.5	40	now on desired course of 350° (mag. var 15°) wind astern. Trying to make most of breeze - to date little strong wind. another night without breeze only 13 miles (estimated).
4	78	60	main ripped at head, sailed daylight hours without it.
5	82.5	64	first 100 miles, but unfortunately on course of 370° (steered 340°)
6	87.5	129	pulley system used "emergency tiller as steering 340° in heavy seas and sails in danger of gybing, a lot of sail change free 4 winds for 24 hrs astern - boat pitching waves. - chafing of booms and had watches - crew sleeping easily. electrical storm squalls 4½ hrs at 4.00 am. put on watch first rain experienced since on yacht [18/11 - 19/11/68] sailed several hrs. with spinnaker only - saving engine ship in Bosun's chair - endeavoured to spear a Bonito under keel sailing with "wing + wing". - Genoa and Mainsail the wind directly astern - new with the Trades, hot 17°C. more sails repaired. Spinnaker, main and Genoa. Slotting from wind gusts causing considerable wear + tear. extremely hard to estimate speed - no change of sails during period. - plain sailing. sails remain unchanged.

Genoa, Jib, staysail, main set with the mizzen furled. Jib between the main and mizzen booms across slip and low.
at 10.00 hrs. sighted first vessel for 16 days.

another isolated storm centre, but passed without incident average being maintained - another 9 days to Antigua?
Spinnaker pole converted to main what as track twisted
Temporary bridge - experience considerable difficulty, att G.
a day of squalls - take up and setting sails, throughout night riding conditions out without taking sails.
changed course to 360° for recovery to 17°N latitude - squall after squall which made our course a dogleg.
now too far South of bed to maintain desired course of 285°

best sailing day ever for "Bettina" N. 6.75k, but we were once again unable to maintain desired course (now 44 m. S of ?)
rain squalls very prevalent.

as we preferred "using before the wind" necessary to make a course slightly out of desired.
on calculations expected to sight Antigua 65m. away at 5.00
actual sight 6.30 am.: boat just on centre of island into fresh 4 wind around stern easterly to English Harbour -
docked at 11.00 am. and finished anchorage 12.25 pm.

Arrived 5th December '63 completed
North Atlantic Crossing   PT.

hitched around Europe and worked as a lifeguard and a film extra before finding Peter in France, and they drove south into Spain in Ellis's Vauxhall. The pair shared exotic tastes and a social curiosity which would take them both down several Iberian rabbit holes.

11 September 1963
On tour, Spain
Dear Mum and Dad,
Touring here is much different to that at home. As this is the first real experience, at this stage it may not be the proper one, still this is the idea – am travelling with Rennie Ellis (a Brighton Grammar boy and agent for John Severson's *Surfer Magazine*, also from the Lorne SLSC and the boyfriend of Carol Silk of Ciro's fame) and a fellow he met in England, Frank (part-time actor and film stand-in man); also two girls (one destined for Madrid who speaks French and Spanish; the other I don't quite know where she lives). The general set-up at this point was to leave Biarritz on 9th September and to arrive in Genoa, Italy, prior to 27th September. The journey is to go as far as Casablanca in Morocco, NW Africa.

I thought that I would be going from Biarritz to Madrid with Peter Viertel – he was the first to introduce surfing to France and is now the husband of Deborah Kerr. He writes novels, movie scripts, etc. Lives in Switzerland, comes to Biarritz for summer surfing, has a bull-fighting stud in Spain, near Madrid, and returns for winter snow skiing in the Swiss Alps (also drives a Porsche, which prejudices me in saying that he possibly lives like most people dream they would like to live).

Instead we left Biarritz at 8.15pm on the 9th and drove to San Sebastian, where we slept in Rennie's car on the stone pebbles near a fisherman's docks (it was this night I decided now was the time and place for me to purchase one of those canvas lilos for £4 19/-, but expect will have my money's worth in the next year or so as to date have spent all but approx 3½ weeks in a sleeping bag anyway). It was also quite interesting to see street cleaners at 5am sweeping around flaked bodies lying out on bare cobblestones in a city of 120,000 people and with a large floating population of tourists. I feel I should note here that to enter Spain was not hard, nor anything special placed in my passport except that one feels rather squeamish when everywhere soldiers are stationed, and all carry rifles, etc. The day was spent in San Sebastian and we both actually caught 3 foot waves in the harbour and afterwards walked along the whole length of the beach to the accompanied stares, giggles, side comments, etc. as we both completed this tour in our Okanuis – never seen before in Spain as I believe nobody ever wears shorts, except on the beach.

We went on a Spanish type 'pub crawl' through the back streets of Madrid as perhaps in Fitzroy. This way we were able to mix with the average poor person of Madrid. I have a problem – every Spanish man looks at me intently and thinks I am a 'queer' due to the sun bleached hair, which they think is peroxide. The señoritas all make comments to each other and the whole time it's like being in a monkey cage. We drank wine and ate a food dish at each place visited – a real gourmet rally – snails, shrimp, octopus, spiced cow's insides, grilled prawns, potato chips with a chilli sauce, cake, milkshake, red wine and some deep sea fish with a white sauce, bread and olives. The 'king' of cheapness here in Spain is wine – a two pint bottle for 1P and you certainly get drunk on that.

The next day we made Cadiz, where Rennie made contact with two Australian girls whom he knew in London and were at this time holidaying in Cadiz (they had won a holiday in Spain for two and accommodation at the most fashionable hotel in the city by the name of Hotel Atlantic, adjacent to the sea). We lived here and were able to have a hot shower, use toilet arrangements, wash hair and clothes, and generally organise a much needed clean up. Whilst here we tried to catch up on a little night life by going to the local young people's club, called the Whisky and Rock, but somehow felt a little flat because the music temp didn't lend itself to our type of dancing and mine especially as I particularly prefer Yatey-style Dixieland jazz of the casual nature. Still it was a night out and as this trip through Spain and Portugal hadn't enabled us to see any Flamenco dancing or bull fighting, I sat and watched the account of a bull fight in a local bar whilst I ate bread and sausage and sipped a red wine. It is worth noting the condition of the £100 Vauxhall Cresta. This is a quote from a letter written by Rennie to the Lorne SLSC fellows: 'Spanish roads are unbelievably bad and our car was suffering. Our rusted chassis was cracked, our exhaust bumped on the ground, we bottomed on our springs every minute, our gears were tied up with wire, our bumper was tied on with string, our jack was broken, and after a blow-out we found our spare wheel wouldn't fit the car. Our brakes failed and but for the good driving of Peter we would have ended up crushed between a truck and a bus – as it was our front mud guard passed under the tray of the truck (my usual trick anyway). We drove for 100 kilometres without brakes. We drove along miles and miles, twisting and bumping through parched semi-desert country travelling on a wing and a prayer, our only friends the lone donkey with peasant we passed on the road. Finally, somehow we made the Spain trip.'

Guess what's happened in Gibraltar? Lots of love, and I apologise for keeping you in suspense but I'm sure you'll understand when you receive my next letter.

8 October 1963
At sea between Gibraltar and Tangiers
I am now a crew member aboard a 46-foot ketch constructed of teak in Djakarta – Tandjing Pruik, Indonesia. The craft was designed and built by Dipling Hans-Werner Vos (naval architect) for the owner Dr Milo M Wolff. The captain of the yacht is John Cronholm, who was previously first mate and captain of the brigantine *Yankee* and is now skipper of the *Bettina*. I signed on as crew 28/9/63 at 9am (5-man crew including captain). The crew is John (captain) who is from California USA and is 35 years old, Mike is Californian and 23, Wayne is Californian and 21, Rennie is Australian and 22, and myself (Rennie disposed of his car to the two English crew who came off the *Bettina* as a result of coming with me merely to see the yacht).

Our proposed course, at present, appears to be Gibraltar, Tangiers, Casablanca, Madeira (Portuguese archipelago), Canary Islands, Puerto Rico, Barbados, West Indies, Bahamas, Florida. This is subject to change as the captain's obligations are only that he has to be in Miami, Florida, before February '64 and that the yacht is continually kept headed in this general direction. For me, this saves at least $150 as that was the cheapest passage available to the USA and also, of course, the luck of being taken on as a ship's hand without experience. Our food, expenses and trip are paid for and the individual bears only personal expenses and expenses he incurs whilst in port of a private nature. On completion, I expect I can reasonably say I will have had ocean yachting experience, and this will then, I feel sure, open up other avenues for travel to such places as previously would not have been feasible.

Rennie was seasick almost all of the way and as he was duty cook he didn't have much success as he couldn't even go below let alone cook. I luckily am a good sailor to the best of my knowledge. I was next on watch and had two hours of duty which brought us into Tangiers Harbour. Very exhausting, often with cramps in the arms from exerting continuous force on the tiller – this was quite another sensation, of having such a big monster not quite wholly under your power because Mother Nature and the wind is always present.

We arrived at Tangiers Harbour at 3pm with six foot of the head of the mainsail shredded from the excessive wind. Is Tangiers a thieving den! We kept watch all day and night on a roster system to prevent any loss of equipment or stealing and I tire easily when I have to stay awake in the night (especially 3am to 5am). Because my first plans were to catch the Yugoslav freighter from Genoa, and now find myself on a yacht. But now it's months since I've had a letter so I still don't know the football outcome (if Geelong were premiers) or any news. Hope you are both well, regards to Nanna and lots of love from your only son who promises to be careful and not fall over the side of the *Bettina* in the mid-Atlantic Ocean to the cry of 'man overboard!'

25 October 1963
Las Palmas,
Gran Canaria, Canary Islands
I will go to the Post Office before we sail to collect any more mail but will not be able to write again until December, so my birthday will be spent on the high seas, in mid-Atlantic, sleeping I expect after a 1am–5am watch in howling winds and rain. Hope you are not too lonely without that 'thoughtless child' around the place, but now comment that the 'travelling bug' is catching! When here, you realise the rest of the world travels; and it is a great pity really from this respect that Australia is geographically situated as such, as I feel our culture is so greatly affected. How's that for spouting off and yet it is so true.

We leave here on the 5th of November and drop down towards the equator to pick up the 'trades'. The crossing without sight of land is 2600 miles approx. and we expect to take 25–30 days before making Antigua? (The question mark Mother Dear is only to signify the uncertainty of the island of destination, not the uncertainty of arrival, one has to have faith.)

Looks as though another rush necessary to be in Hawaii at the New Year, have a few ideas in mind, but from now on – new resolution – will not comment until what takes place, takes place.

Received a great letter from 'Snow' McAlister and am quoting a segment from his letter, for me, an honour: 'Now, Pete, when you get to Hawaii, get your thinking right, it's not old Snow raving now! Surf wise thinking get that state of mind, when if the big stuff is on, tell yourself you can handle it. If you can overcome that, you have beaten the thing most of our riders don't on their first trip. Treat it as Bells or Dee Why Point or any other place you have mastered, try and remember that, and get with 'em.

I'm in your corner always, regards to all friends and good luck, Snow.'

19 November 1963,

At sea

Sailing – in the darkness, the boat seems to gather speed, rushing on madly regardless of finesse, bullocking its way through the heavy irregular seas. A swell from behind will lift the boat high at the stern, and in restless energy and eagerness, as if to make up for our tardy start, the yacht then slows down the face of the swell squeezing great volumes of glistening foam from beneath her belly, the bow dipping in abeyance, the horizon disappearing from view as we plunge from trough to trough. The eerie howl of the wind in the shrouds; the stars, remote and ice-cold, peer at us from the hollow void of blackness – these are our companions at our side during the long night watches. One eagerly awaits his relief and then collapses into peaceful sleep when time and distance slip by unnoticed.

The other side of sailing is emergency spelt in capitals and to relate: 3.30am and becalmed, I called to John (Captain) advising him that we had drifted around in the opposite direction to our desired course – 10 minutes later – 'John the wind!' but John was almost already on deck – 'Goddam it.'

'On deck, hurry!' There was an urgency nearing panic in his voice – this was his way. The wind was raging and with feverish anxiety was plucking at our vessel. 'The main first, Mike, give me a hand, Mike, Christ Mike! Come when I call. This is serious!' We had been on a broad reach and the mizzen and main were sheeted well out. Wayne and Mike hauled on the sheet as Rennie unhooked the preventer. Around us were the sounds of a thousand demons in the air. The rain, thin and biting, attacked us unmercifully. John and Rennie stood on the deckhouse hauling on the main – 'Grab the bugger!'

It seemed to slap back at us in anger, but we snatched back, pulling, tugging and mothering it with our bodies and then defeated, was lashed to the boom with the gasket rope. The sea around us was whipped into a frenzy yet the rain strove to pacify by flattening the windswept crests. Blue lightning gnawed with witch-like fingers as she lit the heavens as would one huge fluorescent light over a road intersection or the arc light over an operating table. Picking out the details of our frenzied struggle – John, his mouth never shut, concern etched in the lines of his face and the wind snatching at his every word. The wind was so cold and the harder it blew, the deeper the penetration. We were now running NE (desired SW) before the storm at a driving 8 knots. Only muscle got the mizzen down, the wind its artful ally picking its pent-up powers against mere human strength. We then set the staysail, and as its purpose was to take some of the wind, we took it as planned. I observed all this, huddled over the compass in the cockpit and wrestling with the tiller, drops of rain glistening in my now ginger beard (two months old in three days). From peering eyes shielded under a yellow waterproof hood drawn tight across my worried and puckered brow, I observed the rest of the crew crawl below decks, freezing, soaking, tired and yet exhilarated after the ½ hour battle against the elements. We are, of course, still soaring the water's crest in the exact opposite direction as to that which was the desired. This is sailing.

Throughout this voyage and now as I near land, accompanied with pent-up personal feelings (which is all one has to be alone with on a crossing as this), intense desire and awareness that now, again, I am to relive those moments I first experienced on leaving home and Melbourne, except that now a 'new world' is opening before me – a world I can as yet merely contemplate and dream of, but shortly to know that I will be part of the long repetitive days aboard ship from where you cannot observe distance by observation, and hence have the feeling that one is like a small beetle on its back, crawling frantically to nowhere. Hence, my ears strain to hear the silent 'Ahoy there, land ahead!' from deep within my subconscious thought (alas, what writing, but it does endeavour to put the feelings of the moment on paper – and these are so hard to relive after the event has taken place and even more so when nothing is recorded).

All the very best for Christmas and a prosperous season over the holidays.

Regards and best love,

Son Peter

The *Bettina* made it to Antigua, and eventually to Miami. It was there that Peter wrote the following on letterhead from The Castaways, 'America's Most *FUN*derful ResortMotel'.

'*This book is a factual account of my travels, my experiences, my feelings and of the quick glimpse I've been allowed to see of this world we live in. I have endeavoured to sow a seed in the minds of those who may risk to venture out and blaze a path into the unknown yet lack the initial breakaway. Perhaps my 'off the beaten track' experiences here will inspire other young men to talk about such experiences, and then possibly set off themselves in search of their own particular 'paradise'. As one reads through these chapters, perhaps this seed will germinate, so that the fruits of the experience of 'travel' can be tasted and savoured throughout the years to follow.*'

It was the foreword to the book of his travels, a book that would be published 50 years and 140 countries later, after Peter himself had passed on.

Troy made it to Hawaii on 2 January 1964, but Hawaii, rather than being the end, was simply another beginning. He made California in March before heading down into South America, where he was warned, 'So primitive is the country en route that Indians may shoot at the train with bows and arrows.' Troy trekked alone through the Amazon, before ending up in Brazil where, in Rio, he commandeered one of the small wooden boards local spearfishermen used to paddle out to local reefs and started catching waves on it, surfing back to the beach, introducing surfing to Brazil in the process.

From South America it was over to Africa, where he surfed Bruce's Beauties long before the guys in the *Endless Summer*, before hitching alone across the Kalahari Desert. He headed north all the way to Spitsbergen, Norway, the northernmost point of human civilisation. He travelled by either hitchhiking lifts with cars or cargo ships, riding motorbikes or simply on foot. Troy eschewed commercial airline travel. He would later speak of his disdain for the steel bird and how it had made travel utilitarian, an A to B exercise that robbed it of rich, spontaneous moments.

One adventure invariably led to another and the years just melted away. He didn't come home until 1966, by which stage Troy and his travels were already the stuff of legend. Peter Troy had blazed a trail for generations of Australians who'd use surfing as a passport. When he embarked on a second odyssey in the '70s, this time largely through Asia on what would become the 'Hippy Trail', discovering the waves of Lagundri Bay before climbing most of the way up Everest, he became something else again.

1964

Phyllis O'Donell

'If it's a northerly, surf here, if it's a southerly, surf down there.'

Phyllis O'Donell remembers the advice well. Standing with her on Manly Beach, Snowy McAlister started at Queenscliff and worked his way down the beach to Fairy Bower, pointing out the different waves and the conditions they broke best in. Manly was Snow's domain. Phyllis had just taken up surfing. Snow suggested Fairy Bower might be beyond her just now. 'I always called Snowy my mentor,' Phyllis remembers. 'He was a great bloke.'

Phyllis was an unlikely surfer, but people everywhere were coming to surfing from unlikely places. The allure of life at the beach was strong, and young people from the cities and suburbs all over the country were being drawn toward the vibrancy of it.

'I lived at Drummoyne, miles from the surf. I don't even remember why I started surfing,' Phyllis says and laughs. 'My sister's boyfriend had a surfboard at the time and that's what made me take it up.' Phyllis O'Donell was a late bloomer. She started surfing at 23. 'I'd go to Manly with my sister and that's where I met Snowy and he helped me get started. He'd tell me where to surf.'

Phyllis's first surf was around the corner at Freshwater and was memorable. 'I remember I was out on a board and I didn't even know how to surf or what I was doing and then someone came running along yelling, 'Shark! Shark! Shark!' and I was panicking. I couldn't even paddle at that stage and I'm panicking thinking a shark was going to get me and I'm trying my best to paddle in.' She laughs with a twinkle. 'Of course it was a *porpoise*!'

The O'Donells lived in a block of flats in inner-west Drummoyne; their neighbour was Dawn Fraser's sister. 'Dawn used to ride down on a bloke's bike to see her sister,' recalls Phyllis. 'Then all of a sudden Dawn was famous!' Nineteen-sixty-four, as it turns out, would be a big year for both of them. Phyllis, like Dawn, possessed a mischievous streak a mile wide that stretched all the way back to her childhood. 'God, I was a little devil,' she admits. 'I had my first cigarette at age five. Mother and Father wouldn't smoke but they kept cigarettes for their friends and they'd leave them around and my sister and I would get the ciggies out and smoke them. Dad was a rubber manufacturer and we lived close to the Dunlop factory in Sydney and we'd hand them out to the blokes who worked there.'

As a child Phyllis had stuttered. 'I couldn't say the teacher's name,' she remembers. "Good morning M-M-Miss ... " but I outgrew it luckily by the time I was 13.' She'd also played the piano and had her heart set on being a music teacher before her mother suffered a nervous breakdown and Phyllis took responsibility for looking after her. Phyllis had been an expressive kid looking for an outlet and, as an adult, she took an immediate shine to surfing once it found her.

Phyllis's surfing blossomed after the O'Donells moved north in 1963. 'My mother and I came up on a little trip and we just fell in love with Rainbow Bay.' They returned to Sydney, convinced Phyllis's father to sell up the family service station they then owned, and they moved into a house at Banora Point, just south of Tweed Heads. Compared to living in Sydney, her surfing life was suddenly easy. The Queensland sand points were long and languid. They were also on her doorstep. 'I'd get up early to go surfing and we had the shutter on the garage door and of course the shutter would lift up and wake my parents. They eventually said it might be an idea if you moved out and that's when I got my flat in Eden Avenue, Coolangatta. I'd just walk across the road and hit the waves.' Phyllis became a regular in Rainbow Bay, easily recognisable. There were only a handful of women surfing, and walking up the point she cut a distinctive figure holding her board on her shoulder. 'My arms were too short to carry it!'

Coolangatta at the time was a small, seasonal tourist town. Jack Evans's porpoise pool out at Snapper Rocks still did daily shows. Billy Rak hired surfboards at Greenmount with the Peterson boys, Mick and Tom, working summer jobs there. The place bustled in the holidays but now belonged to the surfers the rest of the year.

The surfing scene in town was stirring. There were two boardriding clubs in town – Kirra and Snapper Rocks – both of which had just formed. The breakwalls were also being built on the Tweed River, slowing the northerly sandflow, creating waves at Duranbah, while replenishing sand on the points at Snapper, Greenmount and Kirra.

'Would you believe only two of us surfed at D-Bah?' offers Phyllis. 'That was a guy called Del Perriot and myself; only two of us at D-Bah. In the old days if you came from Sydney you wanted to surf the points like Rainbow, Greenmount and Kirra. I've got a great photo of me surfing left at Kirra, you know.' Surfing quickly took over Phyllis's life. 'I'd go down to Byron once a week to surf The Pass, and we surfed Noosa on a cyclone when it was too big here. We'd jump in the cars and surf Noosa and stay with Ma and Pa Bendall.'

Phyllis became secretary of the Kirra Surfriders Club, which was being run by Joe Larkin – who'd shaped Phyllis's board – and Mal Sutherland. Bob Evans called them early in 1964. He suggested they organise a Queensland Titles and select a team to compete in the World Titles he was planning to hold in Sydney later that year. The Queensland Titles were held at Kirra in April after being postponed a week due to a cyclone swell. Phyllis won, and as Queensland champion she was off to Manly the following month.

Flying down with the Queensland team, Phyllis had modest expectations at Manly. 'No one thought Midget and I would win. They thought Linda Benson would win the women's and they thought Joey Cabell would win the men's. Linda was the stand-in for the *Gidget* movies you know. She worked as a stewardess and surfed in Hawaii so she was quite a big deal. I was a nobody from Queensland.' Linda was the only international surfer to compete at Manly.

Phyllis had a few things working for her, though. Manly was her old beach, for starters, and the waves at Manly that weekend were breaking on a sandbar right, not dissimilar to surfing the points back in Queensland. Phyllis was also surfing on her forehand, while Linda Benson would be on her backhand. Phyllis rode a board shaped by Midget in the first couple of heats, 'but I didn't feel comfortable with it so then I got on my Joe Larkin board for the finals.'

Phyllis also had the crowd. 'They reckon there were 60,000 people on the beach. That's what they told me.' The head count may have been generous, but it was clearly a huge crowd, which played to Phyllis's exhibitionist streak. 'They started playing this really groovy music and I totally went along with it,' she remembers. A city radio station was holding a stomp down on the beach, and the music was spilling out over the lineup. 'I forgot about the crowd and the surfing. I was there for fun.' There were some spirited conversations in the judging tent – that would intensify during the men's final – as surfing at that point was wrestling with how to quantify surfing… and what good surfing actually was. Head judge at Manly was American legend Phil Edwards, who'd publicly drawn a line between 'trick surfing' and 'functional surfing'.

'Oh, I tricked around,' remembers Phyllis. 'I didn't have a clue; they just played the groovy music and I relaxed and if they hadn't played the groovy music I don't think I would have won. I was a totally hopeless dancer; it was only on a board. I used to do spinners.' She punctuated her dizzying spins with classic nose rides to the delight of the crowd. Bob Evans wore several hats at the event, including commentary, calling the action for the crowd on the beach. He'd later describe the women's final in the pages of *Surfing World* this way:

> The interest in the Women's event was high and no one could have been disappointed as their display was the best yet seen in this country. One of the impressive performances was that of Victorian girl, Gail Couper. Heather Nicholson of Coffs Harbour came through with her usual confident driving rides, but she has not yet established the fluid body motion in her turns and trimming that will allow her to be our top girl surfer. Linda Benson of the USA and Phyllis O'Donnell [sic] of Australia were performing like the national champions that they are, but where Linda (a goofyfooter) was having some trouble with the white water in the mostly right slides, often grabbing the rail, Phyllis was completely at ease on the swell, which was identical to the Queensland type waves with which she is so familiar. Her placement in the wave was ideal and her trimming and arching through the hollow sections pretty to watch. Though every wave these great girl riders made earned spontaneous applause, Phyllis O'Donnell [sic] was a decisive winner.

Famously, the women's presentation was held first, and Phyllis would in perpetuity be remembered as the first surfing World Champion crowned, man or woman. 'They announced the women's before they should have and I was up there with Linda,' recalls Phyllis. 'They announced that I had won the women's. I didn't win any money for the world title; I won the trophy and a carton of Craven A cigarettes.' She pauses before shooting a sideways glance, 'And I smoked them all! Linda and I went up to the Manly Pacific and we had a couple of noggins to celebrate.'

While Phyllis's world title was big news in the press, not a lot changed for her at home. She returned to Rainbow Bay and her job at the tenpin bowling alley. 'I was the assistant manager there. I used to have to do microphone work telling everyone what to do.' She started writing a column for the *Courier-Mail*. She drove young Michael Peterson to his first surf contest. She kept winning Queensland Titles, won the Australian Title again the following year in 1965, and made the finals of the World Titles in 1966 and 1968.

However, Phyllis's new lofty status didn't make daily life in the surf at Coolangatta any easier, the Coolangatta points becoming busier by the day and dominated by blokes. 'I remember I had a pink rinse in my hair this day,' Phyllis says matter-of-factly, 'and *anyhow* … I'm paddling out and these guys were laughing at me. I went, "What are you laughing at?" They said, "You!" They said, "We haven't seen anyone as old as you out in the surf!" I went, "Old? Old?" I was only 28! They started laughing and I went okay, laugh away. One of them dropped in on me so I grabbed him by the wetsuit and threw him off. I always had fun in those days.'

1964

Midget Farrelly

Bernard Farrelly's first Hawaiian trip in the winter of 1961 had been inspired by an act of big-wave bravado at home. 'Dave Jackman was making it known he intended to ride the Queenscliff Bombora,' recalled Midget years later in *Surfing World*. 'We'd seen Hawaiian surf movies by Bud Browne in surf clubs and the odd theatre, and Dave had seen the big waves and said, "Well, I'm gonna ride the Queenscliff Bombora when it gets big." So Joey Larkin made him an 11-foot balsa board and he was training to do it and the day came and he did it. It was low tide and breaking top-to-bottom and made the front page of the *Sydney Morning Herald*. The next week he was interviewed and asked, "Well, what are you gonna do next?" And Dave said, "I'm gonna go to Hawaii and ride big waves." And we all thought, "Well, we better go with him! So we did, we all bought tickets on P&O and that's how Makaha came about. Everything hinges on Dave riding those waves at the Queensie Bombie.' Midget asked his boss, Barry Bennett, for an advance on his wage, boarded the *Oriana* with Dave Jackman, Bob Pike and 15 others, and sailed off to surf Hawaii for the first time.

Just over a year later, in January 1963, Midget disembarked a Canadian Pacific flight at Sydney airport carrying the Makaha trophy – a Hawaiian warrior and surfboard carved from monkey-pod wood. Australia had a new sporting hero … and a new sport. Australian sporting triumphalism at that time was reserved for swimmers, cricketers and football players, but the young sport of surfing was having a moment in the sun. It just needed a champion. And here he was. Eighteen-year-old Midget was spirited away by his mates from the Dee Why surfing fraternity, who immediately took him to the pub to celebrate.

For Midget, the Makaha win was unexpected. For Australian surfing, it was a new dawn. The Makaha International was regarded as the unofficial world championship, but had only ever been won by Hawaiians. Riding a nine-seven balsa board he'd shaped himself, Midget broke away from the pack in the 10-man final and surfed the inside runners on his own. The Australian's win caused a stir in Hawaii. Makaha wasn't meant to be won by outsiders, especially outsiders who surfed the inside. Midget recalled, 'Three of the judges, Dick Brewer, Dewey Weber and Buzzy Trent, were never allowed to judge again when I won that contest.' The win would cause an even bigger stir back home.

Australia at the time was a young surfing nation desperate to prove itself. 'There was a great want for beach culture,' recalled Midget. 'We all lived on the coast, we all understood the ocean and there was a great want for the connection to be stronger. Prior to that it was unthinkable that an Australian could win in Hawaii. Well, when it did happen it was acknowledgment and confirmation: acknowledgment that we were a water people and confirmation that we were good enough to win.

'Surfing back then was a lot smaller,' Midget said. 'There were far less people, it was a tighter society, we all knew each other. Most of us worked in the surfboard industry or nearby to it. Sydney's northern beaches had surfing populations. Manly to Queensie, Freshwater and it would start to thin out around Dee Why. It was a different world in the sense that it's only so many years after World War II. Australia was a much more basic place and luxuries were very few. Very few people had a car, TV was new and Australia was a conservative Anglo-Saxon place with the White Australia Policy. The church and the state were still telling you how to live.' For surfers 'the state' meant the surf lifesaving clubs. Midget hadn't quite forgiven the surf clubs for their iron rule over the beaches during his early surfing years but, at the same time, he understood that they'd given Australians a connection to the ocean and a reason to paddle out into it. We weren't connected in the same way as the Hawaiians, but Australians belonged in the ocean nonetheless.

But now that surfing had broken free, and with cars and then surfboards being produced in numbers, the Australian coastline seemed boundless. There was a wave of youthful energy headed toward the coast. 'Once balsa came along a father could buy a surfboard for his daughter to put on top of her Austin A40 or her Morris Minor and suddenly gone were the days where you had to be a bronzed Aussie to lift your 16-footer off the roof. So boards were becoming shorter and lighter, clothing was becoming surf-orientated and people were starting to get excited about the idea of surfing lots of different waves.'

Bob Evans, meanwhile, was moving and shaking. Midget wasn't even off the plane before Evans had stated in *Surfing World* – the magazine he'd founded – his belief that Australia should host its *own* Makaha. The very first official World Contest. Evans framed it as wishful thinking, but was already working behind the scenes to actually make it happen. He knew the chances of it happening relied almost squarely on Midget, who was now the face and voice of Australian surfing. Boyish, articulate and considered, he challenged the narrative of surfers being a threat to civil society. More than that, Midget could frame surfing in a way that conservative mainstream Australia could actually understand.

Midget was the perfect frontman but took on the role reluctantly. He cherished his privacy and grew impatient with anything that got between him and his surfing. However, he remained a true believer in Australia hosting a world contest and spent months working behind the scenes to pull it together. 'Once I saw the politics of Makaha, how it was set up, I thought it wouldn't be that hard to do it. Makaha was relatively exciting. It drew publicity and it was known around the world as *the* event. The win there created a heightened sense of interest from Australia and we had structures already in place that meant getting it off the ground would not be a difficult thing to do. The bones of it were already there.' Before Australia could host a world championship, it had needed a national body to run it and Evans helped drive the formation of the Australian Surfriders Association (ASA). When it was formed at a meeting on Sydney's northern beaches in August 1963, Evans immediately nominated Midget as its inaugural president. He was elected unanimously.

The relationship between Midget and Bob Evans didn't extend beyond the professional. 'We weren't friends,' offered Midget curtly. 'Bob fancied himself as a promoter and that's what he could do with surfing. He brought a lot of colour and attention to surfing and in the end Manly may not have happened without him. We were two very different people. Like all of us, he had a passion for surfing and his vision and his ability to say, "I can promote this," was catalytic.' Midget saw Evans forever on the lookout for 'the new surf man' – the next star for his movies, magazines and even his contests. And while for now that was Midget, in 1963 Midget recognised who his successor would be.

Nat Young was just 15 when he won the ASA Invitational at Bondi in November 1963. At the presentation on Bondi Beach, Bob Evans told Nat he'd just won an all-expenses-paid trip to Hawaii. Evans then dropped the bombshell to the crowd. Australia would host the very first official World Surfing Championship in May the following year, over the bridge at Manly. Midget hadn't competed at Bondi but would soon be headed to Hawaii to defend his Makaha title. Nat was coming along for the ride.

In Hawaii, Midget and Nat shared a house on Ke Nui Road, in front of Pipeline, with fellow Aussie Kevin Platt. Midget, as Nat recalls, 'showed them the ropes'. They surfed giant Sunset, lost their boards and were washed in half a mile down the beach. Later that night they were fast asleep when they heard a commotion outside. Arriving from parts unknown, Peter Troy was running around their yard with five angry Hawaiians in hot pursuit. An argument over petrol money apparently. Midget was awake by now, and coolly appraising the situation. He waited until Troy ran past the back door, called him in and slammed it shut before the Hawaiians caught up. Troy woke up on the lounge the following morning with Midget standing over him, arms folded and sporting a look of disapproval.

Nat idolised Midget, but toward the end of the trip they had a minor falling out over money. As Nat's profile rose in the years ahead their rift became a continental drift. The 1963 Makaha contest meanwhile would be a farce. Many of the international surfers who'd travelled to Hawaii weren't allowed to compete, including a bunch of Australians. Midget and Nat had their boards stolen from the roof of their car while they were enjoying a dinner of teriyaki steak and rice in Nanakuli. Midget made the final on a borrowed board but finished last. Hawaiian Joey Cabell won.

Meanwhile, the upcoming World Championships in Manly were generating a huge buzz, not just with surfers. 'There was huge support for it,' recalled Midget, 'so it bloomed very quickly and took off. I was watching the whole thing develop and build and like a lot of people I was amazed at the way it was turning out. It was only a couple of years earlier we were the outcast fringe-dweller nuisances who had to pay to register their surfboards and were under threat of being heavily policed by councils and surf lifesaving. So as this thing progressed and developed it took on this incredible new energy.'

Evans had pulled it off. Ampol petroleum had underwritten the contest. Qantas had flown everyone there. 'It wasn't a huge competing group but it was diverse,' recalled Midget of the World Championships field. 'Surfers from France, South Africa, Jersey, Hawaii, California, New Zealand, it was really the birth of something and because of the scale of the event and the energy leading up to it, the World Contest was born big. It wasn't born small.' There was nothing small about that weekend at Manly. The crowd? Midget judged, 'Conservatively 60,000. Upper end,

80,000.' Manly teemed. Music pumped. Teenagers stomped on the sand. It was an explosion of youth, televised live on Channel 7 all weekend.

'Well, there was no precedent,' Midget remembered. 'We'd never had anything like that, and funnily enough expectations were high even though people didn't know what to expect.' The one major expectation was that Midget would win. The pressure on the 19-year-old weighed heavy. Midget detached from the whole scene, floating through the weekend cocooned in a bubble of private surfing thoughts. 'I looked at the images and in one of them I'm standing there with a canoe paddle speaking to the crowd and I'm thinking, "How did I get that canoe paddle? How did I get it? Why is it in my hands?" I must have been on autopilot only because I just don't remember.'

The autumn surf at Manly delivered. Chest high, light sea breeze, good sandbanks. The judging, however, would be key, but with Phil Edwards acting as head judge the final result came with the imprimatur of the world's premier stylist. The final came down to Midget, Mick Dooley, Mike Doyle, Joey Cabell, LJ Richards and young Bobby Brown from Cronulla. The atmosphere was described in *Surfing World* as, 'gay, but tense'. It was certainly tense in the lineup. Cabell imposed himself on the final, repeatedly dropping in on the other surfers. The aggression sat uncomfortably with Midget. Despite his respect for Cabell's mastery in Hawaiian surf, Midget felt 'rotten'. Midget – riding a 10'0" squaretail he'd shaped himself at Gordon Woods's – surfed classically, banking hard off the tail before skipping up to the nose. Midget flowed. Cabell, built like the Makaha trophy and accustomed to Hawaiian waves, surfed a more modern style, more from the middle of the board. As Midget later put it, 'Cabell didn't walk.' In the shadows of the final Midget found a long, zippering right and surfed across the whole pack. He sensed he was probably trailing. He surfed cat-like, dancing twice to the nose before jamming a cutback that would achieve immortality. The finishing gun went off, the crowd went wild, but would it be enough?

The surfers milled around the beach tent as the sun dipped behind the Norfolk Island pines. Bob Evans grabbed the microphone and cut straight to the chase. No minor placings needed. Midget was the winner. His early minutes as the first official world surfing champion were uncomfortable. 'I was naturally shy. There's a difference between the performance out in the water and the one that begins once you hit the sand. Because there's an event in the water and then another event that starts when everyone comes in for the presentation. That's the fame and notoriety thing and that is a whole different game.' The euphoria over Midget's win was shared all around Australia, and would only die down a month later when the Beatles arrived.

For Midget, the win was an affirmation of what he stood for as a surfer. 'As a kid my parents dragged my sister and I all over the world so I never lived anywhere for too long. I was always an outsider in somebody else's culture. All I really ever had was being true to who I was, and that extended into my surfing. I had to be who I was so that's all I did. I did that at Makaha. In the final I saw the long rides weren't there so I rode the inside and won the thing. It happened. And when Manly came along it happened again. But I was still the same person. I knew who I was, I knew what I had to do, I knew how I wanted to be. I wasn't looking at somebody else, thinking I want to surf like this or that.'

When asked by Nick Carroll much later in life what surfing meant to him, Midget replied, 'Freedom. It's freedom from other people's ideas.' That freedom became harder to find after Manly. Midget's good friend Gary Birdsall noted, 'We all have our good days and our bad days and if we're just a regular surfer we don't give a shit. Midget didn't seem to have that freedom once he became famous, the freedom to surf and frolic.'

Midget engaged with surfing on a level few surfers ever reach. 'You go into oblivion,' he'd wax of the surfing experience. 'Suddenly all your life is there in this long, long, stretched-out wave; you're removed from the past, everything that has been on your mind has become immaterial, everything goes to jelly, and you feel completely removed from the world around you. Nothing matters any longer but you and the board and the wave and this instant of time.' Midget had a pure vision for surfing, but it would be challenged in the years ahead as surfing grew, ironically, as a result of his Manly win.

The win, from Midget's view, was never about him anyway. 'Whatever that World Contest did for me doesn't matter. It just does not matter. What happened was that it took surfing from the back stalls to the front stage in one fell swoop. So this World Contest at Manly was a massive turning point. It was national acknowledgment that surfing was an Australian way of life.'

As the sun went down and the traffic slowly started moving out of Manly, the newly crowned world champ put his board on the roof of the Farrellys' family car and drove home with his parents. 'That's a giggle in itself. They were accepting and didn't make a fuss. They were very down to earth. It was really simple.' As to the conversation in the car, Midget recalled, 'I'm pretty sure my mother would have said to me, "Oh Bernard, that was wonderful."'

The following week Midget bought his own car – a Holden – and drove up the coast with a group of friends. Other surfers from the contest followed in convoy. Linda

Benson, Phyllis O'Donell and their friends drove behind, with Snowy McAlister riding shotgun to keep out unwanted approaches. They surfed Crescent Head before driving north to Angourie. Albe Falzon, Bob McTavish, Bob Evans, Nat Young and Claw Warbrick all soon materialised … as did Joey Cabell. With just a handful of people sitting under pandanus trees to watch, Cabell stole the show. Midget walked down the hill from the car park after Cabell had come in.

'After Manly, it was a relief for Midget,' offers Gary Birdsall of the north coast road trip. Birdsall remembers being intoxicated by the new car smell of the Holden, and also remembers two local kids nervously approaching Midget for an autograph. 'As soon as someone knew he was the Midget who'd won the contest, they were all over him. It was a funny experience because that sort of behaviour hadn't existed in surfing before. Midget was the first guy to experience it and as a representative of Australia, and a champion, we couldn't have wished for a man more suited to the role of being our first hero.'

1966

Gail Couper

Gail Couper was only 16 and had been surfing for just over a year when she qualified to go to the World Titles at Manly in 1964. 'It was a bit of a shock, I can tell you.' Just a few weeks before Manly, Gail's dad, Stan, had received a call from Brian Lowdon, who was organising the first women's event at Bells. He was looking for surfers to compete. 'He called Dad and said, "We hear your daughter can surf, bring her along." Anyway, no one explained to me what was actually going on. I just paddled out at Bells and caught waves. I only discovered later after winning that I was now the Victorian Champion … and that by winning I'd be going to Sydney for the World Titles. I was stunned at first, then a little apprehensive. That just left me four more months to surf and get better.' Gail travelled to Manly and fell just short of making the women's final, won by Phyllis O'Donell.

The Coupers had lived in Melbourne and would holiday in Lorne three times a year, until finally, one time, they didn't go back. Gail had taken up surfing, 'through frustration with trying to become a tennis player. Nobody in Lorne played or coached, and my aim back then was to be the next Margaret Court. When I got to Lorne the boys played footy and the girls played netball. I didn't like netball. I liked my opposition on the other side of the net.'

Gail had taken to the surf after borrowing a board from 'Sharky' the lifeguard. 'Sharky used to set up on the beach in summer and spray suntan oil on tourists with this dreadful machine. He'd also rent Lilos and surfboards and he let us local kids take the boards out for free. There were four of us that gave it a go and I went, I think I've found something really good.' In winter, Sharky would get on his motorbike and

ride to Rainbow Bay, Queensland. 'He was like a drover,' recalls Gail, 'he had all these places and people along the way who'd feed him and let him stay.'

Gail took up surfing at the same time as a whole bunch of local kids, the lime-green runners of Lorne Point perfect for their balsa longboards. 'There were bathing boxes down on the beach at Lorne – not coloured ones like at Brighton – but the Stribling family had one and Wayne Lynch and I used to keep our boards there. I didn't want to carry the boards up the hill to our place in Charles Street because they were so bloody heavy. Wayne was even higher up on the hill in George Street. Then our group acquired Simon Buttonshaw and Murray Walding and we'd sit between the rock walls, which is what you did while waiting for the tide to drop on the point. Lots of talk. It was quite a little scene down there.' As the kids got better, their range extended. 'Our parents were sharing the duties of taking us to surf on the weekend to different places. We'd surf Kennett River, Eastern View; when Mrs Lynch drove us we'd head to Bells.' Gail's father, Stan, was more into the traditional sports of footy, cricket and golf, but he followed his daughter's interest into the surf. 'Surfing was never an interest of Dad's until I started competing.' She recalls and laughs, 'I dragged him into it.'

Even though Lorne was busy in summer and their little surf gang had regular visitors from over east, their surfing developed without a lot of influence from the outside world. 'I'd never looked at magazines,' recalls Gail. 'I wasn't aware of California or people surfing there. I didn't know what style was or how I should surf, but luckily I had Wayne here, the best stylist of all-time to watch and learn from. He was inventing all these manoeuvres and was so vertical in his attack, so continuous in his flow. Because we had our boards down there together on the beach we surfed together quite often after school. Wayne was a little keener. Brian Singer was teaching here in Lorne at the time and Wayne would race him back from Bells in time for class to start.'

John Monie and a group of young surfers from the NSW Central Coast were regular visitors to Lorne, and on one of John's trips he delivered Gail's new board, the board she'd ride throughout 1966. 'Midget had made me a new board. It had three redwood stringers and a big resin fin. The thing weighed a ton. The irony is the board I got rid of was a balsa board that was actually lighter. I was like, what's the deal with foam? I thought it was supposed to be lighter. I'd met Midget at Manly in 1964 and he'd always been supportive of women's surfing. His sister Jane surfed, I think. At Bells he'd always take the time to talk surfing with you.'

In 1966, Gail was in Year 12 and doing her VCE, so – in theory – her surfing career would run second to school that year. Gail laughs, 'It didn't quite work out that way. I was fitting surfing in as fun between all the serious stuff, but then surfing became quite serious stuff too.' Gail went to Belmont High in Geelong; the school bus drove along the Great Ocean Road … and the surf. The bus left at 7.25am and would drop her home again at quarter-to-five. 'My winter surf after school was 20 minutes, but it was so cold you'd only last 20 minutes anyway.' Gail was also into track and field and that year set the javelin record at Belmont High. 'It stood for 15 years. I used to be a sprinter, too, but Lorne Point used to have these little wooden fences that caught the sand and at high tide you couldn't see them. I jumped off my board one day and landed on top of one of those stumps on the arch of my foot. I couldn't run anymore after that.'

Gail won Bells again in '66 although her win was a footnote in the surf mag contest reports. Nat Young won the opens and Wayne Lynch the juniors, and the buzz around both dominated the coverage. 'Surfing journalism was so Sydney-centric,' offers Gail. 'Unless you were a woman from Sydney you got no press. In some ways that bothered me and in others it didn't. I was quite happy to be left alone to get on with what I wanted to be doing, and I hated interviews. I ran a mile from them but it bugged me at the end of four pages of the Bells contest there's two lines saying, " … and Gail Couper won again." That was it. I didn't want to be raved about but they could have at least mentioned the other women in it.'

The 1966 Australian Titles were held in Coolangatta, and the Coupers travelled up from Lorne. Gail as Victorian Champion had a free air ticket, so she flew while the rest of the family drove. 'I'd heard nothing of the place except that Sharky went there every year and there were pointbreak waves and it was warmer than Lorne.' She didn't find too many rainbows in Rainbow Bay. 'It poured rain and the car park where the pine trees are in front of the Coolangatta shopping centre was a metre deep with water. My brother was four and I remember him running madly through the water. It was such a huge storm. They ran the women's in howling onshore waves at Coolangatta, breaking way out. You paddled and paddled and when you got sick of paddling you'd turn around and catch something. That's how I remember the final. It was a terrible easterly mess.'

Gail, who'd finished second in '65, was now finally the Australian champion, beating defending champ Phyllis O'Donell for the title. Snowy McAlister congratulated Gail on the beach. Midget sent her a telegram: 'Congratulations on your convincing win.'

Gail's victory came with an air ticket to California for the World Titles in San Diego later in the year. She went back to Lorne, sat her trial exams, and packed her bags for California. She'd never been overseas, and on 16 September boarded an Air New Zealand flight alongside Nat Young, unsure exactly of what was waiting for her at the other end. The flight was almost empty, and Gail found three spare seats, stretched out and slept.

'We get to California and there's nobody there to meet us at the airport. We all come out of arrivals together but I got out there and went, what do I do now? Thankfully Bob Evans rescued me at LA airport. He'd rented a car and had Lee Cross and Peter Drouyn with him. He said, "Well, you better come with me. We're going north," and I went, "*Okay*!" We drove up to Santa Barbara where he'd planned to meet Bob Cooper. We stayed at the Coopers' that night and went to The Ranch the next day, surfing these beautiful righthanders. Bob got us through the gate. On the way up there we'd pulled up at this house and there's this big steep driveway and this guy comes out and it's George Greenough. We then surfed Small Rincon and Cojo Point. We could see Point Conception but we ran out of time to surf it. That stretch of the coast,' she recalls, 'felt a bit like back at home on the Great Ocean Road.' Gail had taken a camera with her and documented the trip. 'My auntie's husband was from Germany and he gave me a camera that year. It was an Ihagee, made in Dresden, and I took it with me wherever I travelled.

'Heading back south toward Los Angeles was an eye opener. It was just so fast and so new. We surfed Malibu, although I surfed more out the back and around the corner – it was too crowded for me in the inside. Then we came back through and watched the US Titles, which were being held at Huntington. The contest was outrageous. It was so loud and there were so many people. I'm like, what kind of crazy event is this where you wear a helmet and you have to surf under the pier? We didn't do that at Lorne! But I remember as we travelled seeing all the oil rigs pumping away on the side of the road and everything near the beach feeling so drab.'

When Gail got to San Diego thinking a room had been booked, she found her hotel didn't open till the next day. 'I had no accommodation when I got there so I got dumped with Phyllis, poor thing, and then they put us up in the Shelter Island Inn in San Diego while the contest was on. I remember never knowing quite where I was. San Diego was very disorienting. You'd drive half an hour and you'd be looking at the same view you just saw.'

The contest was surfed at Ocean Beach and the waves, Gail remembers, were 'pretty terrible. The points were cumulative and going into the Grand Final I was in second, 12 points behind, so I was in with a chance. Looking at the trophy now just makes me think about how badly I stuffed it up. Everyone else was laughing before the final while I was trying to quell the nerves. I was really self-conscious about people watching me surf, which is why I always did well at Bells because I was way out to sea. In San Diego there were thousands of people on the beach and they were really close. I paddled out and got out-manoeuvred. The smart thing would have been to follow the ones getting the waves, but I got lost out there. I didn't catch a single wave. I got no points for the final and suddenly second wasn't second anymore. I dropped to equal third, which I still thought was all right, but then they came over and said, "Sorry, the trophies for third and fourth are different sizes so we need to split you." They walked away and came back and said, "Sorry, you're fourth." I was suddenly not on the podium and standing on the sand instead, which was a little awkward.'

Californian Joyce Hoffman was the favourite and she indeed won, her second world title in a row, but while Gail may not have won the title she gained a friend. 'Joyce and I met because she was US champion and I was Aussie champion, and by the time the contest had finished she and I had become quite close. After the contest I stayed on at the Hoffmans' for a week.'

The Hoffmans loved the ocean and the pace of life there felt more like home at Lorne. Their house was on the beach at Capistrano with boards everywhere and a small fleet of Hobie Alter's catamarans sitting on a spare block next door. 'Anybody who lived there could take one and try it out.' Joyce's brother-in-law Herbie [Fletcher] would take them down to Trestles and surf. 'We surfed every day, but Joyce also showed me around the city.' That week they visited Disneyland, Beverly Hills and the San Juan Capistrano Mission. Gail and Joyce, although quite different characters, got along famously. Joyce – 'Boo' – was larger than life and a little more 'California' (she'd been the *LA Times* 'Woman of the Year' in 1965), while Gail was more considered and a little more country. They struck up a friendship 'and we've stayed best friends to this day'. The pair travelled together two years later to the Puerto Rico World Titles, and when the World Titles were hosted in Lorne in 1970, Gail returned the hospitality.

Gail's return home was celebrated in all the newspapers, although a newspaper column had her in trouble a few weeks later. 'When I came back from California, the Geelong *Addy* [*Advertiser*] asked me to write a column, and I nearly got sued by the Barrabool Shire. I got called into the principal's office at 9.15 one morning and he goes, "I think you might be in a spot of bother." I asked why and he said that my dad had rung up and the Barrabool Shire wanted to sue me. I'd written a column talking about the lack of facilities at Bells and I'd had a bit of a go at them about the toilet block because it stank. My Dad and I always felt very strongly about looking after the beaches. Anyway, I was my diplomatic self, but there was a sub editor at the paper who'd changed the heading and hyped up the first paragraph in bold and he'd had a real go at the Shire under my by-line. The principal said, "This is a bit tricky for a Year 12 student." Luckily I'd kept the original handwritten column and Dad took that to the Shire and sorted it out.' Gail sat her final VCE exams, finished as dux of the school, and enrolled the following year at teacher's college in Geelong.

Gail continued to win Bells titles (she'd win 10 in all) and she remained in Lorne, worked as a teacher and kept surfing but in the following years saw less and less of Wayne Lynch. 'As Wayne got older and more independent I didn't see much of him. I went to teacher's college and I was stuck in Geelong – we were a one-car family – while he went to Europe with Nat and all that crew and became very famous. We kind of drifted apart a bit. I surfed with him occasionally on weekends but that was about it. I'd see him from time to time, which was great, but I wasn't even aware the poor guy was stuck in all that trouble, being called up to Vietnam. That would have been so incredibly tough.'

1967

Bob McTavish

The cover of *Surfing World*'s March 1967 issue called them 'The Wild and Wonderful Days of Noosa'. The cover channelled album artwork from *Strange Days* and even *Sgt. Pepper*'s. Standing on a wooden boardwalk in the littoral rainforest at Noosa National Park, beamed down from the Crystal Ship above, were John Witzig, Russell Hughes, Terry Purcell, Trish Thomson, Kim Nelson and Bob McTavish. Midget Farrelly later described them as 'the naughty kids on the stairs' but the cover was a statement of the times. This was Australian surfing's 'Summer of Love' and it was the man at the front of the shot, shirtless in sashed white cotton pants with the earnest expression who was leading the movement. 'We were on the cusp of a revolution, a global revolution,' recalls Bob McTavish excitedly. 'This was the year!'

Bob McTavish saw the surfboard as a vehicle for social revolution. A new generation wanted to move through the world more freely than their parents … and if you surfed, your surfboard was how you moved through the world. Having lived with George Greenough for three years in Noosa, Bob had long been inspired to liberate surfing. 'I wanted to go vertical like George, just standing up. I'd been living and surfing with George and I'd see him shred and was keen to exploit his vertical ability on a wave. I'd even made a 4'8". The first time I saw him I made a 4'8" I could stand on, but I couldn't make it work.' Surfboards needed to be shorter and freer, but to do that Bob needed to head south. Noosa was the longboard capital of Australia and no place to launch a shortboard revolution. Bob realised that as idyllic as it was, changing the surfing world from Noosa would be difficult. He needed waves and he needed a critical mass of revolutionary thinking. He also needed guys who'd be able to ride the boards he was envisioning. Bob needed to get to Sydney.

But while the ideas of one American had sparked his thinking – and while a kaleidoscope of countercultural change was coming out of America – Bob felt it was the established surfing order in America that had been holding his designs back. 'It was Miki Dora and Phil Edwards who had us bound up. They were the cultural icons and we couldn't do it back in '64. It took three years to make that break. What happened when we went down to eight-foot in April '67, we kissed goodbye to Miki Dora to Phil Edwards and the entire California hierarchy, the whole structure. We were out on our own. We went, 'no', and it was a brave step. That was the hardest thing. That was the biggest decision; to go contrary to the predominant American culture. It wasn't personal. I certainly wasn't patriotic.' Patriotism at the time was dragging young Americans and Australians into a pointless war in Vietnam. No, it was simply the old ways giving way to the new. 'We shared stuff across the world: Skip Frye became a lifelong friend and we were hanging out with [Dick] Brewer and [Mike] Hynson and Gerry [Lopez]. We were an international set of brothers – Nat, Russell Hughes, Mike Doyle – an international body of experimenters. Nationalism? We weren't into that at all. It was a global brotherhood and the boards reflected that.'

The catalyst for the move south to Sydney was a pitch from a good friend, Kevin Platt. 'Kevin was working for Denny Keogh at Brookvale at the time. He'd been working at Hayden's at Noosa with me and we both got the sack – another story – and Kevin got in touch and said, "We'll get 10 bucks a board off Denny if you want to come down." Ten bucks a board was phenomenal money. Boards cost $70 so I'd be collecting one-seventh the price of a surfboard.' The money was good, but it wasn't the money drawing Bob to Sydney. He had already lived in Sydney in '62 and '63, and he knew the waves of the northern beaches well. 'Moving to Sydney meant more powerful surf than the Sunny Coast. It meant we could get a lot of six-to-eight-foot surf, which you needed to go vertical. You needed the wave face. I was visualising Narrabeen, Dee Why Point, Queenscliff, Palm Beach. I loved big Palm Beach, big rights off the pool.' Bob moved in with Paul Witzig at Palm Beach and got to work at Keyo's.

Shaping work at Keyo's was often performed stoned, in a haze of Afghani hash or bush weed from Newcastle. This would have quite the opposite effect on Bob than it did on everyone else. While most people glazed over and retreated into their own thoughts, a couple of tokes for Bob invoked all sorts of ideas and theories about board design that he was enthusiastic to share. 'It turned out to be the most intense period of pot-smoking and LSD-dropping in my life,' recalls Bob. 'But I was really searching for Truth, and the hippy movement seemed to offer an alternative.' Bob's boards began to reflect his search for Truth.

'The first strike was the Easter of '67,' he recalls. 'I'd made two similar boards. I don't remember the size … I think they were both eight-footers, thinned out with double concaves and a raked Greenough fin. I later called them the 'Genesis' boards. Paul Witzig spoke up for one and Robert Conneeley spoke up for the other but I took them back to take down to Bells. I took those two boards down along with my standard Noosa '66 design, plus an experimental 9'6" wide-tailed single-fin gun, which essentially was a 9'6" version of George's kneeboards. You never took quivers at that time, you just took one board. I got some strange looks when I turned up in the car park at Bells with all these boards.'

'We were all headed to Bells as we did every year but I purposely wasn't going to compete. I was going to surf *around* the event without surfing *in* the event. I was on a bit of an anti-contest protest thing at the time. This was a statement. I was the Queensland Champion at the time and I'd come second in the Aussies the year before in '66, so I was a contender, but I was making a protest. I was trying to embrace some other way of seeing surfing go.'

Bob didn't surf Bells – he paddled straight out at Winkipop, the adjacent pointbreak. At the time the local crew were starting to surf Winki more often as it was faster and steeper, hard work on a longboard but perfect for something shorter. 'I surfed Winki the whole event while they surfed the contest at Bells and I realised short length was happening.' Bob's statement didn't go unnoticed. He got a knock at the door soon after and answered it to find two young Torquay guys carrying beers, keen to talk about Bob's designs and what he was planning next. Doug Warbrick and Brian Singer were young surf entrepreneurs who would, in years to come, make an art of staying ahead of the curve. They left Bob's Torquay unit an hour later with an agreement that Bob would send a consignment of shorter boards to Torquay once he'd made progress.

With typical manic energy, Bob went straight back to Sydney and worked on a board incorporating a deep vee and a wide tail, an idea George had floated past him to allow a board to tip onto a rail and turn up toward the lip. Bob made the board at nine foot to still allow for noseriding capability. The nose concave ran six feet down the board, a deep vee ran six feet up the board, the two overlapping in the

middle third. 'Very powerful, very animal,' recalls Bob. Needing to assume some kind of transcendental state and stare at the board's outline for a number of hours, Bob took the shaped blank home to Palm Beach. As he pulled it out of the car, Paul Witzig took one look at it and exclaimed, 'It looks like a plastic machine.' The name stuck. As soon as the board was glassed and half-cured Bob surfed it at Avalon ... for 10 hours, coming in on dark to a group of surfing mates around a campfire on the beach. They asked Bob how it went. 'Freedom! Speed! Thrust!' was the clipped version of Bob's hour-long, punctuation-free assessment of the board's performance. 'I was convinced surfing would never be the same. Or surfboards.'

The refining began immediately, and first order of business was to go even shorter and sacrifice nose riding altogether. Bob got to work. 'I made myself an eight-two with a deep vee. I dropped the concaves and added some rocker.' Bob took the board up the coast to Treachery and was besotted with it. The phone at Keyo's began to ring off the hook, and soon guys up and down the peninsula were riding Bob's boards. Bob himself wasn't settled, though. He was still wrestling with questions of length. Working late one night Bob stared at a fresh 8'6" he'd shaped, before pondering it over a curry and bottle of red with his gloss coater, John Mantle. He came back, picked up a saw, and took a foot off the nose.

Just up the peninsula and around the bends there was a parallel surfboard revolution happening, more considered and a little less cosmic. 'Full credit to Midget,' offers Bob. 'Midget at Palm Beach meanwhile was doing the same thing. I was living up at Palm Beach, living at Paul Witzig's house and late afternoon I'd pull my board out and go surf Palm Beach and Midget would pull his board out up the beach and we'd be looking at each other... and looking at what each other was riding.' Midget's boards were also coming down in length staggeringly, a separate evolutionary branch but, while they were moving toward a similar point, the way they got there was very different. 'It was a funny juxtaposition though between straight Midget and us dope-smoking counterculture dudes down here. He was determined he'd play it straight and be a winner, and we were determined to go into a new world and see where we were headed. We were doing our own things, but at the same time we had a rivalry going. We were neck and neck up until November that year.'

Meanwhile, Nat Young had returned. 'Nat had fallen in love with a girl who was a snow skier and he'd disappeared into the mountains through winter in '67 – May, June, July, he was off skiing and drinking wine, hobnobbing – and he didn't know the shortboard revolution was happening.' Three months in 1967, it turns out, was a long time. 'He missed those crucial months. He walked into Keyo's and said, "What the hell are these?" He made his own board, of course, because he loved to shape his own boards, and he shaped that at Keyo's. He was away.'

In November, America's Windansea Surf Club visited Australian shores. The club wasn't a local beach boardriders club like they were here, more a social club for surfing movers and shakers in California. By this stage, reports of surfboards drastically coming down in length had crossed the Pacific, and the Windansea crew landed right in the middle of it. They arrived not only with guys like Mike Hynson, Mickey Muñoz and Skip Frye, but also a film crew who would ultimately shoot footage for a film titled *The Fantastic Plastic Machine*. The Windansea crew held an invitational event at Long Reef. 'The Yanks were just blown out of the way because we were all riding the first eight-foot vee bottoms.' Neither Bob nor Nat competed, however – 'an anti-competition stance' says Bob – but judged instead. Midget finished second. His surfing in the event made the cut of the movie.

Long Reef was one thing, Hawaii would prove another. Nat, as reigning Australian champ, had been invited to the prestigious Duke event in Hawaii but had given Bob the invite – and the accompanying plane ticket – thinking he could turn up and get a start anyway. The last time Bob had been to Hawaii he'd famously stowed away on a cruise liner, so suddenly finding himself in the Outrigger Club in the company of Jose Angel, Joey Cabell, Phil Edwards, Mickey Dora, Mike Doyle, Mike Hynson, Paul Strauch and Fred Hemmings, well, he had to take a minute. While the buzz around the shortboard revolution had made it to California, Bob hadn't even been to California and was still largely an unknown Aussie. Bob spotted the Duke, who was sitting regally on his own in the corner and Bob did what any 'surf bum from Australia' would do – he took the Duke over a beer.

Once the Duke contest started, Bob's Plastic Machine got the ultimate test. The board, however, was made for hotdog surf, not Sunset. 'I made two boards for Hawaii but you could only travel with one on the plane. One was a nine-foot Plastic Machine, blown back up from 7'6", scaled up to ride Sunset. The other was an elegant nine-foot gun like a Brewer. In a way, for many years, I kicked myself for not taking the gun, but I had to be daring so I took the Plastic Machine and, of course, it was famous for spinning out at Sunset but, you know, after a while I managed it and made it work.'

There were plenty of establishment crew willing the design to fail at Sunset, but as Bob says, 'It at least got them thinking. On one wave I drove off the bottom and whipped it up to the top of the wave, and I got covered up at Sunset from a bottom turn/top turn snap. There were no photos of that. I got covered up but I wiped out, I got smacked, but the fact that I was actually there was the thing. It impressed Gerry [Lopez] and Phil Edwards on the beach. Phil was judging and had me first in my heat. I checked my judging sheet and two guys had me first and two older guys had me last. I didn't get through. Phil later pulled me aside and wanted to talk about shortboards. The Plastic Machine, the thing that made people pay attention was that they went vertical. How did they do that? At least they were dramatic.'

Bob island-hopped to Maui and rendezvoused with Nat, George and the Witzig brothers, who'd flown across to Maui to surf and shoot. They posted up in Lahaina, an old whaling town transforming into a hippy enclave, and waited for a swell to bring Honolua Bay to life. At the same time, Reno Abellira and Gerry Lopez turned up from Oahu with blanks for Dick Brewer to shape. 'On Maui I hung out with Brewer,' recalls Bob, 'watching him make a 9'6" mini-gun pintail for Gerry.' Famously, once it was done Brewer had looked at the board, looked at Gerry, grabbed a saw and took a foot off the tail. 'He made a 9'6" an 8'6" and that became the inspiration for the spring where 'RB' [Brewer] was doing the mini-guns. RB started with 9'6"s in January 1968 and by December he was shaping 6'6"s. It was unbelievable. You see Reno surfing in Puerto Rico in the World Contest in December '68 and he's riding a 6'6" Brewer. That had all happened in 12 months. It was unbelievable.'

Bob's Plastic Machine surfed far better on the clean walls of Honolua than it had at Sunset, but after seeing Brewer's sleeker take, Bob already felt his design had become obsolete. Things were changing quickly. Bob gave the Plastic Machine to 'some hippy guy' and jumped a plane to California. 'I was never going to go near a Plastic Machine again. Gone.' Bob's mind was already thinking about what came next. In California he was soon in the company of the man who'd inspired the whole thing in the first place.

'George picks me up from the airport in a black Dodge, an old Highway Patrol car,' remembers Bob. Greenough was back in California for the winter, living in the family hacienda in the Montecito hills, surfing and fishing out of his Boston Whaler. With no board, Bob got busy shaping something for the Californian winter of '67. 'I go to Rennie Yater's shaping room with an eight-foot blank and I shaped myself a board for Rincon. The board was 7'10" by 21", *tiiiiny* vee, lower rocker and softish upfront. Little bit of hull in the front but nice tail rocker and nice vee and hard edge in the tail, which was Brewer. It was a Brewer, but more practical. That board just killed Rincon.'

With his boards changing so radically, Bob's surfing needed to keep pace. 'That's the best I ever surfed in my life,' he recalls. 'I was 23 years old, fit as a Mallee bull, I didn't even have a wetsuit and I'm surfing Rincon in winter! It's freezing and I surfed six hours a day, every day. I was fuelled up on Taco Bell, as many carbs as I could get. Roll into Taco Bell, three burritos and out I go again. George and I had the most classic six weeks through January and February. He had a friend who had a house on the point at Rincon so we had private parking. We'd walk through the yard out to the creek mouth, wait for a lull and paddle out to Indicators, where there was only the two of us, me and George. Wait for the biggest sets, take one and pump and drive all the way down to the bowl, where there were 50 or 60 longboarders sitting there. I'm driving and it starts to draw sand and hollow out and you're getting barrelled and popping out and there's guys on longboards in the lip thinking you won't make it. Big roundhouse and then work the inside cove, which is a play wave compared to Indicators. Hit the beach, light a fire, get warm and do it again. I consider those weeks a real pinnacle of my surfing.'

Bob did four months in California, overstayed his visa and got back to Australia in March of 1968. The shortboard genie was out of the bottle and in the following years would go to extreme lengths. It wasn't clear where it was going to end, but what was clear to Bob was that there was now a new branch on the surfing tree. The most revolutionary thing he could do now, he felt, was recognise what they'd left behind as equally valid. 'The first thing I did when I got home was make myself a brand new 9'3" Noosa '66 and a brand new 7'10" Rincon board at Keyo's. I said there's two kinds of surfing in the world now – there's longboarding and there's this thing called the shortboard. I rode both, but soon was the odd man out on longboards.'

Bob was receiving large cheques from a deal he'd done with Morey-Pope in the States, and with those he left Sydney and rented a place at Wategos in Byron. 'In the morning I surfed Lennox. I surfed it on shortboards every morning when it was from three foot to 12. Then in the afternoon, when it turned southeast, it was off to The Pass where I surfed longboards. I clearly drew a line at that point that there were two kinds of surfing now.'

1967

Claw Warbrick

Torquay in 1967 was still Old Torquay. There might have been a thousand people living in town, tops. Pawson's Palace Hotel was still rocking and wouldn't burn down for another decade, and the Boot Hill boys were still singing terrifically bawdy jazz numbers in the bar. Bells was still a longboard wave and the old bakery in Boston Road was still selling pies. The bakery would soon close, however, and a year later be reborn after a bunch of local surfers moved in and started making wetsuits in there. One of those surfers was recognisable around town by his glasses and the gap between his front teeth. Old Torquay would soon become New Torquay and it was the surfers who would change the place.

Doug Warbrick lived at 66 Zeally Bay Road with a bunch of the good old boys, who knew him simply as 'Claw'. It was one of the old quarter-acre blocks with two small flats on it, and framing for two more that had never been completed. The flats had been built originally for the 1956 Olympics, when the exhibition surf lifesaving carnival was held in Torquay. Claw had bought the property for six-and-a-half grand, a decent chunk in those days but even in his early 20s Claw already had a mercantile streak and was spinning a few plates.

Young surfers were fleeing Melbourne for the surf of Torquay, although at that point there wasn't much else to do in Torquay *but* surf. Claw found himself in the rarefied position of being over-employed. 'I had several jobs and several interests all going at once,' he remembers. 'I'd do a bit of work for this bloke or that bloke. One job would run into another in those days.' Claw had already dabbled with his own surf shops in

Melbourne, Torquay and one down in Lorne where he'd employed a local surfer named Brian Singer. 'I'd started 1967 working with George Rice in Melbourne on the surfboard production line, a four-day-a-week commitment before three days down the coast.' Claw's trips back to Melbourne became less frequent and he soon moved to town full time. 'I was working in the surf industry, pursuing the dream of making a living out of surfing. It sounds lofty, but the basics back then were to make enough money on Monday to go surfing Tuesday. We needed fuel in the car to go down the coast and enough for three meals a day and that was it. Beyond that we had no real grand plans.'

Claw's main gig in '67 was working at the Torquay Golf Club. 'It was fantastic,' he remembers. 'First up I was a full-time greenkeeper. I signed on in the morning and signed off in the afternoon and had little supervision but I was quite fastidious in raking the bunkers. They told me that was an important job and if I raked the bunkers they seemed to be happy. I'd mow and tidy up but I also used to leave a surfboard down near the beach at Ben's Moll, hidden in the bush and I'd surf at lunch and after work. Ben's Moll had pretty good lefts and as a goofy I appreciated them. I'd knock off, have a surf after work, change my clothes then go back to the golf club and work in the bar. That was my other job. I'd work till we ran out of people to pour beers for. It was low pay but a lot of hours and meals were included, so I made quite good money. I was in my early 20s so I could burn the candle at both ends. They wanted me to do lots of hours though and that restricted my ability to go surfing.'

Like every other young guy in Torquay, Claw was mostly busy surfing. They'd been drawn from Melbourne to surf Bells, but found Torquay was a good springboard to a whole coastline of empty waves. 'Locally we were surfing Point Impossible a lot at the time. We'd head down to Lorne and Kennett River, which was a secret spot at that point, a new discovery for the Noosa Heads type of surfing. Heading the other way, we'd go all the way to Lonny and we'd started surfing over at Corsair. We didn't have our own boat at the time, although we bought one soon after.'

Claw's EK Holden panel van also disappeared 'down south' to the Otways and beyond, coastline that still felt like a surfing frontier. 'The first jaunt I had down there was to Johanna Beach, and once you're down there, there's any number of secret and less secret spots. We'd occasionally go further – down to Port Campbell, Portland, Port Fairy, Warrnambool – there were plenty of waves down there. We didn't know most of their names and just stumbled upon them. I'm sure they were already being surfed but to us we felt like we were pioneering them as there was nobody around most of the time. There were small communities down there but not a lot of surfers and they were generally pretty happy to see you back then. It was generally big, treacherous and sharky. You wanted some company.' You also needed a campfire on the beach and plenty of warm clothes, because surfing wetsuits were rare and rudimentary. The first locally manufactured surfing wetsuits weren't made in Australia until 1967.

The real scene though was Bells. The annual Easter Rally was now drawing surfers from around the country, and Claw was in the middle of it despite originally wrestling with the idea of surfing competitions. 'I felt surfing was a purist activity and we were free spirits and we shouldn't be in this organised surfing thing. I felt it was quite strange.' Watching Doug Andrew win the '63 Bells contest had warmed him to the idea, and after travelling to the World Titles in Manly in 1964 there was no going back.

'I remember some of the good old boys, Joe Sweeney and Al Reid, were starting the Victorian Surfing Organisation and they convinced me to join. I got membership number 14. I soon became a committee member, god knows why. I wasn't that into it but the contests were cool I suppose. So in 1964 they had the Easter Rally that doubled as the Victorian Titles and tripled as selection for the World Titles in Manly. It was small, sloppy southeast swell and I don't remember what I did, but somehow I made the team … That was another pivotal moment for me, meeting the cognoscenti of world surfing at Manly.' Claw did no good in the contest but did finish fifth in the board race down at South Steyne, which had been won by Nat. 'Afterward I was part of a crew who drove up to Crescent Head and Angourie, which was still a bit of a secret. While we were there Bob Evans turned up with Joey Cabell and Nat Young. Their surfing on the point at Angourie was extraordinary.'

Claw soon became a central player in the running of the Bells Easter Contest. 'I was a big supporter of "Stan The Man" Couper and "The Big O" Tony Olsson in the Victorian ASA. I was probably number three in the organisation.' Claw, at the same time, had never fully cut ties with the clubbies. While in other parts of the country there was a huge ideological divide between the old way of the surf clubs and the new generation of surfers, Torquay was a little small for that. 'In those days we were all mates with the people from the surf club, and there wasn't a huge split like there was elsewhere. I could paddle a surfboard fast, and I loved board paddling. At Torquay Surf Club I used to pace myself against Peter Troy and Terry Wall and I could paddle.' The old allegiance would put him in an awkward spot in 1967. 'One of the surf club guys asked me, "You can paddle a board, can't you?" I said, "Well, yeah." The surfboat captain, I think it was, put the heavy word on me to go, so in '67 I actually competed in the Australian Surf Lifesaving Titles in South Australia as a board paddler. I won a medal in the Taplin relay, which was good … then I pissed off back to Bells.'

The awkward part was that the clubbie titles had been held at Easter and clashed with Bells. It wasn't just any Bells, either. Bells in 1967 was hosting the Australian Titles for the first time. Claw drove overnight to get back. 'I missed two or three days,' he remembers. 'Once I got back to Bells, Stan Couper went, "Where have you been?" He kicked me up the arse and said, "You're our most reliable judge!" The waves were good. It was six-foot-plus at Bells and got bigger. They ran the event over three rounds including a round at Fishos in town and I think a round down at Lorne. Nat was in all his glory. He was the reigning world champ at the time and he won the opens, Gail Couper won the women's while Wayne won the juniors, the first of his four in a row.'

It was early in '67 that one of Claw's road trips saw him land at another pivotal point in surfing time. Claw packed the wagon and drove north to Noosa. As a kid, Claw's family had moved south from Queensland, and he'd been 'up and down those highways all my life. I had family at Maroochydore, which was my old stomping ground, so I saw them first and did a bit of surfing there. I surfed The Bluff, Point Cartwright… I even surfed Old Woman Island.'

Eventually he ended up at Noosa, surfing the points with a loose collective of surfing souls drawn from all over the world. 'It was a real melting pot,' he recalls. 'There were a bunch of Kiwi guys like Wayne Parkes, Al Byrne and Taff Kennings and South African guys like Andy Spengler.' Noosa had become its own scene and, in the middle of it all, sat Bob McTavish. 'Bob was holding court about surfboard design and breaking the shackles of surfing and going vertical, which of course he'd got from George Greenough, who was living there with him on the Sunshine Coast. Every day we'd surf with those guys and every day there'd be a new discussion about where surfing was going and how surfboard design could liberate surfers.'

McTavish would turn up to Bells at Easter that year with a couple of distinctly shorter boards and instead of surfing the contest at Bells surfed the adjacent Winkipop. Boards were already in a transitional phase. By the following year they would be unrecognisable. McTavish would be a key player, but it was in the air. Bob took particular interest in Claw's 9'3" Pat Morgan. 'I had a good board with a shallow vee bottom and a fin somewhere between a Bob Cooper and a Greenough stage one. The board had high-low rails and the boys were quite enchanted by it. I was a kook compared to those guys but I'd get a good one and every now and then they looked at my board. It was easily as advanced as what they were riding at the time, but then Bob was about to make the next jump.'

The conversations became more animated. 'We'd have these round tables after we got out of the surf at National Park, we'd sit there and have these discussions every day. I think we talked more than we surfed. At one point late one afternoon Bob declared he'd had enough of this bullshit, he was going to Sydney to change the world of surfing. "I'm going back to Brookvale," he said, "I've been talking to Denny Keogh and I'm going down to make a new style of surfboard." He wasn't being too secretive; he described it to me and a few others. It was going to be even shorter and with more vee.' He'd convinced Claw. 'I said to him, "Look, I've got to go back to Victoria. I'll drive back through Brookvale in a few weeks' time and if it's all happening I'll talk to Denny to see if we can be the distributor of the board in Victoria."'

By 1967 there was a movement of surfers across the bay from Bells to the racier walls of Winkipop. 'Most of the people who liked a bit of power surfed Bells, but then there were the early adopters at Winkipop,' recalls Claw. 'We'd only go there when Winki was shoulder high but by '67 people had started surfing it on a wider range of swells and tides. The boards could finally keep up with it. They changed the way the wave was surfed. They liberated surfers to go vertical and Winki was a more vertical wave than Bells.'

A few weeks later Claw left the Sunshine Coast and on his way home stopped in Sydney. 'I went in and saw Denny Keogh and told him we'd love to sell Bob's new boards and he said, "Yep, Claw, I like the sound of that." The other Brookvale guys had doubts about where these boards were headed. They didn't think it was going to work. Denny asked me what I thought. I told him that I reckoned he was onto something. Denny said, "All right then, you and your mates can have the agency for the Plastic Machine," which is the name Bob had settled on for the board.'

 Back at home Claw went into partnership with Brian Singer and Terry Wall to sell the boards. One small problem: 'We had no store.' Opposite the Palace Hotel on the corner of Bell Street was a mechanics garage owned by Mumbles Walker's dad, Ted. 'Mumbles was a surfing beatnik,' recalls Claw, 'a great character. There was a small office next to the garage where Mumbles had started a little surf shop selling wax and fixing dings. We asked Mumbles if we could set up on the vacant block next to it and he said no worries, so Brian and Terry went into Geelong and came back with a do-it-yourself tin shed. That was our store. We'd sell the boards out of there.'

Second small problem: 'The surfboards didn't arrive. What arrived was Plastic Machine number four for Wayne Lynch and another one I'd ordered for myself. That was it.' Claw remembers the initial reaction to seeing the board. 'It was a shock. It was fat at the back with a hell of a lot of vee in it … a hell of a lot of vee. Most of your turns were done at the back of the board and it was clear you would be turning from one side of the board or the other. That's how big the vee was.' The long and the short was they had nothing to sell. 'Keyo had hundreds of orders, the thing went ballistic and they couldn't produce them. Bob was away in America taking surfing where it needed to go; he wasn't interested in being a production shaper so we had maybe 30 or 40 orders but no boards.'

Brian took the matter into his own hands. 'Brian goes, "Right, I'm going to Brookvale to get our boards!" Turns out he found another young bloke on the rise who could fill the order of vee bottoms. Shane Stedman had just started a surfboard business and he said to Brian, "I'll make the boards for you." Brian returned home and said, "I've got someone making the boards, now we just need a name."' Starting with the words McTavish had written on an early incarnation of the vee bottom – 'Hot kid, rip board' – they played word jazz using every hip surf word they could think of before settling on Rip Curl.

Local surfer and artist Simon Buttonshaw designed a black and yellow sticker with the lotus flower, and, as Claw puts it, 'We were off. Our first boards were on the way, although as it turns out we didn't get too many of those boards either.'

1968

Wayne Lynch

To Wayne Lynch, 16, his hometown of Lorne was its own tiny, perfectly formed universe. Tucked into a bend in Victoria's Great Ocean Road, nestled between the coastal range and the bay and watched over by sentinel eucalypts, it was far enough away from the madding crowd while still possessing enough life and mystery and surf for a curious young mind to explore.

Wayne was third-generation Lorne, and as a kid the old ways still ruled. Lorne was a hard-scrabble utopia, but the Old World values of the town would soon become the backdrop to some radical New World surfing. Wayne liked Lorne because it felt like a sanctuary from a world closing in, but that world was getting closer. Once everyone saw what the teenage prodigy was able to do on a surfboard – a board he'd shaped himself – Wayne would go from 'local to universal' in a year. That year was 1968.

'Lorne had a very Mediterranean culture,' recalls Wayne, 'and when I finally got to the Mediterranean that year I understood a lot more about my hometown and how it worked. People grew their own food in Lorne. Every backyard had a massive vegie garden and orchard. My family lived on adjoining blocks with Mum's brothers next door and all the backyards linked up. No fences. There were chooks and ducks running free and over the road Mrs Fulton had a cow. My job was to walk over across the valley and get a pail of milk every day. You had to live like that to get by. That wasn't back to nature or country soul, that was *life*.'

'All my family were fishermen – my mum's brothers, my cousin, my dad. Fishing was a hard life in that climate but you had this really productive fishing industry in town. I

think there were 33 'couta' boats on the pier at Lorne – small, 21-to-25 feet, wooden, incredibly seaworthy boats that had originally been sailed. They had no motors in them. The couta industry was huge back in those years – it was the most sought-after fish in the fish shops – and crayfishing and catching snapper on handlines were the other big fisheries. The boats would come in full of fish and quite often a huge variety of species, including sharks, which would get caught in the craypot ropes and drown. But the sea was alive. That bay in my youth was teeming with fish – garfish, salmon, manta rays sometimes and a lot of sharks cruising around because the fishermen would clean the fish in the bay. When the fishing began to die off my dad became a builder. Dad was a good builder, very thorough, so I guess I probably inherited some feeling for things like that when I started shaping surfboards … although I was not very talented at shaping at all.'

Lorne, like most coastal towns around Australia, fizzed with life in summer. 'Lorne would be quiet in winter but it wasn't a town in isolation. It was bustling in summer and you had this great mix of people coming from all over the place; from South Australia, from Melbourne, from up in Wollongong, the Central Coast. There was a venue right on the beach called the Wild Colonial Club, which had been started by the Smith brothers who had a café called The Arab. Also down near the Wild Colonial Club was a huge building with dodgem cars and pinball machines and a big skating rink. My mum was a dancer and skater and she was very good. There were all these activities you could take on and the Colonial Club had the best bands in the country wanting to play there simply because of the location. It was a stone's throw from the ocean. We were too young to get in but had fires burning down on the beach at night, and sometimes the bands would just come down, set up and play on the beach.'

Lorne was a melting pot of different people and backgrounds and surfing was the catalyst for all this interaction and involvement. 'There was a whole group of us who surfed,' recalls Wayne. 'I grew up surfing with Gail Couper and there were a lot of female surfers in town, which was unreal. We all got on together and shared the waves. We were all friends. It was a way to grow up in the spirit of what a community is. For us as kids, fire was central to everything we did. You had your fire on the beach, you surfed, and you'd come in and stand around the fire getting warm, having something to eat, talking to your friends. It helped cement a community and it helped cement friendships.' They were innocent days for a young prodigy, the kind you never get back.

In 1967, Wayne began to shape his own surfboards, but while his hands were still developing, the surfing in his mind was light years ahead. In his mind he'd already seen the board he wanted, he just needed to liberate it from the foam blank in front of him. 'In that period I used to have dreams about surfing. I'd be watching people surf in my dreams, and what's ironic is that they'd be natural-footers, which was weird. Just as I was falling asleep there's a point where you're not awake and you're not asleep, and I'd have these images of people surfing in my head and they'd be doing these amazing things off the lip – what we call today re-entries – and they'd do 360-degree turns, and it was all really fluid and I saw it in my mind and I went, maybe this is possible. I'm a bit embarrassed about this, and I've only just started telling people about the dreams in the last couple of years 'cause people will think I'm weird or I was on drugs, which was not true at all – I was 14, 15 years of age. But I was very self-conscious of it, but I know now it's how you learn.'

The third board Wayne shaped would be the one that launched him into the spotlight. 'That was the board that made all the changes for me and it was quite remarkable it worked so well. It had the wide point back of centre and had a rounded tail. There were boards back in the early years called "teardrops" – very pointed at the front, they looked just like a water droplet. All the width and all the curve was in the tail. I had a mate who would come down to Lorne in the holidays and he had a teardrop and I was astounded at how much better that board felt than my balsa mal. When I started shaping my own boards I never forgot the freedom that board had and the way you could roll into direction changes. The transition from one turn to another was very fluid, and the front, because it was narrow, was light to turn. When I shaped that *Evolution* board I had no set theory at all, and over the years I've gone back to shaping like this, on instinct more than anything. Again, I was so young, 15, and I had no reason behind what I was doing, it was just what I felt. Just instinct. So I can't make any claims … I honestly can't. But the thing was *phenomenal*. What I didn't understand then, and what was key with those boards along with the weight and flex, was the end curve. They just had more curve. So that board let me start surfing a different way, the way I wanted to, trying some new things. I made a couple of boards with extreme vees. One was for doing barrel rolls and 360-degree turns. The board in *Evolution* was actually meant to be a replica of the one I'd made just before it. I made a scaled-down version, then I made the board you saw in *Evolution*. This one was shorter and freer and far looser.'

By 1968 Wayne was already on his way. He'd just won his second Australian junior title, but it was much more than that. It wasn't the fact that he was winning, it was *how* he was winning. On purpose-shaped boards, he'd jam a bottom turn, bury half his board, and train it straight at the lip. 'Those turns were almost accidental,' Wayne offers. 'The board would drive out of the bottom turn and I'd just follow it up into the lip and all the rest just followed.' At a time when surfers had broken free of the longboard and were scribing new lines, it seemed the guy doing it most creatively was a 16-year-old kid. Photos of Wayne in surf mags fuelled the hype. Wayne characterises his surfing in the period leading into the filming of *Evolution* as, 'my board and my surfing catching up to my imagination'.

In 1968 Wayne's horizons expanded in all directions when he travelled the world filming for Paul Witzig's movie, *Evolution*. Paul had been enchanted by the daughter of Jørn Utzon, the Danish architect who was in Australia overseeing the building of the Sydney Opera House. Utzon and his family were living at Palm Beach, up the road from Paul. The Utzons had recently returned to Europe and filming *Evolution* was an excuse to follow, taking Nat Young, Ted Spencer and a teenage Wayne Lynch along for the ride. 'Going overseas back then,' recalls Wayne, 'it was the most exciting, magical moment I'd ever had in my life up until then because you never travelled much. Certainly we never had the money to travel overseas. Only people who were well-off could travel overseas to experience the rest of the world.'

As the surfing culture took root in small outposts around the globe, Wayne began to see echoes of life in Lorne as he went. 'I think I understood the dynamic of Lorne better because I got out to see the rest of the world, and the rest of the world was still similar … where we travelled, anyway. A place like France, for example, you'd go to the markets and the people who caught the fish were the ones selling it. I can't remember seeing a supermarket there in France. We ate at little cafés with good food. The Steakhouse was the place to meet down there in Biarritz. You'd get all these locals and travellers mixing and talking politics. It was quite politically charged back then as well. De Gaulle was in power in France and there were protests and confrontations while I was there. There's a classic shot of the old bunkers on the beach and someone had sprayed "De Gaulle equals Swastika". That tells you about the political dynamic of the time. The social dynamic was quite different; it was really friendly and progressive. There were people like Miki Dora and Keith Paull there at the time, and we met people like the Lartigau brothers, Jean-Marie and Francois, who were wonderful to us.'

While the world was big the surfing world was small, and surfing not only opened doors, it was welcomed with a sense of brotherhood and bonhomie. 'It was a unique time to travel, and it was still that way when we travelled the year after. I'll give you

an example. One time we were surfing down near Biarritz – Ted, Nat and myself. We were heading down to the water near the surf club. Typically, as it was around the world, most surfers were part of a surf club and the local French guys have come down and seen us waxing up. They've gone back inside and come down the beach with these fold-up tables and set them up in a line right near the water's edge. Then they've walked down with chairs. We're watching all this wondering what's going on. Next minute they've come down with a little food and a dozen bottles of wine. They'd heard about us being in town and had come down to watch us surf. They're cheering each wave and they were pretty soon pissed and getting louder. They were so absolutely excited to see us in their country and to see surfing from another country, these people they'd heard about. They're getting pissed and rowdy and loving it and we come out of the water and they're all over us shaking our hands and hugging us, and that was a good example of how it was everywhere we went as surfers.

'We were welcomed for a couple of reasons. Firstly, in places like France they might have heard of us. But then in other places we went like Portugal and Morocco, they'd never seen surfing. We were the first surfers they'd ever seen and they were spellbound by this amazing act of surfing. When we came in they'd invite us into their homes and feed us. We couldn't speak a word of each other's language but it worked. I think we realised at the time it could never be like that again.'

However, the joie de vivre of France soon was a distant memory as they drove down the Iberian Peninsula, en route to Morocco. 'We had to drive through the heart of Spain, which was a pretty volatile country back then. Franco was still running Spain and it was intense. To give you an idea, we got pulled over by the cops at one point because we stood out like the proverbial with our boards on the roof. They wanted to see our passports. They took them and said follow us to the station, which we did. There was a heated exchange for an hour. They wanted a hundred bucks for every passport to get them back. Paul is negotiating with them and I'm just a kid thinking we're going to jail.

'Paul ended up giving them $50 and off we go. Then we break down in the streets of Madrid and there's hundreds of people milling around the car looking in at these foreigners and they didn't seem that friendly. At the time America was hated and you had to really establish that you weren't American. We had to do that a bit. Then we went through Portugal, which was a sort of unknown land. We surfed places I'll never know the name of. There were no other surfers and no names. The people there were really poor and you'd see them on the beach collecting seaweed, some of which they'd eat, some of which they put on the garden. Morocco was another planet, that was my favourite place. Morocco and the people and the culture was completely different to anything I'd ever seen. This was my first Muslim country and I remember listening to the early morning prayers in the streets broadcast from the minarets. It was so poor. People would sleep in the streets, just flop their *djellaba* over and sleep against shop walls ... and people would die in the streets! I remember one morning watching a tip truck come through the streets to pick up dead bodies, people who'd died during the night.

'But they were also the most generous people I'd ever experienced. They were poor people but would give you whatever they had. Every time we went surfing we'd come out of the water and we'd be surrounded by a hundred kids and they were so energised it was almost scary. They'd start throwing sticks and stones, not in a nasty way, but just wild.

'As surfers we were like spacemen who'd landed from another world. That interaction was so direct and raw and natural because they hadn't seen surfers at all, let alone had thousands of surfers travelling through. It was like that in Mauritius and even Africa to a degree. Hawaii, too, was remarkable in those early years. They were so generous. As a kid growing up in the era, especially in a town like Lorne, you had a remarkable respect for your elders, it was almost like an indigenous tribal respect. You understood clearly the elders had the knowledge you needed to learn as you grew up to earn a living and know about your country – "country" as in area, not nation. That was very much part of my upbringing in a place like Lorne. It's a country town and it's a really different cultural existence. When I went to places like Hawaii I understood that straight away.'

On the way home from Europe, the group flew to Puerto Rico for the 1968 World Contest. There was no junior division so Wayne surfed in the opens and was eliminated in the semis, despite being regarded as the most progressive surfer in the field. The contest became an arm wrestle between old surfing and new. Wayne understood how Machiavellian surfing contests could be, and already he felt a mild moral tension between the pure surfing ideal he'd experienced at home and the surfing he'd seen around big contests. 'I was so stoked to get home from those contests because there was none of that where I grew up; it didn't exist. We all shared the surfing and we were overjoyed. It was the best thing we'd ever found. Those aspects of discovery: from surf breaks to what's possible within yourself as a surfer, developing as a person because you're developing your own physical and mental strength, surfing gives you so much. I just saw the rest of it as a distraction.'

Evolution, when it was released in 1969, changed life for Wayne. 'People were very supportive and that film was huge all around the world which was great,' he recalls, 'but it came at a price. My boards I surfed in the movie weren't as good as the ones I had before. They were stiff and sticky and when I watched *Evolution* I'd lost that flowing lightness and that spontaneity. They were gone. I became much more conscious of my surfing. I was thinking about it, I was conceptualising it, and it lost its natural spontaneity. So I see *Evolution* as a downgrading of my surfing. I was trying too hard and the boards weren't working and I had all this attention and I felt my surfing was shithouse. When I was a young kid I was never comfortable being filmed or photographed. I became a bit self-conscious because I got all that attention. I'd only just turned 16 and I felt my childhood got cut off.'

The reaction of both the public and his peers to Wayne's surfing in *Evolution* would shape the wet clay of the kid, and he'd find himself a child star stuck in character. His surfing may have been revolutionary, but what he did next was even more so. 'I walked away from it and people thought I was mad. I'd been part of that era and part of that explosion and the whole scene around it, then walked away from what people would crave—the fame. But I loved my life as it was; *I just loved it*. I grew up in a remarkably beautiful place and I had friends who were very similarly minded, and surfing was the best thing we'd ever found. We all shared surfing and were overjoyed. But then I went out into the big world of surfing with all the intrigue and the politics and the rivalries. I was just a kid and the attention started to be a little too much and I was expected to do amazing things every time I was in the water. I started to feel the pressure and I started to lose the joy of going surfing, of just being a kid and experimenting. But wherever I went I was stuck in this one place in time and I wasn't going to do that. I wasn't going to go out and do 10 re-entries for the rest of my life to please other people. They were well meaning and that was one side of it, but the other side was that I was getting attention and there were people who didn't like that at all. There were some of the fiercest competitors of all time in that era, and they'd do anything to marginalise you and bring attention to themselves, so all these cliques and factions broke out, and let me tell you, it was full-on. In the end – and you'll love this – I just went, "*These bastards are mad!* I don't want any part of this … I'm going home!"' And with that, Wayne Lynch became Australian surfing's first reluctant messiah.

Wayne could always escape back to Lorne but soon even his hometown couldn't provide sanctuary. In 1970 Lorne hosted the World Contest, the contestants marching down the main street. Surfing had followed him all the way back home. Held down at Johanna, Wayne competed for a final time … for now anyway. He didn't attend the presentation night, as there was also the not-unsubstantial matter of him having failed to register for the Vietnam draft. He knew they'd come looking for him.

'I wouldn't have become completely invisible in terms of surfing, but I had to be with the call-up. I just wanted time out. I was 18 and I didn't know who I was, what I was, where I belonged. I needed to sort myself out a bit, and Vietnam just made it more intense, it was another thing on my shoulders, so I really, *really* had to go underground. And I just dove back into my surfing eventually and kept doing what I had to do; found my own little hole in the wall where I lived like an outlaw and really got involved in my surfing the way I wanted to. Surfed the way that felt right to me, not how the collective voice expected or said I should.'

1970

Albe Falzon

Albe Falzon's 1970 was consumed by two rolling creative projects, both of which were set to profoundly shift surfing culture in Australia and beyond. In October of that year, the first issue of *Tracks* magazine hit the newsstands, featuring – with just the slightest hint of irony – the Newcastle steelworks on the cover. *Tracks* was an irreverent, counterculture surfing tabloid modelled on the *Oz*, the magazine that had just been subject to the longest obscenity trial in British legal history. Founded by Albe, John Witzig and David Elfick, *Tracks* was part hippy rag, part radical surf manifesto. It tapped perfectly into the pulse of the times.

Albe's other project was *Morning of the Earth*. Once each issue of the magazine left the *Tracks* office – an old house on Sydney's Whale Beach – Albe would hit the road north to keep shooting for his film. The lines between the projects occasionally blurred but while *Tracks* ran on monthly deadlines, *Morning of the Earth* broke free altogether from the concept of time. The movie was a spiritual trip as much as a surf trip. It showed the world Bali for the first time, but most of the escaping was done on the NSW north coast … and in the minds of the surfers who'd watch it.

'Well, it's all still a bit hazy,' offered Albe later, 'but none of the shooting was ever planned. There were no storyboards or anything, but there'd be times when I'd go up the coast with David ["Baddy" Treloar] and Steve Cooney. They were just grommets and we'd be this triangle of energy. I'd be driving and over would come the chillum and I'd have a toke. It was a fantastic time. I mean, I was in the flow of whatever was happening and those moments were magic 'cause we wouldn't stop laughing all the way up the coast.

We didn't have a plan, so we'd drive out to whatever headland we were at and pull up, make a fire, camp out, smoke a chillum and wake up in the morning and go surfing.'

It was David Elfick, Albe's co-owner at *Tracks*, who tipped him onto Bali, the island at that point unknown to surfers. 'We'd heard whispers,' recalls Albe. 'I think David had heard of it from Russell Hughes, who was a quiet adventurer, a mystery man. Once we got to Bali we camped at Kuta and the swell was flat, but I could see this headland and nobody knew much about it, so I grabbed a motorbike one day on my own and rode out there. I walked along the cliff at Uluwatu from the temple to the cave, along these bush tracks. When I got to the cave here was this perfect little two-foot wave. I didn't have a board with me and I thought, fuck, I wonder what it would be like if it got some swell? As soon as Kuta jumped in size to four foot we thought, okay, this new place might be four foot too. Of course we got out there and it was eight-to-10.'

'Getting from Kuta to Ulu was a trek,' remembers Albe. 'You had to get a bemo out there and then walk in, which was a mission. There were no shops, no tarred roads, women walking around bare breasted, lots of chickens and pigs on the road. Heading out there was an adventure for us. I remember a shot of Steve [Cooney] and Rusty [Miller] walking through the rice fields on the way out there and Steve was so small next to Rusty and he had this tiny board with him. He was a grommet. He was tiny with no leggie but out he went, paddled out at eight-foot Uluwatu, no worries.'

The Bali sequence would shift the thinking of Australian surfers in the years ahead. 'The focus of surfers everywhere at that time was to head to Hawaii,' says Albe. 'No one looked to Asia for waves – no one – and I think the film changed that. Those guys who were really tuned in just went, wow, that island's right there. And there's another! And another! When you went to Hawaii it was already heavily Westernised and not too different from home, but you went to Indonesia and there were different languages, different religions and cultures weaved all through there. You were surfing perfect waves in the midst of this rich culture and that intoxicated surfers.'

While Albe had clear ideals for the movie, much of the shooting came together organically and many of its defining sequences happened by sheer good luck. 'Right place, right time,' says Albe. 'Floated in and floated out again.' The Michael Peterson sequence would, in time, become iconic, but Peterson had simply wandered in front of Albe's camera one day at Kirra in the winter of 1970. 'I can't ever remember having a chat with Michael and orchestrating it. It's funny how Michael seemed to be the only guy in the water. I don't remember it being crowded or other people hassling for waves, but when Michael was in the water really there *was* no one else. He was so dynamic. I had no footage of PT [Peter Townend] or Rabbit from those sessions, only Michael. My camera just went to him every time. I had no choice.'

While being fortunate to capture Peterson in his natural element, Albe would harbour regrets over missing another surfer who, by 1970, was proving harder to find. 'Midget was my idol as a surfer. Midget was radical. I remember pre-*Morning of the Earth*, he came up to the Central Coast one day sporting a Mohawk haircut and I looked at him and thought, wow, too good. He was with the Maroubra guys and his surfing that day was magic. By the time I started filming *Morning of the Earth* though he seemed to be in hiding. I don't know if it was intentional or not, but he didn't want to be there. I filmed a lot around that area on the northern beaches but he was never in front of my camera. That was about the point where there was a clear separation in the tribes. There was a strong leaning toward Nat's aggressive, dynamic surfing, and Midget got left out of the picture, and the further he got left out the more reclusive he became.'

Albe had a saying about sprawling, creative projects, that you never entirely finish them, you simply walk away from them at some point. Into a second year of shooting on *Morning of the Earth*, Albe was close to walking away but still had one great sequence to shoot. 'That session of Nat at Broken Head I just got by the skin of my teeth,' recalls Albe. Nat Young had been invited on the Bali trip but had instead already committed to travelling to South Africa with Paul Witzig to film *Sea of Joy*. He'd been living at Whale Beach at that point, but by the time Albe finally shot the sequence he was living up at Broken Head. 'He was one of the first people to get land up there and I remember staying at his place soon afterward,' recalls Albe. 'What Nat was doing, living on his property up there, building his house and living a simple surfing life, that tapped into the higher purpose of the movie. I remember it was on the back end of a swell, there was no one out at Broken and Nat paddled out for that one session and we jagged those incredible rides for the film. The movie was already done, but it was too good and had to go in.'

That just left the editing, and while the filming had taken almost two years, the edit flowed. Albe crafted the movie in the garage of the *Tracks* house with a mantra repeating in his head. 'Albie Thoms came up to Whale Beach to help me,' recalls Albe. 'I had no idea about editing at all, but I was really interested in putting the pieces of the puzzle together. Albie sat me down and showed me how to work the Moviola. I was living upstairs and I had this little editing room under the garage to cut the film, which was fantastic because I could see the surf from the window as I worked. We started editing and by the time he came up the following weekend I'd cut a lot of the film. Albie was part of the underground film movement in Sydney and they were connected to the San Francisco movement, and one of the guys there was a guy named Jonas Mekas. I tuned into the underground film movement because I loved what they were doing creatively and stylistically. I started absorbing some of that energy, but the most important thing I got was a quote from Jonas – "We are the measure of all things. And the beauty of our creation, of our art is proportional to the beauty of ourselves, of our souls." The surfing and the music in *Morning of the Earth* became merely tools after that, because that quote became the central idea. That was the most important part of the film because for me that said it all.'

The first public screening of *Morning of the Earth* took place at the Manly Silver Screen on 25 February 1972. 'I remember I walked in and looked around and it was like I was looking at a family,' remembers Albe of the night. 'My biological family was there, my surfing family was there, but what was more important was my spiritual family was there. I looked at everybody and I knew everyone and I looked at them all and they were all radiating. I looked at them and I looked through their physical form. The lights went down and I looked over and there was a glow, and I was like, whoa, what is that? And now I reflect back on it I remember that moment so clearly. It was just incredible. We started the film and there was silence in the theatre. It was deadly silence and I didn't know how to interpret that because I had no expectations about how the film was going to be received. I didn't make the film for the accolades; I just wanted to make this beautiful film about surfing.

'Anyhow, during the film I walked out. I walked out of the theatre onto the street in Manly and there was no one around, it was dead quiet, no traffic, and there's Wayne Thomas pacing, smoking a cigarette.' G. Wayne Thomas was a Kiwi musician who'd produced and contributed songs to the film's soundtrack. 'I went, "Fuck, what are you doing out here?" He was the opposite to everyone in the theatre, he was totally anxious about how it was going to be received. He went, "Let's go for a drive" so we drove up to North Head. We got out of the car and leaned against the railing and it was this beautiful starry night and we took a moment to enjoy what we'd just done. It was really poignant. We were young and we were ambitious and we both wanted to create something beautiful. We had no idea where the film was going to go, but we'd created this movie and it was a first for him and a first for me. There was an after party but we didn't go back. We said goodnight and I drove home to Whale Beach and that was it.

'I remember waking up the next morning and there was a clarity and an emptiness and it was amazing. There was nothing there. You know sometimes when you surf you paddle out with a head full of thoughts but each wave washes one of them away till there's nothing left but the waves? You're in a perfect void. I lay there with my head on the pillow and that's exactly how I felt.'

●

Almost 50 years after it was released, *Morning of the Earth* is today revered as one of the purest statements of the surfing spirit. It had a profound effect on surfers around the world, none more so than Albe himself. He's been up the coast pretty much ever since, living on a parcel of hinterland behind a stretch of still-empty coastline and living the ideals of his movie. Albe hadn't watched the movie in years until recently, when he got the news that Baddy Treloar, one of the talismanic stars of the movie, had just passed. Baddy's sequence in the movie had been shot at Angourie Point, where he'd moved soon after and made a life for himself, fishing and surfing. Baddy, poetically, had died shortly after surfing the point, just as he'd done in the movie. He caught one last wave, came in and sat under a pandanus tree, and peacefully called time.

Baddy's passing prompted Albe to pull out the original master and watch the movie for the first time in years. 'I sat here by myself and I just watched this film and it took me into this space. Baddy had died a week earlier and it transported me back. The music was warbly and the original scratches and dust were there and it took me straight back to that time when we were travelling up the coast together shooting it. Baddy and I both lived that life. We both moved up here soon after the film. We lived that life and shared that life over a lot of years. He'd drive down from Angourie every so often and say g'day and we'd surf and talk about life. I thought about him a lot as I watched it.'

'My treehouse is only 40 minutes' drive from Crescent Head, down the back road along the Belmore River. The road comes out near Crescent and it's always been one of my favourite drives on the east coast of Australia. I actually shot a few scenes from *Morning of the Earth* there when we were cruising up the coast with Stephen and Baddy. Even today you'll only pass three or four cars. As you drive at sunrise the light is incredible, the river is alive and there's birds everywhere and animals and there's honesty boxes and classic old farms that haven't been renovated. It's like time has stood still there. That was the attraction for me and that was the attraction for Baddy.

'I had a morning recently where I went down and surfed Crescent on a full moon. It was an hour before sunrise, and the moon was still 30 degrees off setting. There were half a dozen people out already – "The Mushrooms" crew who are there every morning – just five or six of us. It was magic. The surf was phenomenal. It was head high, maybe bigger on the sets, and you'd surf these waves straight into the moonlight. You surfed into the moon and along the path of light across the ocean. It was like being on acid. Then as the moon set and the sun rose and broke through the clouds everything turned golden. Everyone in the water, I looked at them and they were all gold, everything was gold … the water, the waves, the surfers. It was all I could do to stay grounded on my board. It was such a trip.'

1970

Peter Drouyn

'Peter is 19 and walking home alone one night from the Skyline in Surfers Paradise. He's a little bit soaked but Peter could handle his grog. He was walking home on Wharf Road. In those days there were no high rises and he lived with my brother and mum and dad in a little laneway called Sandra Parade. Peter's walking and suddenly this sheet of light engulfs him, encircles him, and there's a misty fog surrounding him. He is totally, like, "What's going on here!?" He was scared. He froze like it was a shark circling him. He could make out the side of a metal object, a curved metal panel and it had lights blazing around it back and forth, coloured lights that came to a single square point and they all slotted into their holes then circled around again. It was completely silent. It just made a shhh, a windy noise. That's why it never woke anybody up. But after three minutes it stays there but no one gets out and nothing happens. Peter feels a bit more comfortable 'cause he's not dead or not being abducted when suddenly it's gone, just a little white speck just shooting off into the sky. Well, Peter ran for his life down the laneway, ran with his shouting waking up the household. "You don't know what's happened! A UFO!" I told Tony and Mum but it was too much for everybody … and too much for Peter.'

The story of Peter Drouyn's close encounter in the back streets of Surfers Paradise would be recounted decades later, but not by Peter. By that stage Peter had reinvented himself as Westerly Windina, a transgender, platinum-blonde Hollywood starlet. Peter was gone, although not entirely; in the recounting detailed above he appears in both first and third person.

The encounter happened in 1969. At this point Peter already felt like he existed on another planet. Five years after coming from nowhere to win the Australian junior title he felt like an outsider in the surfing scene – the 'kingdom of jealousy' as he'd later describe it – his genius on a surfboard not only unrecognised, but actively thwarted. Peter felt badly jilted and as 1970 dawned he found himself at a crossroads. He had two choices – win, or reinvent himself entirely. The reinvention would come later. For now he had to win.

As a Queenslander, Peter already felt like an outsider. The Gold Coast was just stirring to life. The power base for surfing was still Sydney. But there were deeper psychological wounds within young Peter himself. The night before he'd won the 1965 Australian junior title in Manly he'd been beaten up by thugs and had to take himself to hospital. He went to the 1966 World Titles in San Diego but, as Westerly later recalled, 'Peter died in that contest. He was so depressed. It was supposed to be an Australian team but they just left Peter, a 16-year-old, on the beach alone the whole time.' Peter made the Australian team for the 1968 World Titles in Puerto Rico but fell ill, coughing up blood in bed. Again, no one came to his aid. He'd finished second to Nat Young at the Australian Titles in both '67 and '69, the latter after Peter had been handed the trophy and told he'd won, only to be informed that he'd actually lost to Nat.

'Peter was gunned down not just by the surfers but by the judges, by the media, by the public, who all seemed to deny him,' offered Westerly. 'The word had spread that Peter Drouyn was a rebel, a revolutionary even. Peter had been typecast. In those days surfing was a village and the gossip would travel far and wide. Peter would ask, "Why are these people doing this to me?"'

Peter also saw his role in the shortboard revolution as being overlooked. At just 16, Peter was shaping his own boards down with Laurie Hohensee at Mermaid Beach, who recalls Peter's obsession with making boards both shorter and lighter, his teenage hands trying to keep pace with his imagination. 'With Peter you might get one board from six that was ready for glassing. The other five you had to fix up,' recalls Laurie. 'His boards were just so small. He'd taken so much foam out of them.' Westerly remembers, 'Peter wanted a nine-foot board but he also wanted it to be only 16 pounds, which in those days was unheard of. "One layer of eight-ounce glass!? You're kidding!" Peter ended up getting on his knees and begging and they did it … and of course Peter ripped on it. He was tearing Burleigh apart with his power surfing on a nine-foot board. They were all watching Peter Drouyn surf.'

The shortboard revolution would have its totem moment at Honolua Bay in December 1967, with Bob McTavish and Nat Young riding their nine-foot vee bottoms, the torch passing to Dick Brewer and the Hawaiians. Peter Drouyn was also at Honolua Bay in December 1967. In waves three times overhead, Drouyn surfed a 9'3" Atlas Woods 'Stubby' he'd borrowed from New Zealand surfer Wayne Parkes. Peter wrote in *Surfing World*, 'Five boards were broken in half, the other five went in and that leaves me in the end, and that's no kidding. I had it to myself for an hour and a half. It got so big that I had to paddle in after a while because the whole bay was closing out from the left point.' Drouyn was on Maui with Bob Evans, who'd remain a staunch ally.

The shortboard in time would have several fathers, but what couldn't be denied was Drouyn's possession of the archetypal shortboard style. Drouyn merged power with grace, likening himself to a matador. In the week before the 1970 Australian Titles in Coolangatta, Wayne Lynch saw plenty of it. 'Peter's surfing was amazing. It was the most dynamic surfing I had ever seen at that point, and I'd done a lot of travelling very young so I got to see a lot. He put his foot right back and had this low, squat cutback with all this power. It was a pioneering move. The amount of energy he put into that turn was phenomenal and it didn't dissipate, it transferred perfectly, and he'd just drive that turn straight back at the white water. I was just astounded watching it, and I remember Nat coming out one afternoon at Currumbin and you could really see Nat was trying to adopt something of Peter's technique. Nat was much more upright because he'd come off the mals – and he was surfing fantastically – but he didn't have that cutback. Peter and he went wave for wave, while I caught a little dribbler to shore and got out of there! I might have got in the way and there were no beg-your-pardons between them. That's how it was. But I wanted to learn and I could see Nat doing these beautiful turns but Peter's were way more powerful. In fairness to Peter, that Australian characteristic of power surfing, that low centre of gravity, it came from him. Peter made that breakthrough, and Nat and myself and everyone else, we picked up off that.'

Wayne Lynch would win the 1970 Australian junior title at Coolangatta – his fourth in a row – and then it was over to Drouyn. 'I said, "This is it, if they find a way to cut me out of it this year I am going to give it away!" I went the hardest I have ever gone.' After years of close losses, it was now or never. Riding a short, flat-rockered board he'd shaped himself, Peter totalled 276 points out of 300 over three rounds to win comfortably from 10 New South Welshmen. There were calls made for a fourth round to give the other guys a chance to overhaul Drouyn. He fumed. It never ran and Peter

Drouyn was finally Australian champion, the first Queenslander to win it. 'How long could they deny him?' asked Westerly. 'How long could they stop him from winning?'

At the presentation that night, Judy Trim, who'd won the Australian women's title, recalled Drouyn sashaying around with the microphone, singing to the crowd. For an outsider to the scene, Peter was having a particularly good time. A born entertainer, Peter was drawn to the light. As surf contests became bigger and brighter as the decade rolled on, Drouyn would become the headline act at contest after parties, renowned for his Hollywood impressions, phantom race calls, his singing and his dancing. For Peter, the world was becoming his stage.

The 1970 World Contest was held the following month down at Bells Beach. With the Australian title finally his, Drouyn was a strong chance to win. At Bells he was far from the outcast kid who'd kept to himself in San Diego and Puerto Rico. Drouyn had a swagger about him. He'd travelled to Bells with his father, Vic, and was accompanied by a personal attendant, a young guy by the name of Johnny Walker who shadowed Drouyn around in a flat-brimmed spaghetti western cowboy hat, carrying his surfboards. Drouyn himself cut a stylish figure in a suede jacket, collared white shirt unbuttoned to the navel and a dazzling smile. As a child, his parents had owned a clothing store named 'His and Hers' and Peter always dressed for the occasion, although he might have been a touch overdressed for the mud and rain of the Bells car park. It was a strange contest. At the dawn of the '70s a fault line had opened up in surfing. On one side lay a purist vision of surfing and the country soul movement. On the other side was competition. The money and the lights. Drouyn belonged firmly in the second camp. There was no internal conflict with Peter, unlike half the field at Bells who seemed to want to be somewhere else.

Drouyn's rich vein of form continued. The board he'd shaped for the event was a six-foot Hawaiian mini-gun outline, sleek and suited to the push of the Southern Ocean. Glassed light, the board snapped halfway through the event and Peter was forced to surf a back-up. The event was plagued by bad weather and bad surf and ran two days over time. The World title came down to a heavyweight final at rural Johanna between Nat, Midget, Drouyn, Hawaiians Reno Abellira and Keone Downing and Californian Rolf Aurness, the son of *Gunsmoke* actor James Arness. The final was sent out at 4.30pm with barely enough daylight left to finish it. There were just a handful of people on the beach, including a local dairy farmer who'd driven up on his tractor to see what the commotion was. Nat rode too short a board. Drouyn sat on the right side of the peak and, as *Surfing World* reported, 'takes out the prize for the longest rides and the best cover-ups'. Drouyn would finish third, behind Aurness, who walked up the beach the winner, five minutes after the sun had gone down.

In June, Peter celebrated his 21st birthday at the Beachcomber Hotel in Cavill Avenue, Surfers Paradise. He wore a grey suit and tie, but by the end of the night he'd lost his jacket and shoes. The dancefloor was full of sweaty, shirtless surfers. These were all young guys who'd taken Peter's lead into the surf. At the northern end of the Gold Coast, Drouyn was a talismanic figure. Paul Neilsen, flailing wildly on the dancefloor that night, would beat Drouyn the following year to win the '71 Aussie title. Windansea boardriding club meanwhile opened a chapter at Surfers Paradise in 1970, run out the back of the Bikini Empire store on Cavill Avenue. The Californian club was fast and flashy and suited Surfers Paradise. Their president was a longboarder by the name of Darrell Eastlake, who'd eventually leave Windansea for a career calling Rugby League games for Channel Nine.

'Peter Drouyn received an invitation to the Duke's contest one day late last year and the next day he was on the plane and heading for the islands. After an impressive list of contest firsts Peter was pretty well primed for the island contests. If anyone was more deserving of a few wins, it was Drouyn.' The story in *Tracks* heralding Drouyn's triumphant 1970 Hawaiian season talked intimately about Drouyn's competitive psychology. Drouyn was serious. He'd won pretty much everything at home, and that just left Hawaii, which didn't come with the same personal baggage. Hawaii was just Peter against the ocean.

The night before the Smirnoff contest at Makaha, Peter was invited to Buzzy Trent's house, along with Mike Doyle and Nat. The legendary Trent held court, filling their heads with stories of surfing giant Makaha late into the night. The trio slept on couches and the following morning turned up to see Makaha 12-foot and flawless. Drouyn finished a respectable fourth at the Smirnoff. Nat won, the last great win of his career. At the Duke contest soon after – this time held at Sunset – Peter surfed the final and returned to the beach to the backslapping congratulations of friends, only to learn soon after he'd lost the final to Hawaiian Jeff Hakman by half a point. Peter sighed. That just left the Makaha contest.

The *Tracks* report described the Makaha International as 'one of the hardest contests for an "outsider" to win, heavily influenced by hometown politics it is generally biased toward Hawaiian surfers.' The outsider was a role Peter was born to play. Drouyn drove his 'Vauxhall Victor' that he'd bought for $100 across to the West Side to find Makaha 10-foot and firing. 'Drouyn hit the water with only one desire,' reported *Tracks*.

'He completely closed his mind off to everything else. Drouyn is just canny enough to be able to play "The Makaha Game", he waited for the best waves, waves that would suit his determined and aggressive nature.' The *Tracks* report concluded, 'Drouyn's plan worked and he had surfed well. Half an hour after the contests the finalists were summoned in front of the official caravan site. The crowd were as anxious as the contestants to hear the results. A cold sweat ran over Drouyn's body. Third place Jeff Hakman from Hawaii. Second place … Felipe Pomar from Peru. Peter had done what he had set out to do, what he had been chasing for several years.' The biggest win of Peter's career was followed the week after by 'easily the closest call of my life' when Peter lost his board at 20-foot Sunset.

Peter returned home in January 1971. A young Rabbit Bartholomew recalls in *Switchfoot* watching Drouyn soon after, a surfer at the height of his powers. 'The best session I ever saw Drouyn have is one of the best sessions I ever saw anyone have. It was the day he arrived home from Hawaii; he's just won the Makaha International. He arrived home and Kirra was just unbelievable, it was so perfect. I'd been surfing it. There was this buzz, like … "Drouyn's arrived!" I was like, great! I got out of the water, went into the Kirra shed and just sat there and watched. This particular session he was going faster than anyone … he was on this unbelievable narrow little board. It was about 17" wide, this little spear. The way Drouyn surfed Kirra was just extraordinary, he was just so fast, so brilliant. He was at the absolute apex of his career, I reckon, that day.'

After his Makaha win, Peter was openly lauded as the best surfer in the world. The validation he'd sought for so long had finally arrived. So where did Peter go from here? What lay next? After finally winning, Peter would now begin to reinvent himself. In 1971 he enrolled in the National Institute of Dramatic Art (NIDA) in Sydney. Bob Evans paid the fee. Drouyn studied the Stanislavski 'method' style of acting, which he employed not only on the stage, but in the ocean. Two years later Evans and Drouyn would collaborate on his movie, simply called *Drouyn*. It was the role he was born to play.

1970

Nat Young

It's funny the things that stick with you. During the previous
Hawaiian winter, Nat Young had paddled out to surf Sunset Beach. Clean west swell,
light trades, healthy crowd. Nat sat wide and stroked into a peak. He shot down the wave
face but just as he was about to swing down the line, he sensed he wasn't alone. He looked
over his shoulder and there was a guy on his inside, 'a hippy looking guy' with a wide gait
like a cowboy. Nat remembers time almost stopping as the guy whispered, not in anger,
more a flower-power admonishment, 'Hey man, don't bum my high.'

In 1970, Nat took on that mantra. Despite being only 22, by 1970 Nat had spent almost
a decade in the spotlight and was now exploring life beyond surfing notoriety. He'd built
a house at Whale Beach. He'd married his childhood sweetheart, Marilyn, and spent
much of the previous year on an extended honeymoon through Europe. He'd missed the
Hawaiian surf season entirely and arrived home in Australia just before Christmas to be
ambushed by a press conference grilling him about his future, most pointedly whether he
planned to surf the 1970 World Contest due to be held in Victoria, in May. 'Of course!'
Nat proclaimed stridently.

Privately, however, for Nat the idea of another contest season felt dissonant. Contests
were bumming his high. 'I was in a real period of limbo right then,' recalls Nat. 'I didn't
really want to do it, but I knew that was the only way I was going to be able to maintain
sponsorships and credibility and the whole thing. There was a real period for me where
I wasn't getting off on competition, but I was still getting off on the fact that I could surf
and make a living out of it. There was a tension there for sure.'

Nat had questions about life that surfing contests couldn't answer, but he couldn't get off the horse. Not just yet. He was the reigning Australian champion at that point and travelled to Coolangatta in April 1970 to defend his title. He was riding a 5'10" board that would have looked crazy a year earlier, but a space race had developed and now everyone in the field was riding *really* short boards. Nat made the final, but surfed straight over a rock at Greenmount and knocked the fin clean out of his board, knocking himself out of the competition in the process. Nat didn't have a spare board so that was his final, done. Nat unleashed some salty language, unleashed on what was left of his board, and threw his contest singlet away. As he made it to the beach he was ushered to the side by a short man in shorts and long socks smoking a pipe who managed to cool him down. Stan Couper. Nat had to pen a formal apology to keep his spot in the Australian team for the World Contest.

On the way home Nat decompressed in Byron, surfed The Pass, and he and Marilyn discussed the idea of moving north. 'We both fell in love with the place,' he remembers. 'I'd been coming north for a while now and the idea had always been there, but I couldn't really pull it off. We made the decision then and there that we were going to do it.' Nat and Marilyn had just finished their architect-designed dream home overlooking Whale Beach back in Sydney, but the experience had been somewhat spoiled when the house was broken into before they'd even moved in and their wine cellar raided.

Before Nat could move north, though, he was headed south for the World Contest in Victoria. His expectations were modest. 'I knew our boards were too small. We'd gone too far. I had a 6'1" and it just wouldn't go across flat water. It was fine back in the curl, but I just couldn't get over the flat parts. In competitions you've really got to be versatile, you've got to be able to adjust to all the conditions. You surf what you get, and those boards just wouldn't glide.' Nat made the final down at Johanna but it was won by young American Rolf Aurness. It would be Nat's last World Contest.

That winter, Albe Falzon was working on a film project and asked Nat if he wanted to tag along on a surf trip to an Indonesian island he'd never heard of. While Australian surfers were beginning to fan out across the globe, they were still largely oblivious to the waves on their doorstep in Asia. 'I was supposed to go on that trip to Bali with Albe, Rusty and Steve Cooney,' recalls Nat, 'but I was pretty involved with Paul Witzig at that point. Paul was shooting a new movie at the time that would be called *Sea of Joy* and he asked me to travel with him.' Instead of Bali, Nat ended up in Jeffreys Bay.

Nat rendezvoused with Paul, Ted Spencer and Wayne Lynch in Mauritius, before they flew on to South Africa and hit the road south to Jeffreys. 'When we got to Africa though we realised the boards we had weren't working at all, so we went looking for blanks, got into shaping rooms and shaped our own boards.' Nat emerged with a board he called the Big Banana. 'It was seven-foot long and bright yellow,' he recalls. 'It was a classic pintail I'd shaped to go down the line at Jeffreys Bay. I'd had to really lengthen the rail line, which meant I had to really surf it off the tail. It was a good board, but it needed good waves.' This wasn't a problem at Jeffreys Bay. They posted up at J-Bay for three weeks and the waves didn't drop below four foot. 'It was an amazing wave. It was a lot like Lennox Head, really, just better.' They tried their best to leave J-Bay but couldn't, the days melting in a shimmer of Durban Poison with just a handful of local surfers for company.

Their South African chaperone was Ant Van Der Heuvel. 'Ant was great,' recalls Nat. 'He was a good surfer and a lot of fun. He was organising our smoke and getting us out in the water.' The waves and the weed were so good the visiting Australians only vaguely picked up that, socially, things were done a little differently in South Africa. 'Away from the surf the apartheid thing was weird and we sensed that,' recalls Nat. The white Australian surfers would walk in through the coloured entrance at local stores, not so much to make an earnest political point, but more that they were stoned enough to think the idea of having a separate entrance for black people was so bizarre as to be laughable. The Afrikaans shopkeepers weren't laughing. 'They thought it was all deadly serious,' recalls Nat.

The next leg of the trip was to Kauai, which by 1970 had become a fringe outpost for surfers escaping Californian crowds and American society. The Australians rented a small house past Tunnels on Kauai's North Shore and posted up for six weeks. Taylor's Camp – a makeshift hippy commune on land owned by Elizabeth Taylor's brother, Howard – had been carved out of the forest just down the road, and the Australians' neighbour was a wild-eyed young guy who turned up unannounced one day and introduced himself carrying a pillowcase full of peyote. 'This was just around the time when Bunker got all the money from Clark Gable's estate so he was still pretty down to earth,' recalls Nat. 'Relatively, anyway.' Bunker Spreckels was riding experimental craft at the time – cartoonishly short, thick and with hard-edged rails – but on Kauai his boards didn't look out of place. There was a whole group of Californian guys now living on Kauai who'd broken free from established thinking on surfboard design. The surfboards had emerged from a kaleidoscopic swirl of good surf, spiritual exploration and acid. 'It was all in the mix. They'd all take LSD together and either shape or go surf,' recalls Nat. 'Vinny Bryant was a classic, but the real shaping talent was a guy named Bob Smith.' Smith had once been Bob Imhoff but as Nat recalls, 'He said, "You can't drop out if you take everything with you.'" The group were surfing groundbreaking down-rail designs, and that idea soon radiated out across the Pacific. 'When Wayne, Ted and I saw those boards in Kauai, we knew immediately they were onto something.' Nat and Wayne immediately shaped down-railers when they got home. 'And it was all drug induced, you know, and I don't mean that in a flippant way. I think they were doing it quite deliberately. As far as my own involvement with that, that's what we were doing with the peyote. All the time. As soon as we'd run low, Bunker would fly to California or Mexico and simply bring more back.'

When the swell dropped, Nat and Bunker drove to the end of the road where the Nā Pali coast begins and started swimming back in time, Bunker towing behind him a floating container of fruit and peyote. The pair spent two days hiking through the Honopū Valley, 'an amazing place to contact the Hawaiian spirits and explore our minds for the meaning of our existence'. Nat recalls feelings of superhuman movement as he climbed steep volcanic cliffs and swam laps in the North Pacific.

Interestingly, two years earlier two of Nat's heroes – Joey Cabell and Mike Doyle – had swum the 17-mile length of the Na Pāli coast in a state of what Cabell had called 'papaya consciousness' – a transcendental state caused by a hard, physical immersion in nature and a deprivation of any food but the occasional papaya. Before Nat left Kauai he recalls watching a giant swell wrapping into Hanalei Bay with just one guy out, Cabell, surfing the 'White Ghost', a 9'6" down-rail spear. Nat was taken. Nat got Cabell's shaper Steve Teau to shape him two boards before he left Kauai for Oahu and the Hawaiian contest season. Nat won the Smirnoff at 12-foot Makaha on one of those boards. It was his first and last win in Hawaiian waves of consequence and it felt like a departure point.

Nat returned home from Hawaii and he and Marilyn packed up and moved north to Byron. Marilyn was pregnant at the time with their first child – Naomi, 'Pookie' – and Nat immediately set about building a home for the family. 'We bought an old farmhouse in Byron, on Bangalow Road. It needed a lot of work though and my job was then to learn how to build houses. That was just a wonderful thing to do. I'd had a desire to build but I'd never had any understanding about how to do it. The great thing about travelling to America so much though was that you could buy a book on pretty much anything over there. You can learn a lot from books, even how to build a house apparently. I did a lot of work on the farmhouse with Garth Murphy and he taught me a lot about how to pull houses to bits and make things. Garth was a self-taught carpenter while I was only a bush carpenter, but I loved that program, learning what it's like to build. That was part of being a man.'

'The first thing I did with that house in Byron was rip out all the front and open it up,' Nat recalls. 'The old farmhouses in Australia were built to keep out the light. You didn't want the outside coming inside. Those houses were a very European solution to life in Australia; they blocked out the light completely. When we bought that place in Byron I immediately knocked down the front wall and replaced it with glass. Everyone thought I was mad.' The old farmhouses had also been built to keep cyclones out, and when a cyclone dropped down from Queensland the following year Nat was forced to improvise. 'That night the windows were just going crazy and my attitude to that was, I'm just going to open up all the windows on one side, and all the windows on the other side and just let the whole thing go right through. That principle worked pretty well, I must say. You don't fight nature so you might as well just open the windows and get out of its way.'

Once the house took shape, Nat was able to immerse himself in the waves. 'I lived on the ridge there on Bangalow Road just out of town and I'd see the lines of swell and think, geez, I need to go find someone to go surfing with. There were only a handful of surfers in Byron back then, so I'd go and find Russell Hughes. We surfed together all the time. We had our program every morning. When the swell was squarer we'd go to Broken or Lennox; when it was big and from the south we'd surf The Pass.'

Once the house was in order Nat could also focus on making surfboards. The ideas he'd brought back from Kauai soon took form in the back shed – largely, scaled-down versions of the classic, low-rail pintails he'd seen Joey Cabell surfing in Kauai. 'Shaping and glassing, I was doing it all in the shed which felt really good. I'd shape in a pair of shorts and no mask. Eventually I'd farm out some of the glassing and I'd do the shaping, which left me plenty of time to surf. I didn't have to work because I still had money coming from Dewey Weber in America, so the surfboard business was as big as I wanted to make it, really.' Amongst the handful of crew Nat was shaping boards for at the time was Ray Richards down in Newcastle, whose teenage son Mark would turn up occasionally, staying in the Broken Head camping ground.

'It was a wonderful life,' reflects Nat of the time. 'The change in the seasons, the empty beaches, the mangoes appearing on the trees … there are so many things about that time that I remember fondly. We'd have these big tribal gatherings with like-minded friends. We always celebrated May Day as there was a group who'd moved over from Southern California – Bill Engler, Rusty Miller and Garth Murphy – and they made life interesting for us. They had the big concept of what it was like to live an alternative lifestyle with total dedication. It was very, very back to nature. It's the only way you'd put it. I know it's a classic cliché, but for a lot of people in Australia in that period … maybe you can say it was a reaction to the Vietnam War, maybe it was Baby Boomers running away from the restrictions of their parents, or maybe it was just the fact of having marijuana readily available. There were a lot of aspects that came into it, but a lot of surfers were following that route, especially if you had the income already and you didn't have to compromise yourself with work. For me, I wasn't trapped at all. I was totally free.'

The only challenge to Nat's freedom came from the Byron constabulary. 'Someone grew a marijuana plant under the Byron Bay town limits sign out on the main road, which we thought was hilarious. The plant grew to head high before it got ripped out. Nobody really cared too much in the early days, but it soon became very serious. The local police kept a marijuana plant in a pot out the back of the station to show the other wallopers what they were actually looking for. Well, Russell Hughes jumped the fence one night and stole it right from under the noses of the police and we smoked it. They were as mad as hornets. It was a funny period because the police sort of made it very much a 'them and us' situation; they just didn't understand where we were coming from. They thought that we stood for everything they were against. Eventually we got a few police who actually surfed and then things changed, thank goodness.'

The lifestyle was idyllic and mirrored his days on Kauai. Instead of having Bunker and his never-ending bag of peyote, Nat had the bottom paddock that after rain would produce a never-ending supply of gold top mushrooms, which he and his coterie would eat in Vegemite sandwiches to mask the foul taste. On days without swell Nat would swim out alone around the Three Sisters at Broken Head, channelling his Nā Pali adventures. He'd then surf on mushrooms and remembers once pulling into a tube at Broken Head, breaking free of time and emerging to discover the sun had set while he was in there. 'It was a magic time. I'm going, this is the essence of surfing. One time I pulled into a barrel and looked into the wall of the wave and I saw a dolphin looking at me. You to me away, looking me right in the eye. I wondered what it was thinking. What did it think of me surfing alongside it? Was it as curious as I was?'

By this stage Albe Falzon was finishing *Morning of the Earth* and came up to shoot some last-minute sequences of Nat for the film. 'Albe came and stayed on the farm for a couple of weeks and we got some good swell,' recalls Nat. 'We felt like we were living a dream life and the film mirrored that. I think we're lucky we can have things in our life that are bigger than people in everyday life have, and that's the way we felt back then. I'd realised the essence of life wasn't work and it wasn't surf contests; it was family and it was surfing. That to me was it and that became very clear to me in those years.'

1970

Paul Neilsen

In 1970, country soul was in short supply at the northern end of the Gold Coast. The sandy tourist strip was in the process of being reclaimed, carved up and concreted. Meter maids were walking the streets in gold bikinis, the Iluka apartment block was heading skyward on Trickett Street, and old beachfront shacks were being bulldozed and replaced by high-rise apartments. Paul Neilsen was living in one of the shacks, on the beach at Garfield Terrace.

'We were just on the southern side of Surfers Paradise. We had a beach house there we rented, a timber shack called Four Winds.' Paul lived there with Dave Treloar – 'Baddy' – who was still a year away from moving to the country soul of Angourie. 'They were great times with my brother Rick and Dave Treloar in that place,' recalls Paul. 'Dave and I used to surf together in unbelievably horrible conditions out front and train and practise and feed off each other.'

Nineteen-year-old Paul surfed when he could while working in the final year of a carpentry apprenticeship. 'I was just finishing my trade. I was one of those kids. I left school at 15 and my old man goes, "Well you're getting yourself a trade."' Paul's dad, Bill, had been a builder before becoming the first professional lifeguard on the beach at Surfers Paradise.

'I was an apprentice carpenter and did four years of that and you know what? I actually enjoyed it. You think it's sapping your best years but it's really not. All I wanted to do was leave school and go surfing, but the trade wasn't that bad. It gave me a good work ethic. You have a job, you have money, you have a car and then on top of that I was getting money to surf from Ken Surfboards. I was getting $20 a week, which was a lot of money back then.' The Neilsens were a practical mob. Paul would shape surfboards with Ken Adler and Laurie Hohensee, although it would be his brother Rick – a great surfer himself – who would go on to become a highly respected shaper. 'So 1970 was really significant for me in that it was the year when I prepared to go to Hawaii for the first time. I had that on my mind all year. I was due to finish my apprenticeship in December 1970 and I was going straight to Hawaii as soon as I did.' Paul had won the Queensland junior title in 1969 against some heavy competition, which at this stage was largely coming from Coolangatta. 'Michael Peterson was the guy down that end of the coast, with PT and Rabbit not far behind. A lot of those early heats were important to me. I remember a contest at D-Bah, I think it was a Kirra Pro-Am, and my brother Rick and I had spent all week building a board for me to ride. It was small, shitty D-Bah and I managed to beat Michael … and it was pretty rare to beat Michael in those days. I can count on one hand the number of times I beat him and I'd be in a long queue there. It was a strange thing because he was mentally so strong but then fragile at the same time. He was jittery on the beach but of course when he paddled out he was in total command.'

Michael loved winning and Michael loved a smoke, often together. Paul meanwhile played it straight. 'We were trying to get away from the drugs scene in surfing. That was still a time when a 15-year-old kid told their parents they wanted to surf, the parents thought they'd lost you. They thought you'd be brainwashed into that surf cult. But the hippy period was well on the way out by then. It was a turning point right then as that new generation came through – guys like myself, PT, Rabbit and Kanga – we wanted a more straight competitive focus and not the whole other counterculture thing. We all thought how great would it be if you could surf for a living and make a life out of it. That's what we wanted to be able to do.'

The most influential surfer for Paul growing up didn't live in Hawaii or Narrabeen, but four blocks up the road. 'A bunch of us had gone to Bells with Peter Drouyn way back in '67,' recalls Paul, 'and we used to surf together a lot, particularly in the days when he lived in Wharf Road. We'd often surf out the front together at Broadbeach. We saw a lot of him. What an incredible surfer. We got to see him at his best.' In 1970 Drouyn was at the height of his powers, winning the Australian title down at Greenmount. They were buoyant times north of Tallebudgera Creek. Coalescing around the newly formed franchise of the Windansea Surf Club, the power base of Gold Coast surfing had – for now anyway – shifted north.

Paul travelled to Bells for the 1970 Easter Contest and witnessed a generation of his heroes beginning to question where their surfing was headed. 'Peter Drouyn is still on the scene, Midget's on the scene, Nat, Ted Spencer, Wayne, Terry Fitz… it's all that crew. So I go to Bells and all those guys are still there but it's right on the cusp; they're trying to forget about contests and move on. They're there, but they're also very anti-establishment at the same time. They were very much anti-establishment… I didn't know what that even meant! I distinctly remember feeling that as a young guy and sensing there'd be a big generational shift coming soon.' The following year, 1971, Paul would head down to Bells and win the Australian title himself. Peter Drouyn would finish second and Rick Neilsen fourth.

For now, though, Paul headed back to Queensland while the big names at Bells all hung around for the 1970 World Titles, which were being held a few weeks after. 'Thing is,' remembers Paul, 'when all the guys finished with the World Titles in Victoria a lot of them came up and hung out on the Gold Coast. I was living with my brother Rick and Baddy, and all these guys travelled up to the Gold Coast in late autumn and surfed all around here. I was totally starstruck. Gerry Lopez hung with us, Jack McCoy was here, Jimmy Blears, Drew Harrison and Reno, all those guys hung around for quite a while and we got to surf with them. Imagine being a kid and having Gerry Lopez turn up at your place. I remember Gerry surfing on a north swell out the front at Broadbeach, these long lefts running down the beach. It was a huge experience for us.'

'In late 1970 Jimmy Blears wrote me a letter from California,' recalls Paul. 'It's funny to think at the time that was how you communicated. Anyway, in the letter Jimmy tells about this new board design he'd heard about … a twin-fin. He'd drawn a little sketch, like the shape of a bullet with a wide soft nose, a wide square tail probably 15 inches wide with two fins on each edge. He said he hadn't seen one yet but he'd heard of them coming out of California. We were building boards for Ken [Adler] at the time – or maybe with Hohensee by then – but anyway Rick and I built this twin-fin. I took this 5'10" tiny board and rode it at Kirra and it was just mad. It was really quite mad to be riding a board like that at Kirra. It *felt* mad! I'd fiddled around before riding a few guys' kneeboards that had been 6'3", 6'4", and even they had felt tiny. This was something else. When we get the letter from Jimmy Blears about the twin-fin it was a complete blast. It was like that letter had been sent back from the future. I remember before that we were almost nose riding little Kirra. The boards weren't nine-foot mals but they were down to 7'8" and they were changing so quick. Anyway, that letter and that board really fired me up. I was very ready to finish my apprenticeship at the end of the year and go to Hawaii with Rick and another guy, Adrian Hogue. I kept working and glassing boards and saving the money to go, but I was counting down the days.'

Paul finally got to Hawaii in February 1971. 'I stayed with Randy Rarick. Drouyn had stayed with him before me and I think that was the connection. I surfed a lot with Keith Paull on that trip and I surfed a ton of Haleiwa because we stayed in town there. I surfed it every day – big, small, indifferent. I didn't have a car so you surfed where you were at. I surfed Avalanche, all around that area. I headed down to Sunset when I could get a lift.'

Paul also surfed Pipeline. 'Rod Sumpter was shooting a movie in Hawaii that year and was on our case that day, going, "Come on, get out there!" He was making his movie *Oceans* and wanted to get some film of us surfing Pipeline so Keith Paull and I surfed monster Pipeline. I was on a borrowed board and Pipe was really wild. It was a real storm swell and had just started to settle enough to be surfable, but there was nobody out and nobody around. So Keith and I walked down the beach, just the two of us. It was rainy and stormy and the ocean was wild but it was all starting to settle and we were the first ones onto it. There were a couple of waves starting to peel off and hold shape but it was still really big and out of control. We walk down and we're still not sure whether we should be going out or not and I hear this voice yell from the bushes, "Don't do it, you'll die!" I looked around and couldn't see anyone. I looked at Keith and we're like, "Shit, okay..." We kept walking and we heard it again. "*Don't do it, you'll die!*" Paul paddled out and did better than survive. He got a couple of waves that made the movie.

'We went out and it was wild but we got some good ones,' he remembers.

The following winter Paul went back to Hawaii. This time he arrived en route home from the San Diego World Contest that Jimmy Blears had just won riding a twin-fin fish. It would be a breakthrough winter for him. Paul won the Smirnoff contest and made the finals of both the Duke and the Hang Ten, all on a board shaped for him by his brother Rick. 'I suppose you could say I had a good season.'

1971

Mark Richards

'The shaping bug bit early,' remembers Mark Richards.
While other kids were getting pushbikes for birthday presents, Mark was asking for power tools. 'My 13th birthday present was an electric planer. I bugged the shit out of my parents to buy it for me. Well, my dad was pushing hard for it, but mum wasn't keen at all because she thought I was going to cut my fingers off with it. Once I got the planer, though, I was in seventh heaven. I was carrying it around. It was a power trip. I had all these foam offcuts and old boards and fins lying around, and I was just mowing everything in sight until there was nothing left to mow. There was foam dust covering everything. It was like it had snowed. I had no idea what I was doing, of course. I was planing stuff in the laneway on a set of rickety stands in the sunlight, blinded by the reflection. I was carrying the planer around thinking, look at me, "*I'm a surfboard shaper!*"'

Richards Surf – 755 Hunter Street, in the West End – was an iconic Newcastle surf shop. Ray Richards had started it as a car dealership, then it became a car dealership with surfboards, before it eventually became a car dealership with no cars, just surfboards.

The Richards family lived upstairs. The shop became Mark's second home. 'I often used to go to Sydney with my dad to pick up boards for the shop. He had a panel van and in the early days he'd drive down to Gordon Woods and Barry Bennett, fill the car and drive back. They were the first two board manufacturers he started stocking, and from there it was Geoff McCoy and Nipper Williams. At this point I used to tag along for the ride. At Nipper's I used to collect foam offcuts, one-and-a-half to two-feet long, and I'd take them home and set up in the driveway and shape mini surfboards out of them with

a Surform. Academically I wasn't very good at school, but I was good at anything to do with my hands, like woodwork, anything creative, so the whole idea of shaping surfboards appealed to me from an early age.'

By 13, Mark was already winning Novocastrian contests and his surfing leapt ahead once he started riding Geoff McCoy's boards. 'Geoff's boards were the most popular boards we carried. Geoff was the main man at the time. All the best guys rode his boards, everyone else wanted to ride them and his logo was through all the magazines.' With school holidays coming up, Geoff and Ray cut a deal. Mark would spend his school holidays with the McCoys down at Narrabeen, staying with Geoff and his family and doing work experience at McCoy Surfboards. 'I didn't need to be asked twice,' remembers Mark of the conversation. 'It was really my first journey out of Newcastle to another city surfing environment. I'd been to the Goldy twice a year with my parents since I was a kid, surfing Rainbow or Snapper, but this was a hundred times cooler.

'Narrabeen was just this legendary wave at the time. It was the premier wave down there in Sydney and featured in every magazine. You'd always see these lineup shots of North Narrabeen just peeling off, and the Narrabeen guys pretty much featured in every mag. It was in the era when Narrabeen had Terry Fitzgerald, Mark Warren, Col Smith, Tony Hardwick, Grant Oliver. It pretty much seemed like every good surfer in Sydney came from Narrabeen, so for a young guy I was kind of living the dream.'

The McCoy factory itself was in the ancestral shaping heartland of Brookvale. 'I'd stepped into surfboard factories before,' says Mark, 'and I'd seen quick glimpses of people shaping boards and glassing, but to see surfboards being made from start to finish, to see a surfboard emerge out of a block of foam, I recognised the work involved but at the same time I recognised the artistry and the logic involved.' Mark was a quiet kid. He didn't ask a lot of questions … but he watched *everything*. 'I was leaning on a wall or sitting on a stool watching Geoff shape, or Bruce Channon glass, or "Wicka" Hardwick sand, and I think Eris O'Brien, "Dappa" Oliver and Mark Warren were sharing colour, gloss, polish and finish coats. I'd seen all of these guys in *Surfing World* magazine and *Tracks* and here they were, making surfboards three feet away from me.'

The first thing impressed on Mark was that McCoy Surfboards was a slick outfit. 'Geoff was very meticulous with his work. Near enough wasn't good enough. Nothing was halfarsed. He was really quality orientated, and that feeling was echoed by everyone else in the factory as well. They weren't just spitting out numbers. They were going, "We're making the best quality surfboards we can and we're putting everything we can into it." You know, all those guys were great craftsmen. All of those guys were thorough. Bruce glassing, Wicka sanding, Mark and Eris and Wicka, they all carried that sense of craftsmanship.'

Mark, however, was still a grommet, and, 'the thing that stood out and was really cool about hanging out in the factory was that whenever someone came in in the middle of the day and said, "Narrabeen's pumping" everyone downed tools and went surfing. It was like this mass exodus. Everyone just filed out the door. I'm chucking my board in the car thinking, wow, this is like the best life ever! I had the impression up until that point that work was nine to five, no time for fun, but this was nothing like that. If the waves were good they were all out of there.

'There was this funny instance where Col Smith took me surfing one lunchtime. Col used to park on the other side of the lagoon at Narrabeen, near the rockpool, and he'd just paddle out from there. Anyway, this day we've surfed, got changed and driven off and somehow I've left my board behind. I just left it leaning on the concrete wall, full grommet move. It was a brand new McCoy double end single-fin that I'd only had for a few days. In those days you got one board every two years, so leaving it there was a big deal. We ended up back in Brookvale when the penny dropped, and I've gone, shit, where's my board? I'm freaking out and Col's gone, "Get in the car," and we've driven straight back to Narrabeen. The whole way I was freaking out, just going, "Oh no, it's gonna be stolen for sure! Dad paid for it, he's going to kill me." All of that. Col, meanwhile, is playing it cool. "Don't worry, it'll still be there. You were there with me. No one will touch it." He kept assuring me that it had this invisible force field around it because it had been left there in his presence and no one would dream of touching it because I was with him. We got back and, sure enough, there it was, just leaning on the wall.'

Narrabeen was also one of the most localised beaches in the country, but because of the company he was keeping, Mark got a free ride. 'It was amazing. I was completely accepted. I was an honorary Narrabeen guy for a while there because I was surfing with those guys, guys like Col.' The standard in the water was a step up from Newcastle. 'It was way, way more competitive than home. And it was a different way of surfing. The surf was better, and it was a completely different vibe because of the ability of this big group of surfers who were all involved in this great unspoken contest. As well as the big-name guys there were all these other Narrabeen guys, this whole other crew of guys who ripped. It wasn't just like those five or six, there were another 20 guys around that. I thought, holy shit. How good are all these guys? At the time I didn't know who any of them were, but they were ripping.'

Mark did two, two-week school holiday blocks with the McCoys, but also started tagging along on surf trips and contest runs. 'I'll never forget the Phillip Island trip for the Alan Oke Memorial. We were in Geoff's white, pop-top Kombi. Geoff drove, Wicka – as next in the command – had the passenger seat and then in the back there was a comfortable two-seater facing forward which folded into a bed and Mark Warren and Grant Oliver had that. That just left me and I got the shittiest seat in the car. It was this square, fold-out wooden bench with a vertical backrest, no cushions, right next to the little fridge in the very back. It was this medieval torture seat but that wasn't the worst part. It faced *backwards*. The drive was from Sydney to Phillip Island so I looked backwards for a thousand miles. Geoff barely stopped; only stopped for petrol, and I was in the dog box staring at the car behind the whole way.'

Trips north, however, were a little more upbeat. 'Again we were in the white Kombi and Geoff would swing through Newcastle and pick me up and we'd take off on these camping trips to the North Coast. Our first stop would usually be Angourie. We would just camp near that old rotunda thing. The Kombi had a stove and everything in it so we just pulled up and slept in the car park. Then we'd go to Byron and camp at Broken Head. I have these vivid memories of those trips and there being no one around. *Not a soul*. It was just us and the water at Angourie with Baddy and Rod Dahlberg and a few other local guys. Broken Head we'd surf on our own before Nat and Bob McTavish would turn up. I was just like ... I was in heaven, you know? We actually had a week at Broken Head where it was off its nut, four-to-five feet and just peeling. We had it for a week like that with no one around. Just us, Nat, McTavish and the dolphins. We were the only ones camping in the camping ground. You know, looking back and thinking back on it, it was a pretty special time. But we never went any further north. Geoff didn't go past Byron for some reason. That was it. It was like there was a set of imaginary tick gates at Byron that he wouldn't cross.'

The time spent with McCoy was leaving its imprint on the kid. Mark was always going to be a great surfer and on his own he would probably have been a great shaper as well, but that time with Geoff McCoy opened up a path to a higher plane. Mark embraced the idea of the master and the apprentice. 'Geoff was the guru of his generation. He was Australia's equivalent of Dick Brewer. I was lucky that I'd have both McCoy and Brewer as mentors.' The most noticeable aspect of the relationship, however, was that it was never really a relationship. Geoff never tried to teach him anything. Mark wasn't taught; he learned. 'I spent a lot of time with Geoff; staying at his place, travelling with him, surfing with him, and learning the basics of shaping from him. He never actually sat me down and taught me to shape, though. I learned by watching what he did, by watching the process.'

'Geoff was a very, very talented shaper, but more importantly he was also a designer,' offers Mark. 'He had a lot of great ideas. There are leaders and followers in shaping, and Geoff was a leader. He was technically a very skilful shaper, but he was also a great surfboard designer as well. He wasn't copying anyone. He was on his own path with his own ideas.'

Mark's future success on twin-fins was hatched during his time with McCoy in 1971. 'The first boards I rode of Geoff's were single-fins – round nose, round tail, almost like double-enders. Dead flat bottoms with big kick in the nose and that camel hump kind of deck. Then I think an issue of *Surfer* magazine came out with Corky Carroll or Rolf Aurness on the cover riding a twin-fin, and that was the first time I'd ever seen one. There were shots of them trying to do 360s, and not long after, there was a cover of *Surfing World* with Mark Warren and Terry Fitz both holding twin-fins. The first twin-fin I had was from Geoff, and it was that same sort of board – the camel hump deck, flip in the nose, and it was a wide rounded square with a big 45-degree chamfered-off tail. The tail was probably three inches thick. The first twinnie I had from Geoff was a clear board with a green glue-up resin line for a stringer, and it had a bright blue McCoy logo on it. I can distinctly remember riding the twinnie for the first time. It was fast and manoeuvrable and I remember just how much more responsive it felt compared to the single-fins. I was sold from my first surf on it.' Mark was a pragmatic kid by nature but his time with McCoy provided enough bold creative spark for him to eventually pursue the idea of the twin-fin in a landscape populated exclusively by single-fins.

Mark's work experience at McCoy's also landed him on the home beach of the guy who, in time, would see Mark's twin-fin and raise him. 'Simon Anderson was shaping with Shane Stedman at the time, so he was on the other team and I didn't really know him. Shane had Ted Spencer, Terry Fitz and Simon. The first time I actually saw Simon was at the State Junior Titles at Narrabeen. I'd heard about him, because his surfing reputation preceded him, but the first time I saw him I was sitting on the beach and he just wandered past with a board, and some guy said, "That's Simon Anderson." And I just went, "Oh, there's no way that guy's going to be able to surf small waves.

He's way too tall." I just instantly thought he can't be that good … that theory didn't last long.' Mark finished ahead of Simon at the NSW titles that year – both of them beaten by young Steve Cooney, fresh from his Balinese starring role in *Morning of the Earth*. Simon would win the 1971 Australian junior title soon after at Bells.

'That time with Geoff McCoy and the guys at Narrabeen really set a direction in my life,' offers Mark. 'My life would have been completely different without that. Without that initial exposure to shaping and making your own boards and the lifestyle those guys led, I may never have developed an interest in shaping. If that hadn't happened, the twin-fin thing wouldn't have happened for me, and without the twin-fins I wouldn't have won those world titles. Looking back on it, that whole experience, with Geoff and his crew of surfers and Narrabeen and getting to stay with him and travel with him, it set the direction for the rest of my life and I'm forever grateful.'

Mark went home, dragged a table into his bedroom to cut surfboard templates on, painted the wall at the foot of his bed black, hung the templates on the wall and went to sleep dreaming of surfboards moving through water.

1972

Peter Townend

Peter Townend started work at the Coolangatta pie shop at 3am.
He'd picked the job up at 14, when his parents Barry and Hazel told him that if he wanted a new surfboard he was going to have to pay for it himself. Mr Grey owned the pie shop. Mr Black ran it.

On busy Saturdays Ces Black would keep Peter there till 3pm but gave him latitude to surf when the waves were good. Ces Black was never going to stop him. The pie shop was one street back from the waves of Coolangatta and the call was strong. Customers gave a running update on the surf. Peter stuck with the job though; his brother Duncan soon joined him, taking on a pastrycook apprenticeship. But now at 17, PT's world was becoming bigger than pies.

There was a power shift going down in Australian surfing, and Coolangatta was at the centre of it. 'We'd all get pissed off,' recalls PT. 'The swell would come and the New South Wales guys would drive up with the *Surfing World* crew. They'd take photos of their guys and fill the magazines with them and we wouldn't get a look in. The new *Surfing World* would come out and it would be full of Sydney guys surfing Kirra.' Coolangatta, however, would soon be challenging Sydney's northern beaches as the surfing capital of the country.

PT had finished school at Tweed River High in 1970 and was still living with his parents up on the hill in Stapylton Street, behind St Augustine's church. One street over were the Petersons. One street back were the Deanes. It was a 10-minute walk down the hill to Snapper. It was five minutes to Kirra. It was all there in front of him and PT didn't bother getting his first car or a drivers licence till he was 22. 'You live in Coolangatta, why do you need a car?' He laughs incredulously. 'We'd surf the points. You surfed Snapper or Rainbow if the banks were right, or you'd surf Kirra on a swell. Duranbah was there if there was no swell and there was never anyone there.' Burleigh and Lennox were day trips, but PT also travelled to state, national and Australian titles. He'd surfed Narrabeen and Bells and he'd seen what was happening around the country. He knew how good they had it.

The 'Cooly Kids' were becoming known throughout the country and it was largely through the medium of film. *Morning of the Earth* had premiered on the Gold Coast in January 1972. The movie was screened at the local Miami school hall, but the movie's star only made it as far as the front door. Michael Peterson, spooked by the crowd, told his mum he wasn't going in. Michael hated the spotlight; PT was drawn to it. But there was another film released that year that launched the Cooly Kids properly. *In Natural Flow* was made by Cronulla's Steve Core, and it squared off generationally. At one end there was Nat and Drouyn; at the other PT and MP. 'Corey picked us up and took us to Lennox,' recalls PT, 'and in those days you had to park at the fence and walk in. Well, MP and I took a tent and lugged it out to the point and pitched it and we stayed there for a couple of days. It was one of the first times we'd surfed with Nat. We'd surfed *around* Nat at the national titles, but Nat was out there at Lennox. Baddy Treloar was out there too.'

Watching the movie, PT was mesmerised. 'That was the first time we'd seen ourselves surfing in footage,' he recalls. 'It was a bit of a revelation. You had the two contrasting approaches; mine was more the Midget Farrelly/California/Hawaii crossover, while Michael was all animal, pure Nat and Wayne.' As surfers from around the country flocked to Coolangatta it became a melting pot of surfing styles … and style had currency for PT. 'The critical movies before that were *Evolution* and *Cosmic Children* from California and the McGillivray/Freeman films. In those days that was the sum total of the influence you got, unless you had good guys around who you saw surf all the time, and for us that guy was Drouyn.' PT's celluloid ambitions in time – like Drouyn's – wouldn't be restricted to simply surfing.

The key to unlocking his surfing had come from a chance meeting in the red mud of the Snapper Rocks car park. 'I was surfing Snapper; a really fun bank hugging the rock into Little Marley,' remembers PT. 'Burleigh must have been small because Dick Van Straalen was there sitting on his car. I didn't know Dick at the time but I knew *of* him. He said hello and saw I had a Joe Larkin under my arm – the reddish, pinkish one with the bullseyes on the bottom from *In Natural Flow* that I'd shaped for myself at Joe's. The first thing he said to me was, "I heard you're good with your hands," and I'm like, "What are you talking about?" He said, "I hear you worked at the pie shop. Why don't you come up and shape some boards with me?" That's how it started. I used to hitch up to Mermaid Beach every day to Dick's "Spirit of the Sea" factory and shape boards. DVS had flown the coop from Sydney and was part of that movement and he had this whole groovy scene going on at his store, and then at Kirra. His design intellectualism was so far ahead of everyone else's. The only person I reckon who was on his level at that time was McTavish, or maybe Midget. They were at the forefront of design and I went up there and learned to shape with Dick. He was a huge influence on me and allowed me to shape boards to keep up with my surfing.

'The "Joint Effort" board was exactly that. Dick and I shaped it together, then I started shaping that model and selling a few. The Joint Effort was the board that changed everything for me. Joe and Furry [Brian Austin] were great craftsmen, but Dick was an ideas man. Dick had thoughts about the deck and rocker and some concave under the nose. He was into that stuff. The Joint Effort had a diamond tail. He took it too far sometimes though. Dick made me two 17-inch wide stilettos that were like rocket ships. I had to tell him, "Dick, these are too skinny. I can ride them at magic Kirra, but I can't ride these in competition."'

In 1972, MP and PT – Coolangatta neighbours and childhood mates – were the rising stars of Australian surfing. Nineteen-seventy-two also marked a turning point in their relationship as PT, a year younger than Michael, turned 18 and moved from the juniors to the opens, which put him head-to-head with Michael. 'Up until that point there wasn't that competitive friction,' recalls PT, 'but the moment I moved up into the men's it was game on.' The only thing that would make PT feel any better was that Rabbit Bartholomew, the third Cooly Kid and a couple of years younger, would cop it worse from Michael. MP made a habit of winning, while PT placed consistently. In the years ahead that consistency – in all kinds of surf – would become PT's trademark.

The 1972 Queensland Titles finished at Kirra, but it didn't look like Kirra. In May, the Gold Coast City Council had begun work on two rock groynes at Kirra to stabilise the sand flow and counter erosion. The immediate effect was just the opposite and the sand disappeared from Kirra entirely. The Queensland Titles were held in lefts at Kirra, breaking off a reef that had been uncovered with the disappearance of the sand. MP narrowly beat PT for the title, 294.5 to PT's 289.

Surfing those Kirra lefts proved serendipitous. The next event was the Australian Titles at Narrabeen. In 1970 PT had surfed the Australian Schoolboys Titles at Narrabeen, and the following year had stayed with Mark Warren and his parents for a month, surfing the lefts at Narrabeen every day. 'We were ready,' says PT, "we" being the whole Queensland team. 'We had such a dynamic team and the New South Welshmen could feel it.' When it all went down, with the exception of Mark Warren it was an all-Queensland final. MP won and PT – again – got second.

The big carrot at Narrabeen was the upcoming World Titles in San Diego. PT's second place had earned him a spot on the Australian team, and he immediately set about preparing for the world stage. 'This American shaper, Tracy Richmond, who was a good friend of Gordon Merchant – he eventually became Gordon's attorney – I asked him to shape me a California board.' Rabbit had qualified as a reserve and he and PT hatched a plan for San Diego. 'Bugs and I trained at home on the beachbreaks, not on the points. We knew the waves would be nothing like the points. Bugs was in school so we'd meet up after school once the onshore had come up and go surfing. The shittier it was the better practice it was for California. When we got there of course the surf was terrible. Bugs and I couldn't have been happier.'

Qantas didn't fly to LA in those days, so the Australian team landed in Vancouver, en route to San Diego via a PSA flight. The team featured not only the three Cooly Kids, but also Terry Fitzgerald, Mark Richards, Ian Cairns, Mark Warren, Paul Neilsen, Col Smith, Andrew McKinnon and Simon Anderson amongst others. They had high expectations. 'I'd have to say that from the point of view of those old-school world contests,' offers PT, 'that on paper it was the greatest assemblage of Australian talent of any time.' The whole event was stacked with talent, across the Australian, American, Hawaiian and South African teams. 'It was an all-star cast,' recalls PT, 'the only thing missing was the waves.'

The surfers were being hosted at the Travelodge on Harbor Island, San Diego. 'Development on the waterfront? We were Aussies, we hadn't seen anything like it. Even back then just the size of San Diego city proper was pretty mind-blowing for all of us who'd never been outside of Australia. It's not a blue sunshine either, it's got that dullness to it, so for us Queenslanders it certainly didn't feel like home. I think we were pretty wide-eyed, just soaking it up.'

Californian David Nuuhiwa was the star of the 1972 World Titles in more ways than one. 'He was the epitome of a surfing rockstar,' remembers PT. 'He turned up to the contest each day in a white Jaguar with his board strapped to the roof and he'd step out of the car in flares with this glamorous girl on his arm, wearing a fur coat. The first time Rabbit and I saw Nuuhiwa we were downstairs in the Travelodge playing pinball and he pulls up and walks behind us. Rabbit and I both look at each other. Once he was gone we laugh and go, "If that's surf stardom, we want some of that!"' (No grander entrance to a surf contest was made until a few years later, when PT himself would start turning up to event presentations in gold lamé jumpsuits.)

The surfing was far from glamorous. 'The waves were so shitty and people were just demoralised,' remembers PT. 'The only guy who didn't give a shit what the waves were like was Nuuhiwa, who was surfing all over the place on these little fishes.' The Aussie team crashed out, with the exception of PT and his California board. 'The waves were so much slower than at home and not "crispy" like we're used to. Everyone was bogging and digging rails but I got out on that board and it flowed.'

The casualties from the contest all retreated to the Travelodge, where it was every man for himself. 'It was so out of control. There were all sorts of substances floating around and chicks everywhere. As soon as someone got eliminated they were all over it. The Peruvians had brought the good stuff, and that was the first time most people had even seen it. Those guys were outrageous. They rented a boat and drove it into the wharf of a restaurant on the harbour. You've got to remember, this was Nixon-era America. It was a miracle the whole place wasn't busted.'

At the end of the week PT made the final at Ocean Beach with two Hawaiians, Larry Bertlemann and Michael Ho, both of whom were on Ben Aipa swallowtails. 'Michael was just 14 and was lucky to weigh a hundred pounds,' recalls PT. 'The waves were dribbly lefts coming from under the pier. You really needed to get the right one.' The final belonged to Nuuhiwa on his fish, but he got pipped by Jimmy Blears, son of 'Lord Tallyho' Blears, the famed wrestler and surf contest caller. 'The final night we went with the Hawaiians and they'd taken adjoining rooms and filled the bathtubs full of champagne and beer. It was on.'

The San Diego World Titles would be the last before the modern professional era took over … with PT's fingerprints all over it. But while San Diego had been an eye opener for him, it was the following weeks in California and Hawaii that would really broaden his horizons. 'Moggsy [Mark Warren] and I stayed on in California and ended up in Topanga Canyon, staying with Hal Jepson who was filming *A Sea For Yourself*. Jepson picked us up in his Econoline van and drove us to Topanga, where he lived two doors up from the point. A great shaper named Robbie Dick had a shaping shed out the back, while Jepson had his editing studio there. Jepson would play these records at night, stuff like Freddie King, which would then end up on his soundtrack. I'm not sure if Freddie ever knew about it. In those days Topanga was privately owned, so unless you knew somebody you couldn't go surfing there or you got run off. While we were there we met a guy named Mike

Perry who lived on the beach. He was working at *Surfer* magazine and would move to Coolangatta a few years later and we'd become good friends.'

They surfed Topanga and Malibu, but it was a chance meeting while surfing The Ranch that would, in time, alter the course of PT's life. 'We got in and surfed The Ranch and that's where I met Jan Michael Vincent, who was a pretty big star in Hollywood by this stage. At the time he owned a parcel of land there and I got introduced to him. Anyway, he turned up on the North Shore the following winter and we hung out and kept in touch and when the whole *Big Wednesday* thing came up, he wanted me to stunt-double for him in the surf. I'd just become the world champ at that point, and the Stubbies was the first event of the following season and it was just about to start. Hollywood called and said, "We want you to work on this movie." I surfed the Stubbies, got fifth and went, "See you later, I'm out of here!"' PT didn't look back.

In California, PT and Mark were due to fly on to Hawaii, so Hal Jepson drove them to the airport in San Francisco. They stopped and surfed Willow Creek in Big Sur, PT getting 'the shit scared out of me by the sea otters'. From there they stayed the night at Jack O'Neill's place at Pleasure Point before flying out for Hawaii for the first time.

There, PT and Mark found a share house looking directly into Sunset; three bedrooms, three to a room. They shared a room with South African Mike Lamont. The other rooms were filled with Peruvian guys and Brazilian Rico de Souza ... who'd come straight in hot from the San Diego Travelodge. 'Dick had built me this 7'7" stiletto thinking it would work, and I went out for my first surf at Sunset and on my very first wave I dropped in on Ian Cairns on that stiletto and nearly fucking killed him! That thing just wouldn't turn! I realised immediately I needed a new board. I'd befriended shaper Mike Eaton, and he gave me a 7'10" he'd shaped for himself. That's what I surfed in the Duke.' On the back of his world contest result PT scored an invite to the Duke contest, and from a pure surfing point of view the Duke result was the one that got him noticed. At eight-foot Sunset, PT was at one stage running second, before finishing fourth on a countback.

'I'd always been the Cooly Kid who couldn't handle the juice,' says PT, 'and here I was in a Hawaiian final.' He was invited back three months later to surf in the Hang Ten in the spring of '73 and got another third. The following year he made the final of the Smirnoff at Waimea Bay in the biggest waves ever seen in a surfing contest. The world turned quickly for PT. 'Just like that I'd gone from this kid from Coolangatta to making Hawaiian finals. Here I was, an international surfer.'

And international surfers didn't make meat pies.

1973

Michael Peterson

By 1973, Michael Peterson was not only the best surfer in the water at Kirra, he was the best surfer in the country. At just 20 he'd won the Australian title the previous year down at Narrabeen, the start of an unholy winning roll that would last three years. Pathologically competitive, Michael enjoyed being top dog, and as the Precambrian world of professional surfing began taking form, as the contests got bigger and the money flowed, Michael was ready to take them all down. In the Kirra car park, watching the surf in his two-tone grey FC Holden, he made plans. Michael had a wild inner narrative that would only get wilder in the years to come. He pulled a joint down from the sun visor and sparked it. Behind mirrored sunglasses his darting black eyes narrowed and as he drew back, he locked his gaze on the horizon. Without exhaling he let the smoke slowly spill and a cyclone of thoughts calmed.

Nineteen-seventy-three would be the year that Michael Peterson would take his surfing to the world … but first there was business to take care of at home.

Michael's year started with a neighbourhood *coup d'état* in the toilet block at Kirra Beach.

The occasion was an extraordinary committee meeting of the Kirra Surfriders Club, and Michael showed up that January evening with the intention of being elected club president. Michael wasn't good at losing and turned up with a group of heavy characters in leather jackets to ensure that didn't happen. In the confined cinderblock room a fight broke out almost immediately, the tension only quelled after Michael passed around a handful of joints.

The Gold Coast at the time was ground zero for Sir Joh's war on surfers, drugs and good times. Coolangatta back then was still a small fishing and tourist town, but in terms of surfing it had a subcultural gravity. Surfers from around the country were drawn there to surf the local pointbreaks, but as they crossed the border at Coolangatta they were often met by the jackboot Queensland constabulary who either searched and arrested them or promptly turned them around. 'Addicts, Hippies: Surfers Shut Out!' screamed the cover of the *Gold Coast Bulletin*. Surfers were busted. Michael himself had been busted the previous year for a small bag of weed. He had by this stage, on the back of magazine and movie coverage, achieved cult status with surfers around the country and busting Michael – along with Nat Young – had been a top priority for the local coppers.

The background to the coup was that Michael and his crew felt Kirra was becoming too straight. The club had split into factions, the party boys and the pros. Michael enjoyed his social excesses and hung almost exclusively with those who shared his tastes. He had some wild mates from Newcastle and Brisbane who'd joined the club, which had a reputation for being hardcore and underground.

The opposing faction, however, had set about cleaning up the club and distancing it from the drug scene. They saw the Kirra club as a stepping stone to a career as a surfer, and the only mentions they wanted in the *Bulletin* were reports of them winning contests. Michael wanted to win – there was little doubt about that – but he had no intention of doing it straight. The club split hard left and hard right, and the looser Michael's crew got, the more professional the opposing crew became. It was inevitable that it would come to a head.

Peter Townend was the incumbent club president and had grown up across the road from Michael in Coolangatta. The pair were childhood surfing mates but in recent years had drifted. Still on good terms, just in different circles. PT was obsessed with making a career out of surfing and cleaning up the reputation of all surferkind in the process. Michael, meanwhile, was obsessed with beating PT … and Rabbit, and anyone else in the general vicinity. PT was already on a red-hot losing streak to Michael. He'd lost the Australian Title to him the previous year, which made it six second-place finishes in a row to Michael. The presidential vote that night in the Kirra Beach toilet block made it seven. Michael left that night as the president of Kirra Surfriders, although his presidency of the club lasted only a week. 'Too much hard work, Chine. They can have it,' Michael said later.

The vote opened a fault line in the Coolangatta surf community that still exists to this day. The day after the vote, PT met with a bunch of like-minded crew at Mundy's milk bar and revived the old Snapper Rocks Boardriding Club, which had gone the way of the longboard.

Snapper Rocks would become the slick, professional club. Kirra stayed underground. Michael might not have been 'pro', but a short time later, he was a key player in the first professional surfing contest held in Australia. The 1973 Bells Easter Contest had been sponsored by local surf company Rip Curl and was offering a cool $1000 first prize. Michael zeroed in. He wasn't attracted to the notoriety of winning – he loathed it – but the money and the winning rush was another matter.

The '73 Bells contest was also the first in Australia to trial a new judging system out of Hawaii, which instead of giving each ride a subjective number out of 10, gave each manoeuvre a specified value and all the numbers were simply tallied up. Michael thought about the new system long and hard and shaped himself a board he believed would work perfectly – a shorter, more responsive 6'10". Michael's mind was going at a thousand miles an hour but his surfing could keep up with it. He'd fly down the line at Bells racking up scores like a pinball machine.

Michael's only problem was when he pulled up at Bells and stepped out of the car a howling onshore blew through the holes in his old cable-knit jumper. The wind was whipping up a wild ocean, and Michael and his 6'10" hotdogger were promptly lost at sea. He was nowhere on the leader board after two rounds, and it wasn't till the third and final round when Michael surfed an 8'6" that he found some kind of form. Michael thought either Midget, Peter Drouyn or Ted Spencer had won and took off before the scores were tallied and the results announced.

'Jesus, I won a thousand bucks!' was Michael's reaction when told later it was he who'd actually won. He picked up the cheque from the old Torquay Hotel that night, where the party was in full swing. The publican's licence meant he had to feed everybody, so the bar was shut for an hour at 9pm and the lights were turned on while a huge pot of beef soup was brought out. The only problem was that the Rocker Hill boys were all militant vegetarians and beef soup was soon soaking into the carpet. The publican gave up, turned the lights off and reopened the bar.

The Australian Titles were next, over in Margaret River. In those days most of the competitors drove across the Nullarbor but Michael, with a thousand bucks burning a hole in his pocket, flew. He was confident of defending his title. He'd already taken Rabbit out of the game by shaping him a 'special' board half as long as it needed to be for the powerful West Oz swell. Michael was almost *too* confident. When the contest started he got pinged for a drop-in and, incensed, stormed up the beach to confront the judges, who, seeing him coming, promptly changed their mind.

The final was held at Redgate, on a long left-hand sandbank that had formed when torrential rain had opened a nearby creek. Michael fancied his chances. So did fellow Queenslander Richard Harvey. 'Geez, I hope your next wave is really good, Michael,' said Harvey as he paddled past Michael during the final, 'because mine was just a blinder!' Harvey won. Michael stormed up the beach again.

The Australian mainstream press at the time had a particular fascination with surfing and the counterculture aspect of it. 'We also had this ABC TV crew following us around over there filming a story on the Australian Titles,' Harvey recalls. 'We were driving back to Yallingup for the presentation after the final and Michael and a whole bunch of the young crew were on the bus. I'm following behind in my car and Michael is at the back of the bus. The TV car is behind the bus filming and Michael has seen it and dropped his shorts and brown-eyed them. The lasting impression left on the ABC film crew was that surfers were a bunch of bums.' Michael flew out of Perth airport. He boarded the plane, reclined his seat, placed two acid tabs under his tongue and closed his eyes. Later that day at Brisbane airport Michael's board and travel bag was sitting in a corner of an empty arrivals hall, their owner nowhere to be seen.

Arriving home, Michael found the wave at Kirra almost unrecognisable. The rock groynes, which had been built the previous year, had disrupted the sand flow and instead of following the contours of the point, the wave at Kirra had moved out into the bay, forming a deep-water righthander. When the first of the big autumn swells hit, Kirra turned into Hawaii's Sunset Beach, which considering Michael was planning to spend the winter in Hawaii later that year, would prove serendipitous.

Michael would also part ways with shaping mentor Joe Larkin during 1973. While Joe had given Michael his break in the shaping game, Michael was now a big name in Australian surfing and was being offered better deals. Brian 'Furry' Austin had also left Joe's factory and gone out alone, starting up Goodtime Surfboards in Bolton Street, Kirra. Joe had been far more to Michael than simply his boss. Joe had been, in many ways, the father Michael never had, but when Furry offered Michael $30 a board Michael was out the door. Michael would eventually go out alone, shaping under the Michael Peterson Surfboards label.

In September, Michael celebrated his 21st birthday in the backyard of the Peterson's house at 85 Pacific Highway, South Tweed Heads, his little brother Tom walking around the backyard welcoming guests with joints that had 'smoke me' written on them.

Joan Peterson and her four kids had moved from the old family house in Tweed Street, Coolangatta, the previous year. South Tweed at that time was small acreages and not much else, and the Peterson's house backed onto sparse bushland, which Michael and Tom immediately set about re-foliating. Michael's younger sister Dorothy had a horse in the back paddock named Flash, and Joan Peterson began wondering why Michael kept heading down the back paddock to feed it. Michael hated horses. Joan was onto him, and Mick came home from a surf one afternoon to find his mull crop going up in the incinerator, Joan using a broomstick to jam a dozen mature plants into the fire.

But for Michael, 1973 was all about Hawaii. After getting a taste for it the previous year he was ready to get over there and make a name for himself. He managed to do that on the flight over.

Michael, Tom and their mate from Norah Head, Graham Wood, flew over to Honolulu together on 3 November. Michael travelled with a magnetic chess board, and as he and Tom were playing, Michael, without a word, produced a joint and sparked it up at 30,000 feet. You could still smoke on planes at that point; smoking dope however was somewhat less tolerated and the stewardess immediately threatened to land the plane in Tahiti if they didn't put it out. Michael and Tom kept blazing. Soon, standing over them, was the figure of Midget Farrelly, a hardliner when it came to anything to do with drugs. Midget stuck out his hand and said tersely to Tom, 'Give it to me.' The incorrigible Tom looked Midget in the eye, took one last toke, put the roach in his mouth, extinguished it on his tongue with a hiss and swallowed it.

Michael's Hawaiian ticket was booked one-way. He had no intention of going home any time soon. He was there to surf, shape and smoke in that loose order. He had invites into the Smirnoff and the Hang Ten contests and was trying to score an invite to the prestigious Duke, and the best way to do that was to surf the house down … without busting down the doors in the process. For the young Aussie guys, staying on the right side of the Hawaiian locals was a fine dance.

Michael paddled out at Pipeline on a sizable eight-foot day, and when the local guys wouldn't give him a wave, he simply paddled across to the righthander on the other side of the peak that nobody was surfing. Michael didn't know it was called Backdoor Pipe, nor that the reason nobody was surfing it was that it ended on dry reef, but he promptly threw himself over the ledge. Michael's Backdoor waves that day were shot by Hawaiian photographer Bernie Baker and would find their way into *Surfer* magazine in the States soon after. The photos were jaw dropping, but the surfer was credited as unknown. That really pissed Michael off.

It is fair to say that Michael was taking the Hawaiian winter more seriously than Tom. He possessed the brooding intensity; Tommy provided the comic relief. The Smirnoff contest was held down at Laniakea, which was breaking like 10-foot Kirra. Tom and Woody had driven down with Michael's boards and were waiting for him while he had a warm-up surf at Sunset. While they waited Tommy remembered that Owl Chapman had told them the farmland across the road from Laniakea was a choice spot for exotic mushroom picking, so Tommy and Woody jumped the fence and started foraging. They found plenty, sampled a few, broke from linear time and were eventually chased out of there by the farm owner on horseback. They arrived back at the beach to find a commotion. It was Michael. 'Where's me fucking gear!? My heat's in the water!'

Michael blamed Tom again soon after when his sunglasses went missing. In most cases this wasn't a big deal, but Michael's sunglasses weren't just sunglasses, not in the same way they were for everyone else. They weren't windows to look out at the world. No, for Michael they worked the other way; they stopped the world looking *in*. They prevented eye contact. They provided conspiratorial cover. Behind them he was able to observe and scheme. He increasingly wore them inside. They were mirrored aviators, wire framed, and he'd had them since he was 17. When they went missing in Hawaii, all surfing stopped. It took Michael six days to find them and he never lost them again.

Tom and Woody flew home, and Michael moved up to Velzyland with photographer friend Howie Owen. The pair moved into a share house on the escarpment side of the Kam Highway with four Californian surfers. The house shrunk by the day. Michael was particular about his food – he wouldn't touch golden syrup, only honey, and lived exclusively for days off sardines and bread – but seemed more open-minded about food that didn't belong to him. Michael began eating arbitrarily from the fridge; the Californians started labelling their own food. For Michael it became a game. 'Mick would just go straight in there and make a bee line for it and eat the lot,' remembers Howie. 'It caused these huge fights but Michael just didn't care. The Americans were also like, "If you're getting toilet paper make sure it's four-ply, we don't want any of that two-ply or three-ply shit!" Michael just laughed and said, "No worries, chine," then he'd turn to me and go, "We'll just eat their food."'

Velzyland was a rundown estate with tiny knock-up houses and overgrown yards littered with car wrecks and patrolled by chickens and dogs. It was also staunchly native Hawaiian, and it was here that Michael hung out with the local crew. These

ERSON
PACIFIC HIGHWAY
uth TWEED HEADS
N.S.W
AUSTRALIA

EISENHOWER USA
FRANK LLOYD WRIGHT

VIA AIR MAIL
CORREO AEREO
PAR AVION

FRANK LLOYD WRIGHT

MINE THIS TICKET PARTICULARLY THE CONDITIONS
D OFFICE 70 HUNTER STREET, SYDNEY, AUSTRALIA
RT ASSOCIATION

MEMBER OF

Baggage
Claim
SYDNEY

QF 122803

QANTAS

PASSENGER TICKET AND BAG

TOM PETERSON ON A BUMMER!

USA /22c

Mrs. Joan Peterson
85 Pacific Highway,
South Tweed Heads
N.S.W Australia 2413

② Second fold

were the years before the animosity toward Australian surfers got out of hand, but Michael was treated by the Hawaiians as one of their own. At V-Land he'd walk up the road and have huge ping pong tournaments with the Hawaiians that would go for days in between swells. He'd surf and he'd smoke with them. They liked him.

Michael surfed Sunset almost exclusively. He'd walk around from V-Land and surf long sessions. He began to work the place out. He started to take off behind the peak and surf it like a big version of Kirra. He got into a groove out there that lasted weeks, his only problems were that he was running out of surfboards, running out of money and running out of weed. Michael had a plan, though. He called home and asked his glasser, Pete Tracker, to send across his shaping templates. His plan was to shape boards at Reno Abellira's down at Rocky Point, which he'd sell to stay afloat, while shaping himself the perfect Sunset board for the upcoming contests. He kept telling Howie he needed longer boards to surf Sunset like Nat.

Michael and Howie drove to Honolulu airport in the old white Valiant with red upholstery they'd acquired to pick up the templates. Mick was driving and the pair got hopelessly lost as they tried to find the freight depot in the back streets behind the airport. Mick eventually found himself driving up a one-way street the wrong way and being tailed by a Plymouth Barracuda with a blue light on the roof. The Highway Patrol officer pulled Michael over and ticketed him, the scene too good to miss for Howie who whipped out his camera and took what would become an iconic image of Michael and The Law. Mick grabbed the ticket, put it in the glovebox, and drove off to pick up the templates. He drove straight back to the North Shore and started work on a nine-foot Sunset board, sprayed red, that he'd ride for the rest of the trip.

Michael surfed the Hang Ten event at Sunset, and on a 12-foot day caught the wave of the contest. 'He's just come flying off the bottom from behind the peak and pulled up into this massive black barrel,' recalls Hawaiian Louie Ferreira, who was in the channel caddying for Ben Aipa at the time. 'I'd never seen anything like it in my life. He went through section after section and came flying out into the channel in this big shower of spray. I just went, "What da fuck!" I'd never seen anyone ride a barrel like that before.' Michael finished seventh in the Hang Ten but won the best tube ride of the contest for that wave. His prize was a 175cc Kawasaki motorbike, which he duly hocked.

After two months, Michael felt like he was surfing at home. He was surfing Sunset like he surfed Kirra but he was getting a little *too* comfortable. He'd paddle inside a local crowd and start whistling people off his waves. 'He was making a real nuisance of himself,' remembered Wayne Deane, who'd grown up with Michael in Coolangatta and had seen Michael in this frame of mind at home. Deaney remembered having a bad feeling about it. The locals were getting pissed off. He knew there was a reckoning on its way. 'Eventually he's dropped in on Ben Aipa of all people. He'd picked the heaviest guy in the world to drop in on.' The nose of Michael's board speared clean through Ben's board. Ben paddled Michael's board in to the beach and punched the fin clean out. Michael knew he was in trouble, and when he came in and sheepishly walked over to pick up his board he copped an open-hand left hook to the ear.

The blow was more to Michael's psyche. The often menacing exterior that everyone back home saw out in the surf was in many ways a front. MP the surfer was a cold force of nature. Michael Peterson, meanwhile, was more psychologically brittle. The MP act put the fear of god into anyone he was surfing against but it masked a vulnerability that wouldn't fully present itself until a few years later when Michael's schizophrenia became more pronounced.

For now, in Hawaii, the swagger was gone. There was an element of homesickness – this was the longest he'd ever spent away from home – but Hawaii had also slapped his psyche.

He couldn't dominate the scene in Hawaii the same way he could back at home in Australia. Michael wrote to his mother soon after in a series of letters, pleading for help. 'Once again, well the Hang Ten is over, I came either 5th or 7th. But I am still stuck here. Ben Aipa beat me up then later on said he was going to destroy me. For what I don't know. Please send me some money for a plane ticket before I get put in hospital.' With each letter Michael's tone became increasingly desperate. 'I have relized [sic] a lot of things since I've been over here. So for the last time, buy me a plain [sic] ticket out of here back to Australia and back home where I belong. Get me out of here please before I flip out of my head.'

Joan Peterson, as she'd do for the rest of his life, went above and beyond for her eldest son. She went down to Coolangatta Travel in Griffith Street the following day and paid $446 for an open ticket home. The ticket was sent to Barry Kanaiaupuni's address at Sunset Beach where Michael picked it up.

He was home two days later.

1973

Ted Spencer

Ted Spencer's surfing at the turn of the seventies was a window to where surfing would soon go. Low-slung, kinetic, radical, his waves at Angourie featured in the movies *Innermost Limits* and *Sea of Joy* and showed the pinballing potential of the shortboard in and around the tube. Surfing a scooped, soft-railed Greenough-inspired hull, Ted unlocked new parts of the wave … and in doing so, began unlocking new parts of his own surfing consciousness.

Wayne Lynch – who'd travelled and surfed extensively with Ted during the filming of Paul Witzig's *Evolution* – saw the subtle exchanges going on between man, surfboard and wave. 'Deep down I have enormous respect for Ted,' said Wayne in *Switchfoot*. 'His surfing was unbelievable and his contribution to surfboard design was as important as anyone's.' But Wayne could also see the direction surfing was heading – more competitive, crowded, commercialised – and could see that both he and Ted would soon travel another path altogether. 'Ted was a bit like myself, just totally consumed by the surfing way of life and I think we could feel the pressure coming with the changes and you could sort of see that you weren't going to belong to what was coming. It was no wonder so many people split in the late '60s, it just sort of pushed us away in a very natural fashion.'

By the dawn of the '70s Ted was losing interest in the contest scene, despite his contest surfing reaching its zenith. Having won Bells in both '68 and '69, Ted finished second to Nat Young at Bells in 1970, before finishing runner-up to Peter Drouyn at the Australian Titles in Coolangatta. Ted qualified for the Australian team at the 1970 World Contest held soon after in Victoria but the day before the contest was due to start, he drove away. Ted spent the following years surfing on his own terms, even taking a meditative break from surfing altogether. In his absence, he became one of Australian surfing's most elusive and enigmatic figures. Speaking to *Tracks* about this time in his life, he offered, 'I also realised that the pleasure of surfing was something that I projected onto a wave. Thus the pleasure was inherent in me, something I could tap inside me and set free. So surfing became secondary to my concern with advancing spirituality.' The surfing philosophy guiding him was articulated in a short surf parable, *Veruna*, Ted wrote with a friend – 'TKD' – while living in New Zealand in 1973:

> Michael stroked over the first of two waves and halfway up the face of the third, sat back on his board, grabbed the left rail, reversed his board, pulled it under him and aimed it down the face of the wave. There was no need to paddle in this situation. The board was like a dart, and the hand of the wave propelled it toward the target. As the wave lifted the tail of his board, he sprang to his feet and poised in a graceful, cat-like stance. He'd been through it dozens of times, and it was all performed effortlessly with the grace of a ballet dancer. It would not be an exaggeration to say that once he felt the wave beneath him, he could have come to this point with his eyes closed. That is the power of confidence.
>
> A split second later, the bottom fell through and the wave sucked out like a sideways whirlpool. Faced with the vertical throw, his confidence shattered. 'I can't make it!' flashed across his mind. At that moment he surrendered all thoughts of making the wave and his efforts ceased. The wave swallowed his board and spat it out on the shoulder about 20 yards inside. It glided smoothly across the surface and into the path of Veruna, who had witnessed the whole episode. Veruna paddled alongside and laid his right foot on the deck of Michael's board, then, the board in tow, he paddled on. 'Over here!' he called out as he flashed a smile to Michael, indicating that he had retrieved his board for him.
>
> They paddled on in silence and positioned themselves in the lineup, awaiting the arrival of the next set. It was an unusual day; the waves were seven-to-nine feet, the water crisp but pleasant and incredibly clear, clearer than Michael could remember, and he had surfed there for many years. The reef dazzled his eyes now and again as its brilliant colours were highlighted by the autumn sun, which also sparkled on the liquid surface. The atmosphere was alive yet not tense. They were out alone, and the waves were plentiful.

As Michael paddled back out after a nice tube session on the inside, a big set approached the reef. He saw Veruna whip around on the face and nimbly leap to his feet. The peak seemed to leap forward as it struck the reef ledge, and its sudden surge lifted the tail of Veruna's board high over his head. As Veruna plunged down like a fishing bird about to pierce the ocean's surface in pursuit of its prey, Michael flashed, 'He's finished! He'll never make it.'

As Michael slid over the shoulder and down the wave, his vision of Veruna was blocked by the set's second wave. In his mind's eye, however, he could picture Veruna getting drilled beneath the surface, exactly as he himself had been drilled on that first wave earlier in the day. Michael scratched up the face of the second wave and reached the crest in time to see Veruna emerge from the green room and execute a particularly fluid cutback. 'Incredible! He made it! He made that drop!' Michael let out an exuberant scream. He must have come out of that drop like a swooping bird, thought Michael. Like a fishing bird who pulls out of its dive inches before striking the surface of the ocean.

Michael let the remaining waves pass beneath him so he could ask about that incredible take-off when Veruna got back out. 'Unreal!' he cried to Veruna as he paddled up. 'How did you make that drop? You've got to tell me how you pulled it off so I can learn it too!' Although Michael was jacked up, Veruna didn't seem to think there was much concern for excitement.

'Well, I don't really know what you mean by "learn it". I just flowed through the situation without thinking about it and sort of did what was naturally called for.' He stopped for a moment and thought before speaking further. 'Besides, Michael, why do you want to limit your own surfing by copying others? I mean, those days are gone. Surfing is more of a refined experience now. You can't really progress by memory alone because you will always be entering situations that may call for an approach that you just don't have wired. When that happens your mind will baulk, and you'll be defeated.

'A wise surfer is one who applies sensitivity to his surfing. He doesn't rely on his storehouse of past memorised moves. So if you just want to learn a new manoeuvre, I'm afraid I can't really help you. I used to approach surfing like that, but found it to be too limiting. Refining your surfing doesn't simply mean refining different isolated areas and manoeuvres. In a deeper sense it means refining your very self; then everything you do will be refined. There is an old Zen saying that if you want to cook perfectly, you have to be the perfect cook outside the kitchen too. In my own life I have found this to be true. As I become more sensitive, so too does my surfing.'

Veruna fell silent. He looked at the deck of his board and dug his nails into the wax. He half looked up at Michael with a gentle smile on his face and then looked down again at his board. He could go deeper still and in a sense wanted to, but he held back as he abhorred the thought of pressing his views on others. Michael could sense Veruna's feelings and appreciated them. Though he had known him for a short while only, at that moment he felt Veruna to be a true friend.

●

The following morning found Michael and Veruna sitting on the beach after their first surf. The sun was warmer than the previous day and they had their wetsuits peeled down to their waists. The faintest hint of an offshore was blowing and the swell direction had changed, causing the inside to speed up and section at times. You had to look closely to see that the swell had dropped slightly. Even so, it had not lost its power. The new angle it approached the reef from made the whole situation more critical and called for acute sensitivity.

They watched the waves for a long while in silence before Michael spoke. 'You know, Veruna, I've been thinking about what you were saying yesterday. It seemed to come at just the right time – so obvious, in fact, that I wonder why it took your saying it to make me understand. I can really feel that my approach to surfing can't really be separated from my approach to life, especially in regard to the development of sensitivity. I mean, sensitivity is just not the kind of thing you can turn off and on, on and off at will. I guess what I'm trying to say is that I'd like to become more sensitive and aware, but I'm not really sure how. I know that for me, at least, it's got to be an individual experience. I can't relate to religions or organisations. I want something more personal and practical, something that fits into my own life. Besides, the fanatics I've had the misfortune of running into weren't very sensitive anyway.'

'What you're saying is true,' replied Veruna. 'Obviously that is not the solution. If it were, the world would be full of sensitive people, but it isn't.' Michael wanted to hear more, so Veruna continued speaking. 'Being sensitive means having the ability to feel or perceive the force or energy beneath all things, and to avoid conflicting with it. A sensitive person is subservient to that energy. His life complements it. For instance, in surfing there are those who complement the wave, and those who fight it. The insensitive surfer cannot perceive the subtle energy that is causing the wave to move, so he often ends up battling it. He sees only the wave and not the energy. The refined surfer, on the other hand, sees both. He sees the wave but can also feel how the subtle energy is moving, and he can thereby tune into and move with it.

'A sensitive person sees the Essence of all things. He feels himself to be a part of that Essence. The insensitive person sees the external only and does not realise the Essence in himself and all things. To cut a long story short, the most sensitive person is one who knows himself. He understands he is not the body or the mind, but the sustaining energy, the spark of life force within them. Though he is still of course limited by being in the body, his deeper insight helps him to stretch that limitation, to work around it.'

'In a way,' Michael replied, 'I can understand what you're saying, Veruna. I've heard similar ideas before and I believe them to be true, but to bring it all back home, how can I develop that sensitivity? In other words, unless I can experience what you're talking about, it's only a fairy story.'

Veruna looked out to sea and scooped up a handful of sand. As it sifted through his fingers, he looked back to Michael and began to speak in a casual manner. 'There is a simple meditation I sometimes practice; you can try it if you like. Say to yourself, "I am not the body. I am the silent witness within the body. I sit here quietly and watch my body act, but I do not act. I am the witness to the body and the mind." Then go about your activities, but watch yourself do them. Be aware of yourself doing them. For instance, when you are walking, watch yourself walk. Say to yourself, "I am aware that I am walking." Gradually you will experience more and more the separation between you and your body, and your awareness will naturally expand.' He paused, then said, 'Let's have a surf, and you can try it while you are paddling out.' Veruna stood up and stretched, pulled his wetsuit up his torso, and stretched the sleeves over his arms. 'I am aware that I am putting on my wetsuit,' he laughed, then grabbed his board and trotted down to the water's edge.

Michael sat in silence for a few moments, contemplating Veruna's words. As he picked up his board and moved slowly toward the sea, he watched Veruna pick up a smaller wave on the inside. He turned high and raced gracefully across the wall. As the inside section caved in, Veruna dropped with it and drew a smooth arc around the whitewater up into the pocket. There was something about Veruna that Michael couldn't quite put his finger on. It wasn't that what he was doing with the wave was anything exceptional; rather, it was the way he was doing it.

There was a gull overhead, and Michael watched it momentarily. It soared effortlessly. Without a flap of its wings, the gull climbed and dropped, arced and circled, riding the air currents that were invisible to even its own eyes. Veruna's like that with waves and people too, Michael flashed; on the sea and the land.

He pulled the zip on his wetsuit then stepped into the water. 'I am aware that I am stepping into the water,' he observed, and began to paddle out. 'I am the silent witness. I am aloof from the body's activities. I am sitting here watching my body paddle, but I am not the body.' As Michael arrived at the take-off zone, a set approached the reef. The first wave was six feet, and he positioned himself mid-peak and took off. 'I am aware that I am taking off ... dropping down the face ... turning.'

Michael watched himself surf, and as the autumn days went by, surfing took on a whole new colour for him. He no longer felt himself hemmed in or limited by his past conceptions of his own ability. His mind no longer baulked in 'unmakeable' situations. And most importantly, he no longer considered success to be synonymous with making the wave or failure with not making it. Michael's success was no longer visible to the eyes of others; it was an internal thing.

1973

Stan Couper

'Dad was a doer,' recalls Gail Couper. 'He got involved in surfing out of sheer boredom I think because I dragged him around to all these surf competitions. He didn't surf himself but he wanted something to do. Dad always wanted something to do. That's the way he was. It was that era when your parents put their hands up to help out with their kids' sport and referee or carry all the gear. I remember our clothesline at home in Lorne would be full of contest singlets hanging out to dry.'

Stan Couper, however, would take his role of Saturday-morning sports dad to its ultimate conclusion. Stan not only ran local contests for his daughter, he would soon be running the sport across the whole country.

Stan had been a RAAF navigator in World War II before returning home and working a desk job as a chartered accountant in Melbourne, which to be fair didn't quite have the same horizons. Stan played football and cricket, but in 1960 when the Coupers moved permanently down the coast to their annual holiday spot of Lorne, he shifted to fishing, tennis and golf. Stan Couper didn't do things by halves. Lorne Golf Club, mowed from farmland at Allenvale, had only nine holes. Stan thought this was nine too few. 'I remember coming home one day,' recalls Gail, 'and Peter Thomson and Guy Wolstenholme were there with Dad making plans to extend the course. They were drawing bridges over gullies and all these ideas but the most they could get to was 15 holes, so it was scrapped.'

'Surfing was never an interest of Dad's until I started competing.' Gail Couper started surfing down at Lorne Point with the Lynches' young bloke from up in George Street, and just a year later, in 1964, she surprised everyone by qualifying for the World Titles

in Manly. Stan got a close look at how the fledgling sport was being run and quickly realised it was a rabble. He rolled up his sleeves and stepped forward. Officious, by-the-book, conservative, Stan was better suited to the surf club movement, but instead landed on surfing's doorstep at a time when surfing needed someone like him. Stan was the man for the job.

Stan Couper formed a partnership with the equally formidable Tony Olsson, and the Victorian branch of the Australian Surfing Association (ASA) was soon not only the strongest in the country ... it was *running* the country. 'The Big O' and 'Stan The Man' soon lobbied for Victoria to host the 1970 World Contest, the fact that they had no funding and just five months to pull it off presenting only minor hurdles. Olsson got the money out of the Victorian Premier, Sir Henry Bolte, on a promise to keep the titles on the back pages of the newspapers, not the front. In 1970 however this would not prove easy. Inviting a couple of hundred longhaired surfers from all over the world to your town had the potential to go up in smoke. The Drug Squad patrolled Lorne sweating on a bust, the hotel manager effluviated bad vibes, and the American team threatened a boycott after Corky Carroll was suspended for swearing at the hotel manager's wife. The controversy made the front page of the *Geelong Advertiser*.

It was a letter sent to Stan after the World Contest by Wayne Lynch – the Lynches' young bloke from up the road – that would really make him stop and think. 'Dad had a soft spot for Wayne and always wanted him to do well,' recalls Gail. 'Wayne was quiet and didn't mouth off like some other people. He'd just do his thing. He just surfed.' A handwritten letter from Wayne needed to be considered.

'I wrote a long letter to the ASA, resigning, being quite explicit about how I felt about what had happened to Johanna and Bells during the contest,' recalls Wayne. 'They put the road through Bells for the contest and destroyed something incredibly unique. To get to Southside previously you had to walk around at low tide under the cliffs or paddle. The gully at Bells also used to be so private before that. Sometimes you'd stumble on an old swaggie living in there on his travels. Usually they were men who couldn't fit into society; some were war veterans just looking to earn a few bob. The police harangued them but the police harangued everybody back then.

They destroyed all that for this contest and it really upset me. That contest also inadvertently destroyed Johanna. Straight after it there was so much publicity in the local papers in Melbourne and Geelong. A few weeks after everyone left, a bikie group went down there and there was this beautifully made wooden fence designed to keep the cows out of the dunes running from the first to the second car park. Well, they ripped it down and used it for firewood. Johanna was our hole in the wall. That's where I was hanging to escape Vietnam. That's when it twigged with me, how we'd exploited the place for a surf contest. Of everyone, surfers shouldn't exploit a place. It ran against the grain of the way we felt about it.'

The letter got Stan thinking. While a large group of surfers descending on a town could pose a threat to civilisation, the weight of a legitimate surfing body could also be used to protect fragile coastlines from being overrun by development. By now 'Stan The Man' was president of the ASA – Tony Olsson had moved back to Melbourne to look after his business – and Stan took on the mission to protect Bells Beach. He led a group which included Rod Brooks (now his offsider at the ASA) to lobby the Victorian State Government and Barrabool Shire to officially recognise Bells Beach's importance to the surf community and put some formal protections around its natural state. After two years of back and forth, Bells Beach Surfing Recreation Reserve was officially declared in 1973, the first time a surf break anywhere in the world had been afforded that recognition.

'To his credit and my eternal respect,' says Wayne, 'Stan Couper made sure that nothing like that ever happened again and he advocated to protect these places. He used the ASA and its numbers as a vehicle to go to governments and councils and say we want this protected. I always really respected Stan for that and as much as he was part of the crew organising the contests, he saw a way bigger picture. He understood what we were getting at. Everyone else eventually came around to recognise that the coast is fragile and if it's gone, it's gone.'

Stan Couper had a day job with the Lands Department at Barrabool Shire Council, working with local farmers to get rid of noxious weeds and prevent erosion on their property. Through Surfing Victoria, Stan started the annual 'Conservation Contest', a round of the Victorian Titles where in between heats surfers would be asked to take native seedlings Stan acquired from work to plant out the surrounding area at Bells, which back in those days was a muddy mess.

In 1973 the Australian Titles headed west to Margaret River, and would land Stan in the middle of another ideological battle. Margaret River had hosted the 1969 Aussie titles, but the news they were returning wasn't met with universal glee by locals. Margaret River had become an end-of-the-earth refuge for a growing number of surfers from around the globe, many of whom weren't real impressed by the idea of their remote utopia being overrun by hundreds of east coast surfers and TV cameras. *Tracks*, in a column titled 'Paradise Lost', reported an expat American shaper named Tom Hoye asking rhetorically, 'Why do we want another national titles in our surf? Good question … no real answer.' Local resistance grew and after a vote the titles were called off. Stan, as ASA president and at his diplomatic best, intervened and after some heated meetings the titles were back on again.

Stan had it no easier once the contest actually started, making a controversial call to move the event away from Margaret River down the coast to Redgate. As Errol Considine noted in his report for *Tracks*, 'Just a little aside from the actual contest, but still an intrinsic part is Stan Couper … our big boss man ASA El Presidenté. Rod [Brooks] knocked me for knocking Stan in the last article. Don't get me wrong, I think he generally does a good job, but he sure as hell was giving a few guys the shits with his often dictatorial, but unspoken, "this is my contest and we do it my way" attitude rulings. The guy doesn't surf, he doesn't know the coastline … Rod Brooks says Stan is often a victim of his position as president. Point accepted. And he often has to be strong. True too. But anybody in a position of executive authority should be ready to accept the shit as well as the accolades.' Richard Nixon was evoked in the next sentence. Stan was the meat in the sandwich as surfing wrestled about how surfing contests should run … or whether they should even run at all. Surfers themselves couldn't work it out so what chance did a non-surfing, World War II veteran have? Stan couldn't win but he had conviction. Stan was dead-ahead, thick-skinned and phlegmatic at a time when running a surf contest required all of these qualities.

Stan breathed a sigh of relief as the contest at Redgate finally started and things calmed down … only for Michael Peterson, the defending champ, to be scored an interference, running straight up the beach. *Here we go again*. Stan talked Michael down. Stan had actually paid Michael's entry fee at Bells the month before when Michael had turned up short. He never got the money back, even after Michael won the $1000 first prize.

The Bells Beach contest in 1973 had been pivotal for two reasons. Claw Warbrick had returned from Hawaii in early '73 with details of a new judging system the Hawaiians had used that removed the subjectivity from judging scores. The 'points-per-manoeuvre' system gave each move a set score, which was scaled up or down depending on the size of the move. Someone simply sat there and called the moves and someone else tallied them up. Stan – 'unscrupulously fair' as Claw remembers – was a ready adopter of the new system. The only problem was that the new system was incredibly Byzantine, induced headaches, and produced ugly surfing. Michael

Peterson went on to win the contest, his mind and surfboard going equally as fast, claiming later to have 'zigged and zagged between his zigs and zags'. Nat Young, one of the disaffected surfers Stan believed would be lured back to surfing contests by the objectivity and fairness of the new system, bailed him up about it instead.

The 1973 Bells contest more importantly had been the world's first professional surfing event, with Claw's humble surf company Rip Curl stumping up $2500 in prizemoney. There was a clear divide in those days between amateur and professional sport, and many feared going pro would change the character of the event … and of surfing itself. Stan, as president of the ASA – the amateur body – had the most to lose, but the writing was on the wall and Stan acknowledged the change was inevitable and, ultimately, for the better of surfing … which had been his goal ever since he'd taken Gail to her first contest back in 1964. 'Dad's theory was that if you wanted to make a living out of surfing and being a pro, then there had to be some avenue for you to do that. Dad believed in that.'

Stan Couper handled the presentation for surfing's first professional event, held at Torquay's Palace Hotel. He handed Michael Peterson his cheque for $1000 and watched on as the first professional surfing contest descended into an all-in drunken food fight. Stan shook his head. It would soon be someone else's problem.

1975

Terry Fitzgerald

Terry Fitzgerald's connection to the Hawaiian islands dated back to the 1970 World Contest, when his room at the Lorne Hotel adjoined the room of iconic Hawaiian surfers Paul Strauch and Ben Aipa. Young Terry soon found himself adopted by the Hawaiian team and thrown in the back of their hire car for the drive to Johanna. Terry made the semis that year and struck up a friendship with Hawaiian James Jones, who stayed on in Australia after the contest, the pair surfing Winkipop together and keeping warm between surfs with a campfire under the cliff. When James headed home he left an open offer for Terry to stay with him in Hawaii.

Jones was soon picking up Terry from Honolulu airport. While the trip was technically a honeymoon, it would become a seminal trip for Terry's surfing and shaping. By chance he met Dick Brewer on the beach at Rocky Point, the shaping master taking more than a passing interest in Terry's surfboard. 'The irony of my involvement with Brewer was this,' he'd later tell *The Surfer's Journal*. 'Starstruck yokel lands in Hawaii and finds himself in the presence of God, then discovers God needs him as much as he needs God.' Terry spent four months on Kauai, surfing Hanalei and Acid Drops and shaping alongside Brewer, the pair trading design ideas. He'd later tell *The Surfer's Journal*, 'My mind was opened to the whole Hawaiian deal.' Over the next three years, designs derived from those Hawaiian mini-guns saw Terry develop, manufacture and surf his foiled creations featuring wings and single-to-double concaves, in multiples of shapes, from 5'10" all the way up to 8'4".

A conversation with Brewer stayed with him. Terry had just watched Barry Kanaiaupuni surfing 15-foot Sunset. BK was Sunset's premier stylist and Terry had been

taking cues from him. Brewer suggested instead, 'Look, clean up your act, do it your own way and you'll be better off.' Terry would possess a surfing style all of his own. 'Mr Body Torque' surfed with his hips. It was expressive, expansive and *fast*. Phil Jarratt tagged him 'The Sultan of Speed'. Terry owned one of the '70s signature styles, best suited to long runways like Sunset, Honolua, Bells … and, in time Jeffreys Bay. He lost himself deep in the shape/surf/shape continuum. 'The greatest benefit was that if we wanted to develop a certain manoeuvre or a certain style we could actually shape the boards to create that, and in shaping boards to further assist signature moves, your boards accentuated what you wanted to do even more. That was how people developed all these flamboyant individual styles. It was all based on very, very different equipment.'

Terry lived at Narrabeen – arguably the most tribal beach in Australia – but wasn't beholden to tribalism. He had a neat skill for striking up simpatico relationships with other surfing cultures wherever he went. Along with time in Hawaii, California and Bali, he'd also spent a formative year shaping on the Gold Coast. When asked about 'the Narrabeen cult' in 1975 he replied, 'What a colourless place the world would be if we all looked and thought the same.' Terry was open to new ways of looking at surfing, and developing cross-cultural exchanges.

Those early seasons in Hawaii shaped him. With his golden orb of tightly frizzed hair the Hawaiians saw him as a long-lost ancestor washed-up on a distant shore. He told *Bombora*, 'Those first couple of winters I was pretty much the only Australian there so I had this innate opportunity to be accepted as a surfer, not confronted as an Australian.' He received an invite to the '71 Duke and made the final at Sunset.

Returning home from Hawaii, Terry borrowed a thousand bucks and started Hot Buttered surfboards, named after the Isaac Hayes album that he and Owl Chapman had grooved on in the islands. Terry moved the business into an old house at 9 Mitchell Road, Brookvale, then, soon after, moved into the two rooms not assigned to surfboard production. Sons Kye and then Joel made their appearances shortly later. The business was his bread and butter. 'One of the beautiful things about the era we grew up in was that for us to eat we had to do something, and the chosen few shaped surfboards.' By 1975 Hot Buttered really *was* hot. As the ads said, 'Hot Buttered boards are the sum total of every wave ridden, seen ridden and dreamed ridden.' Martyn Worthington's airbrush sprays and a roster of free-thinking team surfers gave the label character, but it was Terry's presence that gave it gravity. Derek Hynd, who rode Terry's boards, described him as, 'the surfer's surfer and the shaper's shaper.'

Nineteen-seventy-five would be the year surfing in Australia would go pro. There'd been professional events for the past two seasons, but they were now starting to coalesce into something bigger. The challenge for the guys pulling it together was to create something that wasn't a total sell-out. No one walked the line between pure surfing and business better than Terry, and no one was better equipped to spell out exactly where that line was drawn. He told *Tracks*, 'The reason we're surfers in the first place is that we don't want to be caught up in the mainstream of regimented, structured life. I think the people involved should be level-headed enough to know what they can get away with.'

Terry's 1975 began with his first Hawaiian win, the Lightning Bolt Pro at Velzyland. He rode a double-wing swallow, single-to-double concave, a design that 'after four years of development was finally starting to reach perfection.' In '75 he'd ride a winged pintail version everywhere between Honolua, J-Bay, Bells and Uluwatu. He'd even shape one as a gift for Brewer.

He then returned to Australia for the pro events, which were beginning to spin in some kind of regular orbit. However, there wasn't anything regular about the events themselves. The different formats, arbitrary judging and contest politics sparked all sorts of skulduggery and squabbling … and made Terry's '75 achievements all the more remarkable. Direct to a fault, Terry would cut through the bullshit about how pro surfing should be run. He half-joked/half didn't to *Tracks:* 'There's only one way to make things better and that's to yell and scream, insult people and stand up for what you think is right. I've done my share of yelling and stamping because I've always believed my interpretation of surfing was the best. Well, it's hard to say the best – there's 50 bests in surfing – but what I'm doing is supporting my own assessment of what is good surfing.'

During the 1975 Coke contest, the Australian Professional Surfers Association (APSA) was officially formed at a meeting of surfers on the balcony of the North Narrabeen Surf Club. The APSA was part sporting body, part surfers' union. It had big visions. 'Part and parcel of the deal,' Terry told *Tracks*, 'is that to be a foundation member of anything one of the decisions that has to be made within yourself is you've got to create a career path or a future'. The APSA was driven publicly by Claw Warbrick, Graham Cassidy, Peter Townend and Ian Cairns. Terry was rank and file (later a vice-president) but played an influential role behind the scenes. He remained in many ways a reluctant public figure. 'I'd get this split-consciousness thing a lot of the time,' he told *Tracks*. 'Up till the last year or so I'd swing more to the business-like approach and thinking, what the hell, and get up there in lights, but now I take a bit of a closer look before I project myself.' He explained it away like this. 'I guess it was more an ego thing too. I'm an Arian and Mars pushes me around a bit.' Meanwhile, Terry was having his best-ever competitive season. He'd finish third at the Coke.

The ASA – the old amateur body – was suddenly being made to look old and amateur. Two days after the Coke contest ran at Narrabeen, the ASA's Australian Titles began down in Middleton, South Australia. The two days didn't leave much time to get from Sydney to Adelaide. Most surfers made it. Michael Peterson, the defending champ, didn't. As Michael simmered in the car park it was left to Terry to cool him down. 'To be honest, I had a lot of feeling for the guy and I guess I was one of the few people he connected with. I remember at that time trying to explain to him what actually happened and explaining to him the common sense in taking his lumps. "It's happened, there's no way you're going to change it." Stan Couper was the guy running the ASA and as much as Stan drew flak he was actually a straight-up guy. Michael needed to accept that. The ridiculous thing, though, was me trying to explain straight-uppedness to anybody.'

The Aussie Titles would be labelled 'the Dribbleton Fiasco'. Five days went by without surf, before they draped a banner saying 'Australian Titles' over the back of the Seaford toilet block and off they went. By the end of the week Terry Fitzgerald was Australian champion, although he'd afterwards claim of the win, 'It doesn't really matter. I think I wanted it badly a couple of years ago but now it doesn't really matter.' The APSA, meanwhile, had created a leader board. It ranked the Australian surfers over the '75 pro season, and at the end of the year Terry Fitzgerald finished first, in front of Michael Peterson and Mark Richards. If the ratings had been accepted globally, Terry would have been the '75 world champion. As with many things, he was a year early. The following year the global IPS ratings were adopted and Peter Townend would be crowned the first professional world champion. Terry's fate lay down another road.

After the Gunston 500 in Durban in July '75, Terry drove south to Jeffreys Bay for the first time. 'My first ride into J-Bay was with Piers Pittard in his *bakkie* [a pick-up truck], overnight from Durban through the newly created Transkei, with a rifle and handgun for no fun. Africa by night, where stars and firewood pilots were guides stoking blind adventure through cold emptiness. A border crossing rite and continue the flight from a sun that seemed to muscle in from the left like an incoming apocalypse. Now dawn is a glory from across J-Bay, lighting the walk through dewed grass and frosted sand, with offshore crispness at your back and sheer delight in your heart.' TF rolled straight into town and straight into a seven-day swell.

'Oh boy, seven days of various surf ranging from almost perfect to past perfect. Three-to-five feet or eight-to-10 feet, slightly offshore or straight offshore, in freight-train waves, where you can go so fast that on a crowded day guys paddling out look like a black picket fence flashing by. You can max out your boards so heavily that the difference between spinning out or not was decided by whether you had had a big breakfast (all that extra weight).' Terry would famously later claim to have survived the week on Sustagen, whisky and penicillin. 'Sustagen for energy, whisky for warmth and penicillin for disease.'

Watching on that week was photographer Art Brewer, who'd later recall to *The Surfer's Journal* the visceral effect Terry's surfing had on him. 'During this single session of six-to eight-foot perfection halfway around the world, it all came together. Surfing like that had been reserved for the gods, and there was Terry Fitzgerald making the 1000-yard run. Terry started up at Boneyards, passed through Supertubes and set up for the impossible section of Impossibles, twisting and power turning through the tube to end up at the Point. I, along with a couple of other people and the sand dunes, got to share in the history as the master of speed and style surfed to a never-before-witnessed level, epitomising grace under pressure, seamlessly synchronising his mind, body and soul. Terry's surfing broke the traditional rules, building his speed by arching and thrusting his hips, symmetrically raising and dropping beyond the fall line. A wrist twitch or an ankle tweak adjusted the speed and edge, always attacking the fastest section of the wave with precise control. He'd then run back to Boneyards and do it again. I'm still not sure how many waves he rode that day, but he didn't stop until the conditions changed.'

Jeffreys Bay would soon call in the way Hawaii once had. Terry would return for decades ahead and be welcomed back – just as he'd been in Hawaii – as a lost son. He'd explain the cultural exchange to *Bombora* this way: 'It was a rewarding ritual in the sense that you would … you know, you would give as much as they would give. Which was a lot. You'd talk surfboards, you'd talk experiences, you'd talk who knows who, what knows what. And even though we'd seemingly be faking it by having this little business thing on the side (which really was the be-all and end-all of it because that kept it all running), the fact was we were very, very lucky in being accepted in all of the places where we ventured. It was based on a shared spirit, the spirit of surfing.'

After moving on from competition, surf adventures provided editorial exposure, intertwined with building Hot Buttered into an international business. Brazil, Europe, Japan … discovery escapades to Tahiti, the Maldives and multiple Indonesian outer islands with Kye, Joel and Liam. Fifty years on, Terry and Martyn are still hand-making gold standard surfboards.

1975

Ian Cairns

'My 1975 began back in 1968.'

At every Australian Titles, the most improved junior is awarded the Duke Trophy, a pan-Pacific tribute to the Hawaiian who'd brought surfing across the seas to Australia, the wide brown billiard table that was, in 1975, challenging Hawaii as the new power base of surfing.

At the 1968 Australian Titles held at Long Reef on Sydney's northern beaches, a tall, serious kid in a tube suit from Western Australia was awarded the Duke Trophy. 'The presentation was held at this weird Chinese restaurant in Dee Why,' recalls Ian 'Kanga' Cairns. 'It was your typical presentation, everyone got crazy drunk. I remember Nat turned up in a paisley suit and Keith Paull and Robert Conneeley were there, the whole space case crew, and I was the 16-year-old kid from Western Australia having his mind blown.'

The Duke trophy held immediate significance. 'Back in those days if you didn't go to Hawaii you were no one,' offers Ian, who at the time had just moved with his family from Avalon to Perth. 'We'd had that indoctrination from Bob Pike at Narrabeen. The whole idea of going to Hawaii was reinforced, as was the connection of the Duke bringing surfing to Australia at Freshwater. It was Snowy who worked me with that one. I was standing on the headland between Manly and Freshwater and he was telling me about the significance of the Duke. Listening to him you just wanted to be part of something deeper, part of this big timeline of history. As a young surfer, who could you model your thinking and ideals on? For me that surfer was Duke Kahanamoku, so getting that trophy

and hearing about those first Duke contests and imagining, could I ever get to Hawaii and surf in the Duke contest? Imagine if you could get in that thing!'

A voracious reader even as a kid, Ian loved sprawling, historical sagas. 'If I had a thousand-page book I wanted an extra 500 pages.' He'd lose himself in the book and as his eyelids drooped he would find himself in the role of the book's hero. Ian visualised. He became Jim Corbett in *Man-eaters of Kumaon*, hunting tigers in colonial India. 'That story was enthralling and it really resonated with me,' he recalls. 'I grew up as a kid thinking the days of Jim Corbett and tigers were gone, but then I discovered surfing and realised they weren't.' He ploughed through Michener's *Hawaii*, fascinated by origin stories from the islands. He buzzed on generational epics and joined the dots between the past and the present.

Ian soon found himself in Hawaii. He'd first visited the islands on his way home from the 1972 World Titles in San Diego, where his Australian mate Peter Townend had promptly faded him at Sunset on his first wave. 'My first day on the North Shore I paddled out at Sunset, looked around and thought, this is just like Margaret River. Then I turned around and here's this massive west set bearing down on me! But I loved it. I'd already tested myself to the limit in Western Australia so what was next? Hawaii. It was like my Everest.' Ian climbed quickly. The following year he won the Smirnoff contest, and in '74 his dream of being invited to the Duke contest came true.

'They had this opening ceremony over at the Polynesian Cultural Centre in Laie, conducted by Reverend Akaka. There were all these discussions of *mana* and you had the *leis* and the *koa* wood bowl of water used for the blessing and you had the sense this was the blend of ancient Hawaiian religion and Christianity. It was uplifting. This was more than a surfing contest; there was a spirituality about this. As a *haole* you're brought into this club and being allowed to be part of this was an honour that wasn't lost on me.' Ian, with Rabbit Bartholomew caddying for him, would finish second in the '74 Duke contest to Larry Bertlemann at big Sunset. 'I did a bunch of swimming that day, but I had the realisation that I could really become part of this great story. To do that though I needed to win it.'

Nineteen-seventy-five began at home in Western Australia. Ian and wife Pat lived at Busselton, north of Margaret River. 'I was a pro surfer by this stage,' he recalls. 'I was doing some shaping but I wasn't working for my parents anymore ... I was too slow for the potato-picking machine.' Instead of potato farming he was travelling around the world winning money from surf contests. 'There was this weird juxtaposition of living in a remote country town. I kind of didn't fit in there, but even around contests I didn't feel I fitted in socially either. I was kind of living these two lives. I was a competitive surfer but I was also a surfer out for adventure because that was the life you lived in Western Australia.'

The southwest corner of Australia in the early 1970s was frontier surf country. 'There were only a handful of people surfing and George Simpson and I would go bushwhacking in my old Landcruiser and we surfed all these breaks that didn't even have names. I'd drive to Cowaramup and decide whether I went north to Yallingup or south to Margaret River. One look at the ocean and you knew which way to head. I surfed The Box on my own and had North Point, one of my best ever days with just one guy sitting on the shoulder. It was mind boggling how good it was.'

This frontier life in WA sat at odds with Cairns's vision to turn surfing into a global major league sport. The plan for surfing to go professional was well underway by 1975. 'This was the same time that James Hunt and Niki Lauda were competing for the world Formula 1 title, and I was asking why don't *we* have rankings? There was some pretty wacky bullshit going on with surfing at the time. Others didn't share the vision but we were like, what if this was organised?' A meeting of surfers was held during the 1975 Bells event and the idea of the Australian Professional Surfers Association was sparked. 'Sid [Cassidy]with his media angle, Claw with the business angle, PT with his typewriter and me with my Formula 1 ideas. Can you picture that room?' The APSA would bring together the four Australian pro events under the one banner, create a ratings system, and hatch a plan to chase sponsorship and media coverage. 'It gave it form and purpose and, more importantly,' recalls Ian, 'it gave us proof of a concept to do the same thing globally.' The genesis of the world tour happened in Australia, in 1975.

In South Africa that year the discussions to take pro surfing global began. How could they bring together the gypsy tour under one banner and make it work? 'A patchwork quilt when it's all put together makes complete sense,' offers Ian, 'but there's all of these individual patches that you look at and go, how does this match up with that and that and that? That's the magnificent thing of taking a diverse group of people with different ideas and aligning them around one big inspirational idea that everyone can agree on. That's what that time was like. Everyone wanted something more … but no one knew what more was.' Hawaiian Randy Rarick was in South Africa, and it was agreed he'd take the idea to Fred Hemmings in Hawaii. A year later a professional world tour became reality with the formation of the International Professional Surfers (IPS). Peter Townend would be its inaugural world champion. Ian Cairns would finish second.

While he was in South Africa, Ian took a flight and visited his brother in Rhodesia. 'He was living in Salisbury and working as a geologist. He was working for a big mining company and would go out into the bush cracking rocks, which is what he'd done in Western Australia too.' The vast, ancient African landscape Ian encountered came straight out of a Wilbur Smith novel. 'When I was there I went to the Zimbabwe ruins. These people had built this civilisation, these granite fortresses on hillsides with farms in the flats. I loved the history of the Matabili and the Zulu. This was the fabric of my life on the tour,' he offers. 'To travel to all these amazing places and just sit on a beach and go surfing would be a travesty. I wanted to explore culturally as well as surf.'

In Hawaii that year Ian was staying with a South African guy named Al Paterson up at Sunset Beach. 'Al was actually from Zambia originally and he could remember being on the roof of his house when he was younger with terrorists trying to kill him. He got driven out and moved to South Africa and that's where he started surfing. Eventually he'd landed in Hawaii. Al was a waiter at Turtle Bay but had helped start the Beachcomber Bills Grand Prix series that ran in parallel with the IPS for a few years in Hawaii." Fred [Hemmings] hated it,' laughs Ian of the Grand Prix. 'Fred wanted control.'

In between surfs Ian watched American football on TV. He saw more than the game. 'I liked American football and I liked it because of its skill but also its structure and organisation. Aussie rules was more fluid; I liked structure. My dad was an engineer and I visualised things like machines. Surfing contests are huge machines and each machine needed to be put together, oiled and fuelled up. Everyone had jobs and responsibilities to make it run.' Beyond the Great Machine, Ian saw great opportunity. 'What appealed to me about sport was the democratic chance for people who have nothing to rise on the biggest stage through their own ability. It's that blue-collar democracy where you can rise to the level of your talents.'

Ian had won the Smirnoff contest in '73 on a board he'd shaped himself but had a sobering realisation soon after. 'I realised you can't be a great surfer *and* a great shaper. It's just too much. I surfed Sunset most of the time and the most inspirational person out there was Barry Kanaiaupuni. He shaped surfboards and I thought okay, maybe this guy has a special formula for his boards. I bought my first board from him in January 1974. That was the beginning of that relationship. Barry's rockers allowed you to take off and jam it mid-face, which was the special surfing innovation I copied from him for surfing Sunset, Haleiwa and those kind of waves. You need to get going

down the line. By the time you were at the bottom of the wave you've missed it … it's already happening down the line somewhere. You needed to drive across the face and Barry's boards had that unique curve in them that allowed you to do that.'

Kanga's secret weapon for the 1975 Hawaiian winter was a narrow 8'6" BK swallowtail, white with a black lightning bolt shooting down the stringer. The board was designed, Ian remembers, 'for shortboard performance surfing in giant waves'. Ian was hardly running low on confidence heading into the '75 Smirnoff. 'I'd surf out at Waimea recreationally on big days, and on those days I'd be too deep, always. That's how I surfed it; I'd stand there and take it like a man.' In the end he was a little too confident. 'In my mind I'd already won the Smirnoff, but then Mark Richards comes along and beats me. How did that happen? I underestimated him, which was his way. He snuck up on you. MR was quietly brilliant.' The Duke contest was next. 'I'm like, that's not happening again. Bring on the Duke.'

The final of the Duke was held at maxing Waimea. 'We rock up and we're standing there in the parking lot and the ground is shaking and the street signs are rattling and it's so noisy and everyone is looking at everyone else. The contest director goes, "If someone wants to go out we're running," and I'm like, "We're running!" I'd waited my entire life for this moment. Everyone else meanwhile is screaming and yelling at me, "Fuck you, Kanga!" It didn't occur to me that anyone else *wouldn't* want to go out there. If you ever wanted a day to hold the Duke this was it. This represented the *mana* of what I believed this event was all about. It was closing out Waimea. I could paddle out there and put my name alongside Hawaiian royalty like Eddie and Clyde and Barry. I felt we're all part of this long story, these people regardless of race or colour who were all connected by this spiritual love of surfing and this desire to raise ourselves up … and raise everyone in the process.'

Waimea was boiling. 'You'd look up toward Shark Cove and these things are 30 foot and pitching onto bare rock and you've got a minute before that set gets to you and you're trying to position and everyone out there is going, "You want this Kanga?" and I'm like, "Yep!" The dynamic of competition was flipped on its head. No one wanted a piece of those waves. I went out and charged. I was super deep. I'd do a bottom turn and try and go off the top. I saw Waimea as a performance wave and because I had the board for it and because I'd learned from Barry to bury the rail mid-face I could take off deeper and surf it like a smaller wave. There's a great photo from that day of Hakman in a power crouch and I'm doing a bottom turn behind him, looking to head up toward the lip.'

In the dying minutes of the Duke final, Kanga found himself leading comfortably when the biggest set of the day rolled through. 'I went for that wave and thought I could do no wrong. Waimea at 20 feet is just a big peak, but at 25 feet the top of the wave jacks when it hits the reef, it jacks higher as you're paddling and you get sucked up backwards and that's what happened to me. I went over the falls; had the massive wipeout. I came up barely before the next wave. I was looking down a black tunnel and there was a tiny pinhole of light at the end of it. I could see peoples' arms moving, I could see their mouths moving but I couldn't hear anything … and then the next wave hit me and washed me in. I won by default that day. Waimea won. But I feel like I was chosen to be in the Duke event, to be in that place at that time … and to be the champion. That's the spiritual nature of that event.'

The presentation that night was out at the Kuilima where Ian was handed the perpetual Duke trophy, the heroic denouement of his own surfing epic. 'And of course at that point I change back into Ian Cairns and I'm like, "I'm the champ!" The whole persona of what everyone chooses to believe I am took over. You had the juxtaposition of this typical larrikin Aussie with someone who had the depth of feeling to understand what the Duke event represented. Those two storylines ran through it … but everyone saw only one.'

It wouldn't be until the following season in 1976 when Ian returned to Hawaii and found his BK Lightning Bolt boards had been impounded that he began to twig that something was wrong. 'There's always tensions there in Hawaii, I just didn't realise it'd be as bad as it was. We talked it up big and acted brash like typical Aussies. Where you come from in Australia, to rise to that level takes a ballsy bloke. I mean, how else can these dreams ever come true? The backlash that occurred in Hawaii the following winter was over the top but it also suited an agenda. And for me, well, rather than feeling like I was part of this long historical line of people honouring the Sport of Kings, I was an outsider again.'

1975

Rabbit Bartholomew

Tracks: 'What's the biggest wave you've caught?'

Rabbit: 'I guess it would have been Waimea. It was just pretty big, you know. Like you just have to take off on the set. I wouldn't take the first wave in case I didn't make the drop and I got fucking pummelled by the next lot so I took the fourth wave, which is usually a better wave anyway. The last wave I had before I left was a pretty big wave because I dropped in on José Angel and he fucking ate it going down the face.'

Tracks: 'It was a big wave, eh?'

Rabbit: 'Yeah, it's only the drop. It's a pretty easy drop.'

Tracks: 'Did you only have one real session at Waimea?'

Rabbit: I've only surfed once in my life there. I've caught seven waves there.'

It is fair to say Wayne 'Rabbit' Bartholomew had a large bit of teenage swagger to him at this point. He'd just got home from the booming Hawaiian winter of '74/'75, had a breakout season, surfed big Waimea, surfed Third Reef Pipe and had been a whisker away from getting an invite into the Hawaiian events. At 19, 'Muhammad Bugs' was ready to make a statement. The *Tracks* interview titled 'Run Rabbit, Run' caused a stir, although it was more his colourful assessment of the Queensland Education Department that raised eyebrows. His fade on the legendary José Angel and his conquering of Waimea, well, they'd be filed under 'youthful exuberance' and allowed to slide. For now.

The Hawaiian contest season that winter was split in two either side of Christmas, so Rabbit found himself back on a plane to the islands in January 1975. Hawaiian surfing icon George Downing ran the Hang Ten and Lightning Bolt events, and Bugs was so confident he'd score invites to both he went down to the bank before he left home in Coolangatta and got a loan for $200 to pay his entry fees. He got to Hawaii and the $200 was promptly stolen after a break-in.

But Rabbit got entry into both events and scrounged the money. The Hang Ten was held at solid Sunset. Shaun Tomson won. The win was a breakthrough for Shaun but also for Rabbit. If Shaun could win, so could he. The Lightning Bolt was next. 'They held the Lightning Bolt at Velzyland,' recalls Rabbit. 'That was the only event I'd ever surfed at Velzyland and there was a real fun vibe to it because it's such a hotdog wave.' V-Land was also a local stronghold but Bugs had been welcomed, largely due to his friendship with Michael Ho, but he was on good terms with most of the Hawaiian crew at this point.

The Lightning Bolt was held over two rounds. Terry Fitzgerald won. 'The first round I got tenth,' Bugs recalls, 'but the second round I won. I came third overall and that paved the way for the following winter. I was guaranteed of getting invites to the Smirnoff, the Pipe Masters and Haleiwa when I came back later in the year.'

Rabbit's result in Hawaii had been big news back home on the Gold Coast. He'd made all the newspapers, however it wasn't universally celebrated. A news clipping of the Rabbit story had been cut out of the paper and pinned to the wall at Michael Peterson Surfboards, with the word 'Bullshit!' scrawled underneath by the proprietor. MP had barely lost a heat in Australia in two years but had struggled to win in Hawaii. The fact that 'Chine' had jagged a result in Hawaii had pissed him off.

'Here we are, *bang*. Me and Michael. We were into a fierce rivalry by then. What had happened in the Queensland Titles, I'd won in '73 and '74 and at the time they were the big events on the Gold Coast and there was no way he liked it. In 1975 what happened – and there's footage of this, Dale Egan's got this on film – the Queensland Titles had been at Burleigh and I was in one semi-final and MP was in the other, and in those days the hooter finished one heat and started the next. Bang, you're on. This wave came and there's seconds left and I look down the line and MP's paddling for it because he's in the next heat. The hooter goes and we both get up. I drop down, he drops in on me, he tries to fade me, I pull in around him into the barrel and suddenly we're both in the same barrel together. We're in the barrel together at Burleigh and I see it's closing out down the line so I jam out through the doggie door, MP gets spat out down the line and we turn around and shake our fists at each other. And we both got scored! It was so epic.' The swell jumped the following day and the final was held at giant Kirra. Michael won the '75 Queensland Titles in double-overhead sand tubes. 'It was masterful,' recalls Rab, 'one of his finest moments.'

Nineteen-seventy-five was a banner year for swell on the Gold Coast. 'It was a big freesurfing year,' Bugs recalls. 'That was the year of the 28-day swell at Burleigh. The thing with that was that MP and I didn't turn up at Burleigh until the 27th day of the swell. What had happened, they'd built the Kirra groynes at the end of '72 and during all of '73 and '74 Kirra didn't break. There was no sand. It wasn't till '75 that the sand made it around the Big Groyne and that swell actually built the bank at Kirra. While everyone else and all the photographers were up at Burleigh, day after day MP and I were watching the Kirra bank get better and better. It went from the Big Groyne for a hundred metres then down to the shed to the Butterbox section. MP and I weren't talking much at this point, but out there we looked at each other and knew we were killing it. They could have Burleigh. There was no way we were leaving Kirra.'

By the end of the swell Rabbit was cooked. 'I wasn't even surfing after that; I didn't need to. The only thing I'd do was paddle out and surf this guy's kneeboard at Greenmount. It was so much fun, this 22-inch wide kneeboard. Guys came up from Sydney and wondered what we were doing but we were that burnt out from surfing Kirra that we were riding these weird boards. It was just playtime for us. We'd been paddling for two months. We were so frazzled we couldn't even turn anymore.

'Those months of April and May were so amazing. I was hanging out with Shane and Dale Egan, who lived in this little cottage at Rainbow Bay. They were colourful cats. Shane was the artist, so eccentric. It was a magical time around here. I'd go down to the Coke Classic and I'd stay at the Egans' place at Warriewood and there was just a beautiful vibe about that year for me.'

The Australian pro contest season came and went for Bugs without much success. MP won Bells. Wayne Lynch returned from the wilderness to win the Coke. Terry Fitz won the Aussie titles. Bugs was content. He'd had a year's worth of surf already and there was Hawaii still to come. Nothing could knock Rabbit off his cloud, not even travelling with Keith Paull and having to bail him out of some outrageous predicaments, like driving his car up the stairs and into the Pearl Hotel at Caloundra or streaking naked through the Torquay Hotel in just army boots and a Russian Cossack hat.

As the days melted away in Coolangatta, Bugs got lost in his own fantasy surf epic. 'I was reading *Lord of the Rings* that year and here we were; we lived in this magical place and we all thought we were Hobbits in the Shire. It really felt like that. Here I was, Frodo Baggins. It sounds weird but it was exactly how it was, and for me leaving here at the end of the year to go to Hawaii was like leaving the Shire to go to Mordor!' Rab laughs, 'It *really* turned into Mordor for me the following year.'

Shaun Tomson turned up to Hawaii on 1st October that year, and it pissed Rabbit off no end. 'Shaun and I were really vying to be recognised as the leader of the new guard and Shaun had beaten us to the punch by getting there on the 1st. It was so early in the season. Me and Ian Cairns got there on the 20th of October and there'd already been an Off The Wall swell and Shaun had secured cover shots of *Surfer* and *Surfing* before we were even there!'

'Me and Ian, we took our own path. The very first surf we had in Hawaii that year we walked down the beach at 10-foot Pipe. It was a bit raggedy but it was solid. Ian turned around and said, "Right, we're going to make a splash here … you can't go left!" We went out there and surfed Backdoor and took some horrendous beatings. We were just pulling into these big closeouts. Ian hit the reef and ended up with a big chunk out of his arse. It was all-time. The attitude was to paddle straight out and take your beating, get it done, and cut a lot of corners. It'd take you a month to get there otherwise.'

'The gnarly thing was that we came in from that and the adrenaline was pumping. It was a hairy couple of hours. We're sitting there on the beach and José Angel has walked down past us with his board under his arm and kind of looked at us out of the corner of his eye. He gave us the once-over. José's the full Hawaiian legend, and he's paddled straight out through Backdoor, where you should never paddle out. It's dry reef. He's paddled out and made it just before a huge set rolled through. Well, he's paddling up this wave, paddling vertically up this mean wave and halfway up it he spun around, did a no-paddle take-off, free-fell to the bottom and just got annihilated. No leggies of course so he's swum in, grabbed his board and then walked straight past us without saying a word. He was bleeding and had this big chunk out of his cheek. But didn't say anything. He didn't need to. He was such a macho surfer, and we knew we'd just been trumped.'

The previous winter in Hawaii, Rabbit had caddied for Ian Cairns. 'Ian had pretty much taken me under his wing, because I recognised him as Australia's best big-wave rider. In '74 I was his caddy and that was a good introduction because he was a gnarly guy to caddy for. You did a lot of swimming. I remember one time at Sunset he took off on this mean wave that doubled up and the lip landed on his head and pushed him straight through his board. He came up and insisted I swim in and find both halves! He was yelling at me. He was doing all this gnarly shit and because I was his caddy I was dragged into it as well. My pay was a smorgasbord at the Kuilima, but after a day's caddying I was so exhausted I couldn't put my fork to my mouth. But it was a great learning curve. I was watching everything; watching the currents and the sets and so by '75 I was ready to have a go myself.'

Rabbit's first Smirnoff event was held at good 10-foot Sunset. Rabbit made it to the final, only for them to announce they were holding the final off until the following day. The final six were Reno Abellira, Jeff Hakman, Ian Cairns, MR, Shaun and Rabbit. 'It was a classic final. The Hawaiian champions against the newcomers.' The swell spiked overnight and the following morning Rabbit was staring at 25-foot Waimea. 'It wasn't as big as the Smirnoff the year before on Thanksgiving Day. I mean, that day was pretty much 40-foot, but we were looking at 25-foot Hawaiian. I felt ready to have a crack because the year before on that Thanksgiving Day, after the Smirnoff final, a bunch of us young guys had paddled out.' This was the Waimea session Rabbit mentioned in the *Tracks* interview. 'Bruce Raymond, Simon, Shaun and me, we all paddled out, so at least the following year making that final I had that under my belt. I'd surfed it at that size.'

MR won the Smirnoff with Ian Cairns second. Bugs got third. 'It ended up being one-two-three and that was the big moment,' recalls Bugs. 'When we went one-two-three at Waimea, that was the changing of the guard right there.' Ian Cairns then went and won the Duke at out-of-bounds Waimea and the shift could no longer be ignored.

Bugs topped an epic season of waves at home with an epic Hawaiian winter. 'I'd won 1200 bucks and that allowed me to stay till February. Though it was early in my career it was a peak. It was a good year; a lot of Sunset, a lot of Off The Wall and so much west Pipe. Bill Delaney shot the final sequence of *Free Ride* of me and Shaun when we were the two best backside guys at Pipe. If you've seen *Free Ride* you know how good the surf was. It was a memorable season.'

The zenith of the '75 Hawaiian winter was a 12-day swell in December. 'It's such a rare thing,' says Rabbit, 'a 12-day west swell at Pipeline culminating seriously on Christmas Day. By then everyone was cooked. I was so tuned in. I'm riding a 6'8" out there, which back then was a really short board to ride. The big day, Christmas Day, was a solid 12 foot with hardly a soul out.' Rabbit was dating Michael Ho's sister, Debbie, and had been invited to Christmas dinner with the Ho family down at Waimanalo on the other side of the island. 'Well, we surfed Pipe in the morning, we surfed it again at lunch, and when I got ready for Christmas dinner there was Michael with his board under his arm and he looks at me and goes, "Brah, it's just too good. Let's get out there." We surfed till dark and got down to Waimanalo and everyone was pissed off with us. Michael made up all these excuses and we were forgiven.' After months in Hawaii Rabbit was comfortable in Hawaiian surf. He even had a pass to surf V-Land. He got a little too comfortable, calling a guy out who got slapped by another local as a result. The mood with the local Hawaiians was shifting without Rabbit knowing it.

For now though, the Hawaiian winter was all sunshine. 'I started out staying with Jeff Divine,' recalls Rabbit, 'but as the winter went on I split and I ended up staying in The Barracks on the beach at Rocky Point. It was low rent, a mattress on the floor, but it was a classic. I was staying with Doris Eltherington and there was this young Californian kid staying with us. I didn't know who he was. No idea. He was a great kid though and he became like my caddy. We'd get up in the morning and walk down to Pipeline from Rocky Point and I'd get down there and it'd be bigger than I thought and I'd ask this kid to run and get my 7'10". He'd trot back to Rocky Point and come back with my board. Anyway, it went onshore this day, in between swells, not much happening, and someone suggested we go skateboarding in town. They had all these drains which were makeshift skate parks and we ended up at this place called "Uluwatus". Bertlemann was there, Buttons was there, this other kid, Roy Jamieson, who was the best Hawaiian skater. They were all there this day. It was amazing. Well, all of a sudden this Californian kid who was staying with us gets in there and just starts *ripping*. It turns out the kid was Tony Alva. He was the best skater in the world and we had no idea. Doris barks, "I'll have a go at this!" and he grabs the skateboard and drops in and hits the bottom awkwardly and his leg snaps. Doris went down and I went, "Nah, I'm not getting on that thing." Doris was in a cast for six weeks. That was his winter done.

'Seventy-five for me was an incredible year because it was my last year of real freedom over there for a long time. I didn't get my mojo back until '82, '83, and even the years in between I never had that same freedom I had in '75. I still had to dodge and weave a bit.' Bugs returned to Hawaii on 1st October 1976. 'I wasn't letting Shaun beat me there. I went back on 1st October to do what Shaun did to us the year before. Little did I know I was Mr Magoo going over there with no idea what I was walking into. But I wasn't going over there to take on the Hawaiians; I was going there to take on Shaun, Ian Cairns, Mark Richards and PT. They were the ones I was competing against, not the Hawaiians. I just wanted to get over there and establish myself and get some cover shots at Pipeline and that was my plan … but of course it came unstuck in a spectacular way.'

1976

Mark Warren

'I remember 1976 was a good year for me competitively, because I won the Aussie title at Point Leo. The final was a real beauty. It was at Gunnamatta and the surf was just shit. It was onshore slop and I remember Rabbit was having a bad session. Suddenly he paddled in yelling, "Shark! Shark!" No one else saw it … but I suppose it was possible. So, we went in and I remember giving him the eye and going, "I don't care, mate, let's run it again." So, we ran it again and I ended up winning.' It was fourth time lucky for Mark, who'd surfed three previous Aussie title finals. 'For me, 1976 was a pretty formative year,' he recalls. 'The Aussie title gave me a lot of confidence.'

Mark Warren, however, was never short on confidence. Having grown up in Narrabeen, he was a competitive animal, but he was a *good-looking* competitive animal. Sharp, well-spoken and with hair that never moved out of place, he was well equipped to make an impact in the first full year of pro surfing.

It was pro surfing by name, but not yet by pay packet. 'None of us were making any money,' remembers Mark, 'there were little pots of prizemoney here and there but by the time you paid everyone you owed money to, you were broke again. The airfares were expensive, the cost of living was high.'

In early 1976 Mark was approached by Sydney sports journo Mike Hurst, who'd previously managed Sydney punk band Radio Birdman. Hurst hatched a plan to create a marketing troupe of pro surfers. He'd already signed Ian Cairns and Peter Townend, the two guys who'd willed the pro tour into existence. The 'Bronzed Aussies'

would revolutionise the way the newly professional sport of surfing did business. 'So I signed on and we actually had Mark Richards interested there for a while. I distinctly remember having a conversation with him and I said, "Mark, you'll be missing out on a great opportunity." He knocked us back. "Nope, I just want to surf and shape."'

Part *Countdown* glam rock, part corporate hustle and with the surfers sporting matching outfits, the Bronzed Aussies 'really went out of our way to promote surfing. We were going to the media rather than the media coming to us. The surfers would largely ignore the straight media yet we did the opposite. We actually went out and hunted the media down. Mike pitched this idea about the BA's Surf Show to Double J radio in Sydney and we did that for probably a year, which was actually really hard because we'd have to go out and get the interviews. I remember going to a Jackson Browne press conference and Mike, at the end of it, goes "Hey, would you like to do an interview with some surfers?"'

'We also got onto this idea of doing clothing, which nearly took off. That nearly happened, and Quiksilver were actually interested in sponsoring us at one point. Alan Green was half-interested, he heard us out, but I think his colleagues at the time saw through it and went, "Nope, we're not sponsoring those dudes, we're going to stay cool."'

The Bronzed Aussies copped a lot of shit as sell-outs. 'It gave Phil Jarratt so much ammunition in *Tracks*,' laughs Mark. 'I remember the *Tracks* cover where he had a box of Corn Flakes with me surfing on the front. I got kind of offended at the time because I was pretty easy to offend, a bit of a softie, but it was like, "Oh, c'mon, we're not that bad." We were just fodder, weren't we?' More pointedly, however, the Bronzed Aussies failed to make any money and Mark would leave the following year.

Mark, at this point, had his own side hustle going. The idea of making surf wax had come about when Mark's dad, who kept beehives behind the garage, had wondered aloud what to do with the beeswax after he'd spun the honey out of it. 'So we made surf wax. Dad was very clever,' remembers Mark, 'because if you melt the wax and take it above its melting point, it sets really brittle and hard. He used steam to melt it. We had a little bit of beeswax in there but not much; mainly it was a petroleum product. I remember us making the wax and I've heard him swearing, "Fucking bees! Fucking things!" We'd just poured a couple of hundred blocks of wax and the bees could smell it, and they were coming out and landing in the wax and sinking. He was picking them out, and I went, "Nah, nah, leave a couple in there!" People loved the idea. The bees dragged all their dead outside the hive, so I was going out, picking up the dead bees and plonking them in the wax. It was a real backyard family business; it gave my dad a bit of a lift because he was retired, and we employed my sisters and my cousin.' Mark had the sales pitch down. 'It was a huge block. It was value for money, and it smelled amazing. It had the honey scent in it as well.'

The smell of honey-scented surf wax was the smell of summer for grommets right around the country, but the wax proved popular with all ages, for all kinds of reasons. 'The funny thing was I remember going over to the south side of Sydney and finding this company that brought in the first zip-lock bags. I took over my artwork and they made the bags for us, and zip-lock bags were really new then. Anyway, a few weeks later this guy comes up to me, whacked to the eyeballs, and he goes. "Yeah, man, your wax is cool … but this bag is so handy to keep my mull in!" I was fully anti-dope at that stage, I was really straight, and I was horrified. I laughed about it eventually but I felt at the time like I was contributing to the drug trade.'

Mark Warren's 1976 was capped off with a memorable win at the Smirnoff in Hawaii. 'That day with the Smirnoff, it was just beautiful, beautiful Sunset. To be out there with just six guys in the water was a blessing and I thrived on that. I just had one of those sessions where I got any wave that came my way. It was a real privilege to win that event. Eddie Aikau was in that final, MR got second and PT was there too. I was very lucky, of course, but I just had a great day at Sunset.'

The Smirnoff, up until 1976, had been regarded as an unofficial world title but was superseded that year by the first IPS pro tour ratings. Most guys on tour were in the dark about how the ratings worked, Mark included. 'It was retrospective. The tour ratings started that year except it was like, "Hang on, we're going to go back a year and count all these events."' PT and Ian had almost willed the new system into being. PT would eventually be crowned world champ, with Ian second. Mark would finish 1976 rated fourth.

Mark won the Smirnoff on a 7'8" McCoy, whose boards he'd ridden since he was a kid working in the McCoy factory as a finish coater. 'It was a green board. My colours were green and magenta, because I'd worked with George Greenough and he said, "Mark, if you want to stand out, you've got to paint your fins white and you've got to have contrasting colours." Because George was a cameraman, he goes, "It'll catch the judge's eye, you've got to do this." I actually got a couple of jobs with George. I remember one he was shooting in Hawaii for Coca-Cola Japan. He needed to get a shot of someone going over the falls at inside Sunset, and because I'd worked in the media I knew the shot he needed to get, so I paddled out and got smashed. George was great. I remember going to Turtle Bay once with him and we had to find him some shoes because he was barefoot, and his pants were held up by a piece of rope tied at the front. Then I mentioned to him, "George, your hair's a bit long." And he went, "You know, you're right," so he picked up a knife off the table and just cut a hunk off his fringe, right there.'

The 1976 Hawaiian winter was a nervous time to be an Australian surfer on the North Shore. It was the 'Busting Down The Door' winter and Mark's fellow Bronzed Aussies, Ian and PT, were in hiding from some very angry Hawaiians. 'That was pretty heavy, that whole thing, that was really nasty … and really quite unnecessary in hindsight. Everyone was bloody scared.'

Despite the association, Mark was fine. 'I got on with everybody. The funny thing was, Leonard Brady and Bernie Baker – the Island Style photo guys – they actually said to me, "You're *too* nice, Mark." Anyway, I remember I did a photo trip with them and MR that year, we went over to Molokai looking for surf. We didn't find anything good, went to the wrong places. We came back to Honolulu [it was Christmas Eve] and they offered for me to stay at Leonard's place in town. I said, "Oh, no, I want to get back to the North Shore, there might be waves tomorrow." Leonard goes, "I want to give you this gift." It was all wrapped up, and I picked it up and he went, "You can't open it till tomorrow … you've got to open it in front of the BAs, all right?" And I went, "Oh, okay," and they said, "Put it in the fridge." I had no idea. I was so naïve. I said, "What is it? It's too heavy to be chocolates."

'I got back to the North Shore late and I put the package in the fridge. The next morning I got up, and everyone's opening Christmas presents. Anyway, I go, "Oh, I've got this gift in the fridge," so I go and open it up. Well, mate, you should have seen everyone's eyes when I opened this thing up. Here's this gun with a box of hollow-point bullets. It was a .357 Magnum, a big beast of a thing. Leonard came out to the North Shore in his Corvette later, and he goes 'Right, we're going to go and shoot the gun." So we just drove into the sugarcane fields on the other side of the road from Turtle Bay, up this dirt road to buggery at the foot of the little hills. We put six bullets in the chamber and he goes, "Right, hit that sign over there." And the sign, dead set, was 15-feet away and it's about six feet by 10 feet, this big rusty sign. I pull the trigger and the gun explodes and bucks in my hand and my ears are ringing. Leonard then goes, "Empty the chamber!" I emptied the chamber and didn't hit the sign once. I could have thrown the gun at it and hit it. I remember on the flight home a few days later my ears were still ringing.'

Mark doesn't remember much about the night he won the Smirnoff in 1975, but he does remember the night he won the Duke contest in Hawaii a few years later in 1980. 'We're all there celebrating at a party up at Turtle Bay in one of the condos, and someone comes in and says, "Holy shit! John Lennon's just been shot!" It just put such a dampener on everything. Everybody went home after that. But you know what they discovered? The guy who shot him had bought that gun in Haleiwa. I'd gone into that hardware store to buy resin to patch dings, and I remember looking at all the guns in the cabinet wide-eyed like a young Aussie. We never saw guns at home, and the guy behind the counter comes over, sees me and hands me a gun and goes, "Here you go, hang onto that fella. How's that feel?" And I'm like, "Err, have you got any surfboard resin?"'

1977

Col Smith

Col Smith had just been asked in a 1977 *Tracks* interview if his surfing revolved around pulling off 'gravity defying stunts'. Col wasn't sure if the interviewer was taking the piss. 'Well, let me put it this way … ' After a weighty pause Col told it straight. 'There are certain manoeuvres that are near impossible … *and I'm going for those manoeuvres*. I don't really like going for tubes all the time. If there's a tube there and I can't avoid it I'll go for it, but there's nothing very difficult about getting tubes. I'm not going for the packet of hundreds and thousands … I'm going for *the big one*!' This wasn't a hollow boast. Col Smith might have been ancient at 28 … but he was the oldest, most radical surfer in the world.

Going for the big one had recently landed him in hospital. 'I was always trying to do stuff that no one else could do,' Col remembers today, 'and the thing no one else could do was a barrel roll. To turn around, upside-down *inside* the barrel and land it. The first guy I ever saw do one was a dirt-bike champion named Herbie Jefferson. He did a barrel roll on a kneeboard at Angourie and made it. I went, that looks good. If he can do it on a kneeboard, I can do it standing up. So this day at Car Park Rights at Narrabeen the waves were just phenomenal. I dropped down this wave on my backhand, jammed a turn and went right round inside the wave. I made the barrel roll, I was 99 per cent there, but came down and fell off the front of the board. It whacked me in the mouth. The nose of the board hit me and snapped off in my face. I pulled this bit of fibreglass out and went, what's this? I pulled it out and my bloody top and bottom lip nearly fell off! I got a hundred stitches, but I'd been pretty close to making it.' To this day no surfer ever has.

Col Smith's radical streak had started early in life. Soon after moving to Narrabeen at age 10, he'd taken his mother's wooden ironing board, stripped all the metal fittings off, cut his jeans down into shorts and gone surfing. A couple of years later his brother brought him home a 10'6" balsa noserider from the States, which Col had no intention of noseriding. 'Chris Crozier and I cut three feet off it and that was our shortboard.' Col was a child of the shortboard revolution and like most of those kids would almost immediately take it too far. 'We made them smaller and smaller and smaller to the point where I ended up one year riding a 4'10" board at 15-foot Margaret River. Very hard to get into them, but once you got up you were fine. Boards just kept getting smaller and all different styles. I made a board that nearly looked like a football, only five-foot long, super-round, but you could sort of hang ten on it.' As a kid Col also rode skateboards for the Midget Farrelly skate team. 'I remember I did a demo at Dee Why and another out at Ryde where the big shopping centre is. It was a bit scary, downhill racing at Dee Why in bare feet and a see-through skateboard.'

Maybe the biggest influence on Col Smith's surfing, though, was a kid his own age. Col doesn't remember ever actually surfing with Wayne Lynch, but in those years before Wayne stepped away from the spotlight he was kind of hard to miss. In particular, it was Wayne's backhand re-entry that caught Col's attention. 'Many times I'd watch him and think, gee whiz, I'd like to do that.' If Wayne was the first to train the board vertically at the lip on his backhand, Col was the one who took it past its physical limit. 'It got to the stage where I thought, look, most of the surfing contests are held in righthanders, I'm going to ride rights better than I can ride lefts. And that's exactly what I could do.' Narrabeen was the best left in Sydney. Col preferred Car Park Rights, just down the beach.

However, the biggest influence on Col was Narrabeen itself. 'As a kid you weren't allowed to surf Narrabeen until you were good enough. They were the rules. It was strict.' Young Col worked his way up the beach from Waterloo Street to The Pines and eventually to The Alley. Col remembers the 'Log Mob', a hardcore group who hung around a log that had washed up on the beach. Before it was Narrabeen against the world, it was always Narrabeen against Narrabeen. 'It was ruled with an iron fist,' recalls Col of the Narrabeen scene. 'Very strong but very close. It's probably the closest community I've ever been involved with.'

Throughout the '70s Col Smith was the alpha male at North Narrabeen ... the most alpha lineup in Australia. Col had the women. Col had the soul patch beard and Col had the cars. He'd do burn-outs in the Narrabeen car park in his FJ, smoking the place up until the diff blew. He would occasionally paddle out with a cigarette in his mouth and drop in on someone with it still alight. He'd scold the local grommets for not hitting the lip hard enough. 'All the competitiveness was out in the water,' Col recalls. 'It didn't matter who was who; you were going out there to surf … you weren't going out there to make friends. It had a reputation for that.' At a time when it seemed every surfing beach had their resident surfing animal, a wild man in and out of the water, Narrabeen had Col Smith.

Just surfing Narrabeen wouldn't be enough for a competitive animal like Col. He needed other outlets. A natural athlete and all-round sportsman, he excelled at everything he turned his hand to. Col was a great tennis player, footballer and ice hockey player. He'd never ice skated before but was playing Sydney first grade within nine months. The physicality of ice hockey suited him perfectly. 'That was to learn how to fight,' he laughs. 'Every time you go on you're in a fight. I remember this guy smashed me into the railing so I let him have it. And that was my career in first grade ice hockey. Straight into the sin bin. But I loved it. I used to do barrel jumping on the ice. I could jump 10 barrels. If I took something up I wanted to get full-on into it.'

Cars were his real vice. Col was a car guy. 'Was I ever. I put a 351 Ford into a four-cylinder Transit van. Mate, that was the fastest thing on the planet. It had four wheels on the back and I could wheel spin them up to 60 miles an hour. Then I bought myself a '66 Pontiac GTO, two-door, two-speed powerglide, a hundred mile an hour in first gear. I also had an old Ford Fairmont station wagon that I had lowered with all the whiteys on them.' Col helped build the fastest sedan racer in the country, and although he didn't race it himself, he was a demon behind the wheel. He recalls driving north on a surf trip to Newcastle and being overtaken by another car doing 80 miles an hour. 'This car shot past me, blew me off the road. I've tightened the seatbelt up and then took off after him. It felt like the car was floating. I looked at the speedo, which went up to 120. The needle had gone past that and was almost back around at zero.' When asked how it ended, Col replied, 'The car in front blew up.' Col's driving was a bit like Col's surfing – not exactly refined, but always in the red.

Col earned his living shaping surfboards. His shaping reflected his driving. 'I was a very, very fast shaper. I could turn out a board in 12 minutes. They weren't real good but I was still getting them out.' Col had got his start at 18, when Denny Keogh offered him a job down at Brookvale. 'I was a carpenter before that. I could cut the outlines out nearly perfect, but the rest of it was pretty bad. I ended up with a lot of wafers and this side's thicker than the other.' He laughs. 'But after doing twenty or thirty thousand I got there eventually.'

At Keyo's he shaped alongside Geoff McCoy and discovered Narrabeen competitiveness didn't stop at the tide line. 'Geoff and I were mates, but I'll never forget he said to me, "I'll never ever show you how to shape a surfboard." And I went, "Why not?" He goes, "Because every board you shape is one I don't!" I've never forgotten that. Every time I see him I remind him.'

Col shaped with Terry Fitzgerald at Hot Buttered before going out on his own in 1973 with Morning Star surfboards. 'The idea never entered my head, but one day Wayne Warner said to me, "You want to make surfboards?" I said, "Oh yeah." He asked, "How much money you got?" I replied, "Maybe 150 bucks." And he said, "Well I've got 250. Let's go make surfboards." So we ended up making 'em in his garage in Garden Street and that was our start.' Morning Star moved to Darley Road, Mona Vale, then opened a shop at Dee Why. Col even employed a young Simon Anderson. They then opened a surf shop in the Western Suburbs. 'Nat, Wayne and I went thirds in a shop out there ... which was about three kilometres from Bankstown Square. There were no other surf shops for 25 kilometres in any direction out there. We were only open 13 hours a week, but we took more money than any surf shop in Brookvale. We had 'em lined up going down the street to get in.'

The '70s was the golden age of surfing in Narrabeen. Guys like Terry Fitz, Grant Oliver, Mark Warren and Simon Anderson were winning contests all over the country, and in time, all around the world. Col's dominance of the Narrabeen lineup never translated to wider contest success. He never won a major title outside of Sydney. He'd been to Hawaii but rarely received invites to the contests there. He actually did receive an invite in '76 but nobody told him. Judging through the '70s also favoured numbers of turns, not one big radical turn. Hundreds and thousands, not *the big one*. 'Even though I might only be doing one manoeuvre,' he told *Tracks*, 'that's got to be better than doing a dozen other less radical ones.'

By 1977 the most radical surfer in Australia was getting on. Col was 28, married with a two-year-old daughter, not surfing as much and working long hours at Morning Star. He was, however, keeping the faintest hope alive for a major contest win. Pro surfing had arrived but he felt like an outsider to it. He was being overtaken by younger guys. In 1977 he surfed all four Australian pro events but only managed to finish mid-field in all of them. When Col looked at the ratings he saw his name respectably high. Then he saw his name again, way down the list in the same ratings. The guy higher up was Col Smith, a radical young goofyfooter from Newcastle. Col Smith from Newcastle had only surfed one event and was way ahead of Col Smith from Narrabeen, who'd surfed four. Narrabeen Col bristled, taking some consolation that at least a Narrabeen surfer – Simon Anderson – was leading the ratings.

Simon had been a Col Smith protégé, a role now being filled by 16-year-old Tom Carroll. Despite living up the peninsula at Newport, Tom was a regular down at Narrabeen. Col was shaping his boards, and when Tom got a start in the 1977 Stubbies at Burleigh – the first event of the first full professional season – he jumped in the front seat of Col's FJ. 'It was cool,' recalls Col. 'I was the oldest so I always used to have to cart everybody around. I took Tommy to his first surfing contest. That was the Stubbies that Peter Drouyn ran. At 10 o'clock in the morning the surf was going off and Drouyn would go, "Okay, contest over for the day!" Everybody lost it. He said, "Don't worry, the waves are going to be better tomorrow." He did this for 11 days and every single day the surf got bigger. It was absolutely phenomenal. Tommy had to go and surf against Shaun Tomson, who was the biggest surfer in the world at the time. I said, "Shit, mate, you want me to come down and stand on the rocks with you?"'

That just left the '77 Australian Titles, due to be held at Narrabeen. Col had flirted with the Aussie title in the past, having finished 10th, 9th, 8th, 7th, 6th, 4th and 4th. The past two Aussie titles had been won by Narrabeen surfers – Fitzy in '75, and Mark Warren in '76. Col Smith's biggest threat in 1977 was Col Smith. The two Cols – who didn't really know each other at the time – ended up surfing against each other in the final. 'That was fun,' recalls Col Smith from Narrabeen, who won. 'Col Smith first and Col Smith second and the write-up in the paper going, "This is not a misprint."'

For his win, Col was supposed to receive an airline ticket to Brazil to compete in the pro event there that year. The ticket never turned up. The pro tour took off without him. 'It was a bit hard because I had the family. I went to a few contests – I could've gone to a lot more – but I would've been away from home too much. I'd have to leave the kids behind and find somebody to do the shaping. I was getting too old and it was getting too expensive and I wasn't placing as high as I should. So, yeah, I gave it a miss after that.'

Col did the *Tracks* interview the week after his Aussie title win, sitting on the bonnet of his FJ. Tied to the roof racks was a set of snow skis. 'I just spent my first three days in the snow and I'm afraid of it! You see, if I get to like it, and I am *stoked* on it, I might have to give up surfing for a while. I've been thinking about it since I got back. It seemed to me that I learned more in the three days I spent there than guys who've been skiing for a couple of full seasons.' For the next five winter seasons, Col – forever obsessive – would make 20 trips a year down to the snow. In years to come snow skiing would be replaced by fishing and, later, by Ceroc jive dancing.

1977

Simon Anderson

When Simon Anderson says, 'Well, I suppose you could say I had a brief moment in the sun' you need to read between the lines. Sarcastically dry and comically loaded, it's often hard to know exactly what Simon's saying. How brief was the moment? Was the sun even shining? Simon, however, is also dreadfully humble, and as it turns out his brief moment in the sun was a whole year, a breakout year where he went from working-class Narrabeen surfing hero to world-class, working-class Narrabeen surfing hero.

When profiled by Phil Jarratt in the May 1977 issue of *Tracks*, Simon's reluctance to bask in his emerging notoriety was clear. 'Simon Anderson is dressed, as he always is for social occasions, in his wall-blending uniform of brown and white short-sleeved check sports shirt, fawn jeans and desert boots. The preservation of ordinariness was one of his prime concerns in life but tonight he faces an uphill battle.' The night in question was the presentation for the 1977 Coke Surfabout, which Simon had just won on his home beach of North Narrabeen. Simon accepted the trophy and thanked a table full of his well-oiled Narrabeen brethren. 'They are especially proud tonight,' offered Jarratt of the rabble sitting around the table at the back of the room, 'because one of their own is receiving the accolades. Not just another surfer from Narrabeen, but one who shares their no-nonsense creed of mateship, beach, pub, snooker and marrying the sheila you duff. Simon is, as he professes to be, just an ordinary bloke.'

Simon's ordinary blokiness was about to be tested. Nineteen-seventy-seven was the first fully fledged year of surfing's pro tour and it arrived with considerable hype. Peter

Townend had been retrospectively crowned 1976 World Champion, although as Simon remembers, 'that first year happened without too many people knowing it was actually a tour. I certainly didn't know there was a world tour going on. But '77,' he offers, 'was the ground floor of professional surfing. It was quite a big deal.' Some guys saw the tour as a ticket to surf the world. Some guys saw it as a ticket to stardom. Indeed Peter Townend would depart soon after for Hollywood to work as a surfing extra on *Big Wednesday*. Simon remained a little more grounded, a little more Narrabeen than Hollywood, and he saw the tour more as a test of both his surfing and shaping skills. 'The tour came and I guess I went into that year with open eyes, just to see what it was all about.' He pauses and quips, 'We quickly found out.'

The 1977 world tour opened with the Stubbies Classic at Burleigh Heads. Under a blinding Queensland sun, tens of thousands of surf fans turned up to watch the world's best duke it out. Burleigh pumped. Wrestling champion Lord Tallyho Blears provided blood and thunder commentary. Women in crochet bikinis paraded the point. Blokes drained XXXX tins under the pandanus. It was quite a scene. 'As for the crowds and the hype,' harrumphs Simon, 'well, it was the Gold Coast being the Gold Coast.'

If there wasn't enough buzz around the event, the Stubbies was also using a revolutionary new contest format devised by Peter Drouyn. Man-on-man surfing played to Drouyn's flair for the dramatic, and employed 'effective cheating' where surfers were encouraged to drop in on each other. If they happened to collide violently, then the cameras would be rolling to capture it. While effective cheating resembled everyday life in the water at North Narrabeen, Simon was after a purer challenge. 'Drouyn's original idea was a little gladiatorial, although that wasn't necessarily everyone else's vision. I know, personally, I was more interested in a fair competition and the opportunity to let your surfing decide the outcome rather than all the hassling.'

Simon was playing it low key. He'd driven up to the Gold Coast in his grey Holden, with mate Dave West riding shotgun. Once he got to the Gold Coast, instead of renting a condo like many of his peers he crashed on the floor of Phil Jarratt's room at the two-and-a-half star Classic Motel at Mermaid Waters. Simon arrived carrying his surfboards and three trays of sausages. He normally would also have arrived with a case of Toohey's New but in preparation for the tour he hadn't had a beer in five weeks, which for Simon was quite the sacrifice.

Jarratt's contest report in *Tracks* captured Simon's Stubbies regime. '*It's worth digressing here to explain the strange psych-up programs that pro surfers subject themselves to. Some of them drink heavily, others don't drink at all. Some of them read heavy literature and go to bed early, others watch television and eat sausages. In Simon's case the program seems to be working. He's surfing better than ever and we think we know why. After 15 solid hours of television watching can you imagine the energy and frustration that boils up inside the head and has to get loose? It's a frightening sight. Halfway through* Days Of Our Lives *I can see it coming on. The living room is quickly vacated as Simon drags himself up from the sofa, grunting, his nostrils twitching. His giant arms flail madly for the* TV Week *that Holmes has used to wrap the rubbish. I know that something terrible is about to happen. The grunting and groaning is getting louder. Now the vertical hold has gone. More groaning. With a gnashing of the teeth he tears through the skin of the last remaining sausage and pushes the plate aside. Even more grunting and… yes! A word. "Surfboard!" He said "surfboard". With sweating palms we thrust a surfboard in the general direction of the maniac and within seconds the old grey Holden is burning rubber to Burleigh where Simon will crush and kill and get his own back on Bert Newton and the rest of the bastards.'*

Simon would return from Burleigh and take up residence in front of the TV. The Centenary Ashes Cricket Test was on and Simon watched as David Hookes pummelled the Poms. At night, after a dinner of more sausages, Simon eschewed the lure of the Gold Coast nightlife to watch *Pot Black* or *Blankety Blanks* before regular programming was exhausted and the test pattern filled the screen.

Simon was a little overwhelmed by the scene on the hill at Burleigh. His equilibrium was already a bit wobbly. He'd picked up an ear infection while swimming as part of his preparation for Burleigh – 'that'll teach me to train' – and although he got past blond hotshot Cheyne Horan, he lost in the next round to South African Shaun Tomson. Simon and Shaun would shadow each other for the rest of the year; one a bona fide surf star from central casting, the other fighting the idea tooth and nail.

Bells was more Simon's style. The mercury hung in the low teens and there were no crochet bikinis to be seen as Simon swept through the trials, rolling into the main event. The Bells contest adopted Peter Drouyn's man-on-man format, but diluted the drama by running it over as many rounds as the Southern Ocean would allow. It dragged on for days. Drouyn was unimpressed, especially so after winning the first round. The pure vision of his format would have seen him ringing the bell. Instead it went into a second round, and halfway through this second round Simon couldn't be beaten. 'Bells was my big break,' recalls Simon. 'That was my first big contest win so for me personally that really proved something to myself.'

The win presented a fork in the road. Simon still considered himself a surfboard shaper first and a professional surfer second. Surfboards were his bread and butter, while he was simply moonlighting on the pro tour. Two years earlier he'd borrowed $3000 from his brother and started Energy Surfboards in a converted cottage in Carter Road, Brookvale. The Energy logo was a cosmic radiating sun inside a triangle, drawn by *Surfing World*'s Hugh McLeod. The reality of Energy was something more prosaic. 'No one at Energy could reasonably be called a space cowboy,' claimed *Tracks*. 'They're just blokes, ya know.' Simon shaped eight boards a week and the orders rolled in by word of mouth. Energy weren't even listed in the phone book; Simon's growing profile did the job.

'The thing about the Narrabeen area is that it has always been about surfers and surfboards,' says Simon. 'At that time everyone surfed and was involved in the industry somehow, whether they were a shaper, or a glasser, sander, a finish coater. All my mates worked in the industry in some way. Back then we had Geoff McCoy and Terry Fitz and Col Smith so we had three world-class board makers in town.'

For Simon, daily life was spent wearing a path back and forth between the Brookvale factory and the waves at North Narrabeen. 'I was working pretty hard. But back then I was pretty fit so I could surf in the morning, shape all day, then surf again in the afternoon. So that was kind of no problem. It was horses for courses.' But winning Bells shifted Simon's outlook. 'I didn't take the tour all that seriously up till that point, and if I could go back and do it all again I'd take the tour a lot more seriously. I'd be far more professional and wouldn't do all that shaping. I wanted to win and did everything I could to win and be ready for each event, particularly ones I was excited about like the Stubbies, Bells and the Coke.'

The Coke contest followed on from Bells. The Coke was the richest surfing event in the world at that point and Simon fancied his chances – it was being held at North Narrabeen for starters. That home advantage was countered by a lack of swell. Simon remembers, 'It was one foot for most of the contest.' At 6'3" Simon was the biggest guy on tour, riding the biggest boards on tour. 'Most guys had dropped in size to six-six by that stage, but being slow on these matters generally, I was still on a seven-foot board. The other thing was that they'd reverted back to the old points-per-manoeuvre scoring system which again didn't really work for me and my seven-foot board.'

The points-per-manoeuvre system however scaled up the points depending on wave size. Bigger waves scored bigger points. 'And then they had this stupid rule where it was first to your feet had right of way. I just went, thank you. I'd been surfing the bank at Narrabeen and knew what was going on. I sat out the back on my bigger board and took all the sets, which were scored higher according to the system. It was clean Narrabeen so I had no problem surfing a bigger board in smaller surf.' Simon wiped the floor with the field. *Tracks* asked, 'How could a big guy pull off the same radical stunts in three-foot Narrabeen dribblers as he did in eight-foot Bells boomers? How could he manage to tuck his huge frame into tiny two-foot tubes on his backhand?' As Simon told *Tracks* later, 'They wanted tubes so I stuck my head in anything that came along.' In one round he jumped from 19th to 1st and stayed there. Again, halfway through the event he had an unbeatable lead.

That was when they called the meeting. 'I think Paul Neilsen might have asked them for a meeting halfway through the event and they changed the rules. They threw in some other categories which kind of backfired and actually made it harder for anyone to catch me. They basically handed it to me on a plate, which was great. Thanks very much fellas.' Simon celebrated his win according to Narrabeen tradition with a keg for the boys. 'Simon's refusal to accept star billing hasn't gone unnoticed amongst his mates,' offered Jarratt in the profile piece following Simon's Coke win. 'They're totally loyal to him. Sometimes it seems that while he's publicly one of the boys, privately he's the subject of some adulation.'

After the Coke Classic, Simon found himself rated number one in the world, in front of Rabbit Bartholomew and Shaun Tomson. While Rabbit was turning up to events in fur coats and mirrored shades, Simon remained in his Narrabeen uniform of tight boardshorts, polo shirt, tennis visor and thongs. Simon spent most of his time either locked away in the shaping bay, surfing Narrabeen, or drinking at the Royal Antler Hotel. He was still living at home with his parents down the road at Collaroy, and his sudden notoriety hit him for six. Simon's dad, George, even called former Aussie cricket captain Bobby Simpson for some advice on how best to manage his son's growing sporting profile. Simon meanwhile wasn't so keen on anything changing much at all … least of all him. His closing line in the *Tracks* profile said as much. 'No image, that's my image. I don't like the idea of having an image. I don't want to create one and I don't want to change in any way just because I won a couple of surfing contests. Success can't last forever and I think I'm handling it okay.'

In the space of a month Simon had won $10,000, which represented a good year in the shaping bay at Energy. Suddenly this pro surfing game was starting to look pretty good. He paid his brother back the $3000 he'd lent him to open the doors at Energy and then booked himself flights to follow the tour for the rest of the year, starting with South Africa.

Simon was a 'reluctant jetsetter' and flew into Johannesburg not knowing he was even in Johannesburg. The one thing he was sure of was that he was no longer in Narrabeen. The culture shock of downtown Joburg was clear immediately when a black porter picked up his bags at the hotel. 'I haven't given the matter too much thought,' Simon told *Tracks* later when asked about South Africa's apartheid policy. 'That's the truth. I haven't stopped to think about it as a moral issue but on principle I suppose we shouldn't be going ... As far as I'm concerned I'm just a surfer competing against other surfers, and I don't care what they are, black or white.'

Simon's connecting flight the following morning took him to Durban, where he'd surf in the Gunston 500. Simon made himself at home in a cheap hotel a block back from the beach, where, much to his delight, the room cost only $10 a day and included three square meals. 'And they were good meals too.' Simon didn't win the Gunston but finished a respectable fourth. Shaun Tomson won, taking the ratings lead from Simon in the process. The judging was a little provincial, but Simon wasn't one to complain. 'There was a week between events so we drove a Kombi down to J-Bay. It was six-to-eight foot and just perfect. I got this fabulous barrel down at Impossibles that I was in for 80 metres. It swallowed me at the end and I tried to squeak out but the lip landed on top of my head and just flattened me onto my board. I stretched ligaments in both knees so that kind of put me behind the eight ball. With a ligament strain like that you need a month at least. Shaun actually put me onto this guy who looked like Colonel Sanders who took a look at my knees, jabbed a knife into my kneecap and said, "There you go." It didn't do much good.' Simon lost in the first round the following week at Umhlanga Rocks, again in small surf. The tour certainly wasn't a Big Man's World, certainly not a big man with two crook knees. Simon flew to Brazil soon after and lost the first round at Arpoador to Peter Drouyn, who he was staying with. 'It was one foot. Maybe less. That was the end of my year pretty much. The world title was done.'

The historic value of a world title wasn't clear at this early point in pro surfing, but while disappointed, Simon shrugged his shoulders and moved on. He still had a day job. 'Maybe the top three or four guys might have been making money off the tour but generally we weren't really making a living. Shaping was a necessary thing that I had to keep up. It was still my primary income source. But 1977 was a pivotal year because I had success on tour and it forced me to concentrate more on making it work.'

To make it work, Simon sold Energy Surfboards to Steve Zoeller, who promptly re-employed Simon as a shaper and designer. Free of the business side of things, Simon was able to simply surf and shape. 'I'm still gonna work for a living,' he told *Tracks*, 'it's just that I'm not going to let it interfere with my travel. I'm having a good run in contests and the time is right. Being a winner this year has really changed my attitude. I've got confidence I never knew I had before and I reckon I'm going to do okay.'

The 1977 season finished in Hawaii, which remained the supreme test of surfer and surfboard. 'In the beginning of my surfing career there were the Australian events, and then you'd go to Hawaii and prove you were a man and that was about it.' There were still some lingering bad vibes in the islands after the 'Busting Down The Door' winter, and the Australians were treading lightly. Simon's low profile kept him safely out of trouble, and in what would become an annual ritual he would remain out of trouble, posted up out at the Kuilima condos. This was as much for the colour TV as for the feeling of sanctuary away from the hectic Pipe-to-Sunset stretch.

'I had a pretty good board that year and I broke it,' remembers Simon. 'That was my all-purpose seven-six … seven-six was the go-to size back then. Terry Fitzgerald advised me to go and see Jack Shipley and make a board to replace it. So I went into Ala Moana to the Lightning Bolt shop and I fronted Jack Shipley. I'd never met Jack before in my life; this was Terry Fitzgerald's idea. Walking in there asking for a board was the last thing I wanted to do. Anyway I walked into the shop and Jack's standing there and I say to him something like, "I'm Simon Anderson, I'm in the Pipe Masters, I need to make a surfboard. Terry Fitzgerald said you might be able to help me." I remember Jack kind of looking anywhere but at me, thinking it over and then going, "Yeah, all right. Get a blank, the shaping bay is on the North Shore, then take it to Jack Reeves to get it glassed. We'll pay for it."'

The shaper in Simon had always seen Hawaii as much a test of a surfboard as it was a test of a surfer, and this was his first opportunity to shape a board in Hawaii, for Hawaii. 'So I ended up in a shaping bay at the back of Rocky Point in this wooden shed. I remember it was nothing like my shaping bay back home and the planer I was using was a big, ugly Skil thing with this life-and-death cutter that I'd never used before. The planer was impossible to man-handle but the blank was pretty good. Back then it was difficult to get good rockers for bigger wave boards in Australia so I always struggled trying to make a decent board for Hawaii. But, obviously, they had the rockers and the blanks and everything worked out pretty good in Hawaii. So I shaped this seven-six board and it worked beautifully as it turned out and I made the final of the Pipe Masters in my first year. I've still got the board today. I think as a shaper and surfer, that was my greatest achievement – to shape this board in someone else's shaping bay, surf it, get through to the final.'

Simon's moment in the sun, for now, was brief. While he finished the '77 season in third place, the following year he dropped to 19th, winning just $775 in prizemoney. Losing the title and travelling the world to surf waves so bad he wouldn't bother with them at Narrabeen had taken the shine off the pro tour dream. He was also wrestling with the competing demands of tour life and his development as a shaper. The two streams of Simon's surfing life would famously come together once again four years later in 1981, when he surfed his three-fin Thruster design to victory at both Bells Beach and the Coke Classic, the wins validating the design that still dominates the surfboard landscape today. Simon, being Simon, remained gloriously unaffected by the success.

'If I'd have lost at Bells that day in 1981? Yeah, I dunno, the Thruster wouldn't have been such a great story then, would it? How would things be different if it hadn't taken off then? I'd be poorer. I'd probably be happier,' he says, deadpan. 'That's hard to imagine, isn't it? I'd be just in the same place I reckon. It was one good idea. I was lucky. It was right place, right time. If I hadn't come up with it at that time six months later someone else would have come up with it and that would have been fine. I'd still be where I am now, here on this beach … only you'd be around the corner with the other bloke interviewing him.'

SKOL. At the bottom of every great tan

1978

Tom Carroll

'I remember I was just spewing. Like, speeeeewwwing. I'd won it the year before and put too much pressure on myself and bombed out early. Couldn't get my shit together.'

Scrawny, freckly 16-year-old Tom Carroll had just lost his Pro Junior crown at North Narrabeen, bombing out and finishing 13th a year after winning it. To make it worse (or better, he couldn't work out which) Queensland's Joe Engel, who was staying on Tom's couch in Newport, watching *M.A.S.H.* on his TV, went on to win it. The pair were the two best young surfers in Australia at the time and would dominate the Pro Junior for four years. Tom won two. Joe won two. The pair would shadow each other for the next few years.

'The following year in '79 I got second to Joe in the final,' recalls Tom. 'I was really pissed off again, but he was an incredible surfer. He was the first guy at that original Pro Junior who made me stop and go, fuck, how's this guy! He was surfing Alley Rights and was going three or four times faster than everyone else doing these big hacks. I'm like, this guy is out of hand. We were pretty close, Joe and I. He reminded me a little bit of Ross [Clarke-Jones] just with this crazy energy. He'd be bouncing around everywhere, but he had this paranoia that Ross didn't have. It was a great time though. It was a time when we didn't have any big goals. It wasn't like, "We're going to be doing this, we're gonna make it!" We just lived moment to moment, doing it.'

Tom might have been the best junior surfer in the country, but in 1978 he was also an apprentice panelbeater. He'd finished school at Pittwater High the year before and got a job fixing smashed cars. 'That was my trade,' recalls Tom. 'I did a year at tech and got a job with Wayne Smith down at Narrabeen. I put myself through the Wayne Smith school of smash repairs, which was brutal. That was a year spent realising what I *didn't* want to do in life. Al Hunt was working next door doing the quotes and then we'd just bog them up. It was pretty gnarly watching those guys at work – it was full Narrabeen – but the upside was that I got to surf Narrabeen at lunchtime. The other upside was that they let me have time off work to surf contests. That's really why I did it.'

The Australian Titles at Margaret River were next; the first time Tom had been thrown in the deep end with big, powerful surf in a contest. 'That's where it really clicked for me,' he recalls, 'the first time I realised I could do this. That it felt natural. Even though I'd always loved heavy surf here on the east coast when we got it, to head over west and paddle out at Margaret River it was like okay, this feels totally different... but I loved it.'

'I'll never forget that year; my gun was a 6'0" pintail single-fin and we had to paddle out at massive Margaret River. It was the first heat they ran and I'm looking at it going, shit, they're sending the juniors out? I was this weedy 16-year-old kid who'd never seen waves like that. It was dark, overcast, offshore Margarets and I paddled out into these giant lefts. Joe Engel was in my heat. The other guys were messing around on the inside and to my surprise after a little while I found myself catching waves and enjoying it. I came in and I'd won the heat and I'd beaten Joe, and that win started kicking me into gear a bit.'

Tom won the Australian junior title – edging out Joe again – and on the flight home from Perth he was seated next to Newcastle's Col Smith, who'd just won the men's. 'He was filling my head with all these stories from Hawaii,' remembers Tom. 'He'd won the Pro Class trials in '77 to get into all the North Shore events and he was giving me all the Hawaii stories. I remember him going, "Fuck, grommet, you straighten out on a Pipe wave and lay down on your board it's like getting a fucking V8 up your arse!"' Tom's laughing now but wasn't back then. 'I'll never forget that! I was like, Jesus! I was shitting myself by the time I got off the flight. The funny thing was when I eventually got to Hawaii that year I actually *did* shit myself! I wiped out at Inside Sunset and I was thrown over the falls and actually shit my boardies!'

Tom was a 'competitive little mongrel' because his home beach of Newport had evolved into its own self-contained competitive universe. 'At that stage Derek Hynd was the best surfer on the beach at Newport and was doing well on the tour. He was the driver of the crazy mindset at Newport. Derek was Derek – a unique character –

and he was driving this collective competitive mind that was manifesting itself through Newport Plus boardriding club, which we'd all created around that time, '77, '78. Club rounds turned into this monthly beat-up where we tried to kill each other out in the water. There was always a fight out there and Derek was full-on with it. There were no parents there, it was just us. Our parents were as far away as they could get. We were this mongrel lot getting more mongrel by the minute.'

Surfing tribalism was particularly strong on the northern beaches at that point, and the only beach to rival the intensity and ability of Newport in that era was North Narrabeen. 'The funny thing was though that we were actually quite well accepted down at Narrabeen. We used to surf Narrabeen with Derek quite regularly. He used to get his boards from Terry Fitzgerald and I was getting my boards off Col Smith at that stage so we were pretty close to those guys. We tied in really well with them and there was never any real animosity. We'd turn up and they'd go, "Where's ya fucking visa! You come across the bridge you need a visa! We'll Grommet Pole ya, grommet!" But that was about it. We were lucky. Others weren't.'

Tom, as the best junior in the country, scored invites into both the Stubbies and Bells pro events in 1978. He beat Peter Drouyn at Bells before losing to Hawaiian Dane Kealoha, but despite getting a taste of a pro career, it still didn't actually seem any closer. Tom, like all the young guys at that point, just jumped from opportunity to opportunity. 'Once we hit the '80s it was on,' he remembers. 'The 1980s reflected our inner vibrancy. We were young and full of life and it was all there for the taking, but in 1978 it wasn't quite there yet, especially for a kid my age. That's what I wanted to do – go surfing – but there was no real career path. I was still working eight-and-a-half hours a day and getting $50 a week and paying $10 a week board at home. Today it's hard to imagine what it was like back then. It was so different. We were just doing it. We just loved surfing but being paid to travel the world and do it was still a crazy idea.' In an interview with *Surfing World* that year, the first surfer to ever sign a million-dollar contract (albeit a few years down the track) said, 'Surfing's a thing that you just can't think you're going to make millions out of.'

'We definitely wanted to travel though. A few of my friends were going to Bali but that's not where I wanted to go. Not yet. It looked incredibly enticing and I knew I'd get there one day. I finally did in 1980 and it was with Joe again. We had a mushroom omelette together in Bali. I thought I was all right but it turned out to be a fully psychedelic one. We got the fuck out of Kuta somehow when it came on and Joe's come back to the *losmen*, just hanging on, and ends up tearing his room apart. I go,

"Mate, you gotta get out of there!" Jim Banks just happened to be staying in the same *losmens* and he saw it all. Anyway, at the time I didn't want to go to Bali … I wanted to go to Hawaii.'

Tom started saving. He got some travel money from Rip Curl and Quiksilver, but he needed Hawaii boards. He was riding Col Smith boards from Morning Star at the time, but Col suggested he get Simon Anderson to make him some Hawaii boards. 'The golden thing for me was the Narrabeen connection,' says Tom. 'Simon made me two boards for Hawaii, a 6'8" and a 7'2", which were my two longer boards. I also had two Col Smiths, a 6'3" and a 5'8". All single fins. No such thing as a thruster back then and twinnies were cheating. That was our mentality. So Simon shaped me two beautiful pintails, and through that I ended up getting an offer to stay in Hawaii with Simon, Al Hunt and this guy, Greg Hodges, who was running the NSW Surfing Association at the time.'

The reality of Hawaii didn't quite match the brochure. It was a wet winter, and Tom got six weeks of rain and weather and three weeks of good surf. The vibe in the water wasn't much better. The dust was still settling and a young Aussie guy trying to make a name for himself had to be careful of making too big a name. 'For this little *haole* Aussie kid it was quite intimidating,' recalls Tom. 'It was a hostile place at the time. It wasn't pretty.'

The Narrabeen guys were only marginally safer. 'I stayed with Simon and Al for a couple of months out at the Kuilima. I was this full grom, figuring it out with the Narrabeen boys leading me places and just dropping me cold. If I didn't come out of the supermarket quick enough I was left there to hitch back to the Kuilima on my own.' He laughs. 'The duty of care wasn't really big at that point.' Simon and Al were, however, once you got past a little ritual grommet hazing, good company and they knew the North Shore. They couldn't have been too bad … Tom stayed with them the following winter as well.

After years of sitting in movie theatres, mesmerised by 16mm slow motion cuts of Gerry Lopez at Pipe, the day finally came for Tom to paddle out to Pipe. 'I remember the day super clearly. It was the first time I rode the 7'2" that Simon had shaped for me. I was about 4'2" at the time and weighed seven stone and I felt tiny walking down the beach. There was nothing of me. The funny thing was that Joe Engel had surfed it that morning. Joe came up and went, "I surfed Pipeline this morning and it was 10 foot!" I'm like, "Fuck! What do you mean you surfed Pipeline?!" I was bummed he'd beaten me out there so I knew I had to go that afternoon.

'I was frothing but shitting myself at the same time. It was 10-to-12 feet *mega* Pipeline. Just after lunch we walked down the beach and I've got no wax on my board and I'm looking at it and everyone was out there – Shaun was out there on that pink Spider Murphy board, Lopez was out there, Rory Russell, Jackie Dunn – all of them. I got to the beach and put my board in the sand and Critta Byrne comes running up. He'd already surfed it a couple of times that day and he was mad as a cut snake and he's straight back out there. He threw the bar of wax at me and he goes, "Here ya go. Now just paddle out in front of the break. See ya!" And he was gone. I'm there waxing up alone and I reckon I used the whole block of wax because I was just watching it, wondering if I'd even get out. I'm thinking I'm going to have this big board ripped out of my arms and I'm going to be washed in for sure. I'm fucked. But whatever … here we go.'

'I get sucked straight out, no worries. I remember paddling up the line looking at it, and seeing these massive barrels. I'd never seen anything like it. They were all backlit and I'm like, fuck, have a look at the size of these things! So I'm hanging down the end taking it all in. The first wave I get was an insider, and as I dropped into it I distinctly remember thinking to myself *this just looks like a big version of Narrabeen*. It's just like Narrabeen! I dropped in and did a turn and stood there in the curvature of the wave while it did its thing and I whoop-de-dooed a bit and kicked out and I'm thinking, wow, okay. The board felt good. I could actually turn a 7'2". It's a super clear imprint in my memory. Wow, okay, I can do this. I was frothing. It was a pretty quick transformation. I didn't go out to where the big guys were, I just watched those guys and what they were doing, but it was amazing to watch those guys attack it. I'd never seen waves like that before, let alone guys attacking waves like that. It blew my mind.'

The other thing that happened on that trip was that Tom got into photography, a hobby he'd develop into a low key artform in his travels over the years. An Aussie photographer named John Borland had met Tom and knew he was interested in photography, so he left him a camera to use. 'He said, "Look, I'm going home, I'll leave this camera with you. Just bring it back." And I went, oh my god, I've got a camera! I had no idea what I was doing but it started there and it drew me in. I remember looking through the viewfinder and I realised I could focus on something and I could frame it up and I remember thinking this is it! I live in this little square! It felt like this tiny little world in there.'

Tom's first trip to Hawaii had made an impression. 'I got a lot of recognition on that trip as a young Aussie guy coming up. I got some photos in the Aussie mags and in the American mags as well which was pretty cool.' He'd also made friends in the islands. 'I became good friends with a Hawaiian guy, Louie Ferreira, who actually ended up coming and staying with me at Newport. The Newport Plus guys fully adopted him. We had a bunch of guys from overseas who came to Newport and hung out with us. Ketut Menda from Bali was one. He stayed a while. We nicknamed him "Male Member". Louie got the nickname "The Black Piston" because he used to pull all the chicks and Newport was the whitest suburb anywhere in Sydney. But I made a lot of friendships on that trip, guys who are still friends today.'

But after nine weeks, Tom was homesick. 'I remember Christmas was on a Sunday and my flight was a Friday. Well on the Thursday afternoon my passport, the camera and my travellers cheques were all stolen out of the back seat of the car at Ehukai. I had to make a police report, get a new passport and make an insurance claim all the next day. I had a full meltdown. I felt like I was never going to get home. It was a full rookie move and a wake-up call to look after my stuff. I'd just turned 17 and your head is all over the place. You just don't think much about things like that.' He made the flight.

Tom got home just in time for Christmas. His older brother, Nick – who'd win his own Aussie title the following year – hadn't been to Hawaii yet.

'Nick'd just got *Never Mind The Bollocks* by The Sex Pistols, and he was listening to it at full volume in our grandmother's ground floor flat. He's playing it as loud as it goes on Christmas morning. I'm like, "What the fuck is that?"'

Nick could only listen to so many of Tom's Hawaii stories.

1979

Pam Burridge

'Girls Can Be Grommets Too!'

The full-page story in the March 1979 issue of *Tracks* was remarkable in a couple of ways. It was a full-page story on a girl who surfed, for starters. This was 1979. Lineups around Australia were patrolled almost exclusively by blokes in nut-hugging, scallop-legged boardies. 'Chicks don't surf' was a mantra for teenage boys. Girls in bikinis outnumbered girls on boards a hundred-to-one, so a girl scoring a full page in a surf mag was pretty remarkable … but even more remarkable was the girl herself. Blonde, tanned and with a high-voltage smile, 13-year-old Pam Burridge was already a star in the making.

However, it was the surf shot at the bottom of the page, taken at Avalon, that drew you to it. Pam zooming out of the page, her tiny McCoy board throwing sparks, eyes down the line, top teeth biting bottom lip in anticipation of the next section. She'd spent hours that summer up at North Narrabeen sitting on the beach watching Col Smith surf, taking notes. The way she held her front hand like a kangaroo paw and the way she surfed behind that front arm, that was all Col Smith.

Here was a teenage girl who didn't surf like a teenage girl. This girl could really surf and the guys knew it. 'When I started they used to think I actually *was* a guy and I got a hard time,' said Pam in the *Tracks* interview. 'I guess they thought I was just another little trog in their way.' Now at 13 things had changed. Her cuteness was simply cover. Pam was a bigger surf rat than any of the boys on Manly Beach and she'd arrived at an important time. Women's surfing was struggling for any kind of

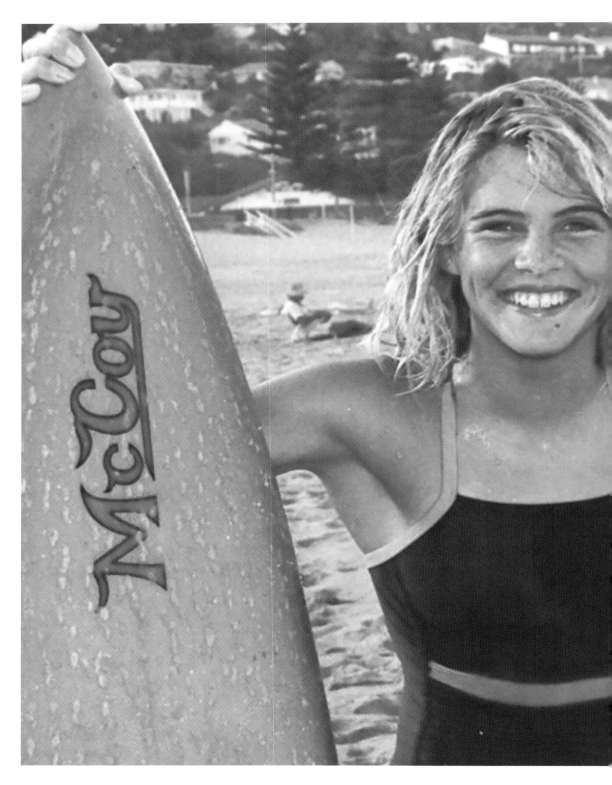

recognition, but suddenly here was Pam Burridge whose only problem in the years ahead would be *too much* recognition. At just 13 the papers were already calling her 'the Great Blonde Hope'.

Pam, like many kids of her generation, wasn't born into a surfing family. The Burridges lived at Clontarf, 15 minutes up the hill from Manly Beach. Instead of the surf, Pam was thrown in the pool. Pam's elder sister, Donella, would compete at the 1984 Los Angeles Olympics in synchronised swimming, but despite Pam being a natural in the water she hated the whole idea of water ballet. Pam had a rebel streak. The pool was uncool. Pam despised team sports and was hard wired to do her own thing. 'That was one of the appeals of surfing for me, that individual nature of it. At school I could only play netball and I hated netball. I fucking hated it. So when surfing came along I dropped everything else.'

Pam enrolled in the Warringah Shire Council's surf school at Freshwater. The school was run by a guy named Bill McCausland, who'd become a guiding figure in Pam's career but for now 'did all the talking and told all the jokes'. He also had some handy offsiders working at the school. 'Nat Young worked there as a coach for a while,' recalls Pam. 'So did Mark Warren and "Wicko", Tony Hardwick. No such thing as accredited coaches back then, just surf stars.' Pam got good, quick. By 13 she was the one doing the coaching.

Pam fell hard for surfing. 'Mum and Dad – mostly Mum, God love her – would drive me to the beach before and after school and on weekends. She'd drive off and grab some shopping or something and then come back. She'd wave this big towel for me to come in … and that was my cue to look the other way and keep surfing. "Sorry Mum, can't see you."' Besides surfing before and after school, on the weekends she spent eight hours a day in the water. 'I'd surf a rip bowl and just go into pure fantasy land. I didn't like sitting still, so I could catch waves in a rip bowl, be carried straight back out, then catch another and another. You'd paddle back out and there'd be another wave there and you'd just spin and go. I'd do this for hours.'

Pam remembers her first custom board. 'It was a Barry Bennett. It was right when the lawyers from Lightning Bolt started to enforce the cease and desist with anyone using lightning bolts on surfboards – they were on the deck of pretty much every single board being made at the time. So, I ordered my board with the lightning bolt and of course when we got it, the lightning bolt had the big Barry Bennett diamond in the middle of it. Legally it wasn't a "lightning bolt". I remember I really loved that board.'

For a young girl surfing on her own, Manly Beach was a wild savannah. Pam remembers, 'Like every grommet I had to keep my head down. Grommets were always getting a flogging, and as a grommet you knew your place. I was a full tomboy though. That's how I got away with it … in disguise. I think I might have been 12 when one of the local rippers on the beach came over to me and said, "Hey mate, you should get a haircut." I'd been surfing out there with this guy for a year and he didn't even know I was a girl! I don't think he'd ever seen a girl surfer and wouldn't know what one looked like.'

Surfing for Pam was never social. It was never a scene. Pam had been the only surfer in the whole school at Balgowlah Heights Primary, and one of just a handful at Mackellar Girls High. On Manly Beach, Pam was on her own. 'I was a bit of an outsider. I didn't really have a surfing crew. My friends didn't surf. My girlfriend group at school, nobody surfed. I can barely recall seeing other girls surfing at the time. I wasn't really hanging out with anyone and I didn't really *know* anyone. I didn't even know anyone's name. I'd surfed at Manly every day for five years with this same guy on this same yellow board, but I didn't know his name and I'd never talked to him. But that was also my personality. I was a bit of a boundary rider. I developed this kind of individualist identity around surfing. "I am a surfer and I'm different."'

One of the few people Pam would talk to was an old bloke in a white terry towelling hat, who'd sit on the wall at North Steyne and point out where he reckoned she should surf. Pam, for the most part, was blissfully unaware of Manly Beach's status in Australian surfing, and it didn't click for a while that the old bloke in the hat had once been the Australian champ. 'Snowy would tell the story from time to time, you know the old story of Snow and the last wave he surfs all the way to shore standing on his head. The wave washes back, he's still standing on his head, and the judge comes down, taps him on the arse and says, "You won, mate." So the story goes. In hindsight I was like, wow, Manly was a pretty significant place to be surfing and growing up, but as a kid I had no idea.'

The 1978 Coke Surfabout was hard to miss. Pam took days off school to watch what would become, in time, one of the most fabled surf contests ever held in Australia. 'North Steyne was just pumping,' she recalls. 'I don't think I'd ever seen it that good. I remember the crowds being down there and I remember the girls were surfing in that contest too, which was pretty incredible back then.' Amongst the women's field were Pam's two favourite surfers – Margo Oberg and Lynne Boyer – who she'd never seen outside of surf magazines. 'Margo and Lynne sort of seemed interchangeable for me because they were both world champs. They were the girls, but I couldn't quite relate to them because they were riding these big waves in Hawaii.' In her *Tracks* interview, Pam recounted seeing them surfing at the Coke. 'I like Margo's surfing the best. She was unlucky to get beaten in the Surfabout – she sat too far inside.'

Pam had started surfing contests at 12. 'My first competition was with Manly Pacific Boardriders, which was probably on its last legs at that point. I won the girls division and made the *Manly Daily*.' What really put Pam in the spotlight, though, was competing against the guys at the '78 Golden Breed Pepsi Pro Junior, held up the road at North Narrabeen. The Pro Junior was a big deal, attracting the best male grommets from all around the country, but they were scratching to get the numbers to fill the girls' heats. Organisers had put out a call for, 'junior geniuses of the juice'. One of the girls who responded and who would surf against Pam was 14-year old Nell Schofield from Bondi, who a couple of years later would star in *Puberty Blues*.

At Narrabeen the girls' heats were barely noticed, but Pam also surfed against the guys. She finished fifth from six surfers, but the fact she hadn't finished last drew as much media attention as if she'd won the whole contest. Pam, by this stage, was regularly surfing against the guys simply for the competition. It was great for Pam's surfing, while at the same time soul crushing for the egos of the guys she managed to beat. Pam summed up their responses as, 'somewhere between aggression and embarrassment, depending on how well I knew them'.

But 1979 was the year it all clicked for Pam. In February she won the Moovin' On junior series, sponsored by Moove flavoured milk. She backed that up by winning the NSW women's title. She was just 14. Her star was rising, and she was offered a spot on the McCoy surf team. 'My surf idol back then was Cheyne Horan, and he was surfing McCoy boards at the time so riding for McCoy was a pretty big deal for me.' Geoff McCoy made Pam a new board – just the third surfboard she'd ever owned – and she was off and running.

While women's surfing in Australia was struggling for any kind of profile, 14-year-old Pam Burridge was everywhere. 'I was getting write-ups in the *Manly Daily* and the Sydney papers. My parents – mostly Mum – told me you've got to do the press stuff if you want to get sponsors and get noticed. I didn't really want to do it. I was really shy, so I had to be coerced a bit, but I got used to it.' Pam recalls a TV crew turning up to interview her about working as a surf coach. The interview never happened. Pam was stung by a bluebottle, Pam's mum thinking it might not have been an accident.

Pam soon lost her coyness. In the summer of 1979 she signed on to do a campaign for surf brand Crystal Cylinders, who were huge. There were ads in surf mags but also TV ads as well. Pam was suddenly on television sets and movie screens right around the country. She became the face of the Australian summer and was paid thousands of dollars. She talked about buying an MG when she got old enough. 'It happened so quickly,' she remembers. 'And it just seemed to never stop from that point. I was pretty stoked, but I think my ego got a little wild there for a time.'

Pam got her first taste of rock stardom. Bill McCausland was also doing surf reports for 2SM at the time, and the radio station organised touring American rocker Eddie Money to head over to Freshwater and go surfing with him. Eddie got to the beach and immediately had eyes only for Pam. In return for the surfing lesson, Bill got tickets for Eddie's show at the Hordern Pavilion, where he was supporting Bill's favourite band, Santana. Bill and his wife took Pam along, the three of them scoring front-row seats. Bill, also a photographer, got a backstage pass to shoot the gig. As he snapped away, Bill watched Eddie Money walk to the front of the stage, lock eyes with Pam and sing *Two Tickets To Paradise* to the 14-year-old. Bill bravely took her backstage after the gig. Through the smoke, Eddie zeroed in on Pam, while Eddie's entourage was busy zeroing in on the tour stash. Bill looked around in horror and remembered assuring Pam's mum he'd look after her.

In May 1979, Pam travelled to the Gold Coast to surf in the Aussie titles. Held at Duranbah, Pam finished fifth against the best women in the country, winning a leg rope and a board cover. It was the biggest contest she'd surfed, but she distinctly recalls the women's heats being thrown out amongst a merciless weekend crowd at D-Bah, who surfed straight between them like they weren't there. 'It was huge, but we were clearly an afterthought to the men's.'

The Australian Surfriders Association ran the sport nationally but the women had long regarded it as a boys' club. The blokes got the best waves. The women got what was left. The women got shitty surf and no billing. 'I don't even know if it was a conscious thing,' offers Pam. 'I'm sure the guys in charge probably never even thought about what was happening with the women, which I suppose was our point.'

In a bold move, the women broke away. The Australian Women's Surfing Association was formed, the AWSA running as a rebel organisation to the ASA. Every top female surfer in the country jumped ship. 'At first they were happy to be rid of us,' recalls Pam of the ASA's attitude. "Go do your own thing. Off you go, have a play, whatever."' Pam recalls it being 'very political at the time' but with the significance of what was really happening – and her role in it – sailing over her head. She was still only 14, and 14-year-old surf rats had little time for anything else. Pam was too busy surfing to realise she now really was 'the Great Blonde Hope' of women's surfing in Australia.

The first AWSA contest was held in August 1979 at Newport Beach, sponsored by CBC Savings Bank. Pam won by a single point from Wollongong's Sharon Holland, who'd finished seventh in the professional ranks the year before in between shifts at her dad's trucking business. The AWSA event made all the Sydney papers. The women's lib storyline got more column inches than the actual surfing, but their point was being made loud and clear.

The following year the AWSA held their first standalone Australian Titles on Pam's home beach at Queenscliff. Pam – still just 14 – beat a field of over 50 women from around the country to win her first Australian title. The contest was as much a statement as it was a surfing contest. The matriarchs of Australian surfing presided. Phyllis O'Donell judged, while Pam was handed the trophy by an elderly lady in a tweed coat and bowls hat. 'That was the first time I'd met Isabel Latham,' recalls Pam. 'She was living in Foam Street up in Freshie at the time, and she'd been invited to be one of the patrons for the new association. There are these fabulous photos of me getting my trophy from her wearing my Seafolly sausage-leg trackies. All very cool.' In the years ahead, Pam and Isabel would become close. Pam would name her daughter Isabel. Her son, meanwhile, would get the middle name Snowy.

Pam's 1980 Australian title doesn't appear in the record books. The official ASA Australian Titles that year would be held in South Australia with just a handful of women competing. After the AWSA Titles in Queenscliff the women met to discuss the idea of re-affiliating with the ASA. The reason for the meeting was the upcoming amateur world titles in France. The AWSA women weren't eligible to go. 'We thought, shit, we need to be able to go to World Titles.' The women met on the beach at Queenscliff but voted to keep doing their own thing. Gail Austen, the AWSA founder, told the *Sydney Morning Herald*, 'We reckon that in the past two years we've done more for women's surfing than the ASA achieved for us in their 17 years.' The AWSA wound up the following year, but by then they'd *definitely* made their point.

Pam's win at Queenscliff, while it didn't get her to France, did earn her an invite to surf in the 1980 Hawaiian pro events. 'I was talking with Geoff McCoy and ordering boards to go to Hawaii and my mum asked him, "How much time do we need in

Hawaii?" Geoff answered straight up, "Six weeks." I just went, "Yes!" Mum was in shock. In the end we compromised and stayed for four-and-a-half.' By competing in the Hawaiian pro events, without it really clicking at the time, Pam Burridge officially became Australia's first female pro surfer. She was still just 15. Her world would move quickly. By 16, she'd finish second in the world.

But for now, the Great Blonde Hope still had to scrap to get a wave on Manly Beach. 'It wasn't a place for any kind of weakness,' recalls Pam, 'especially if you were female. There were Agronauts everywhere and I'd still get dropped in on mercilessly. Cold to the bone. I'm Aussie champ by then but I had to fight for my waves. No one was giving an inch. If a guy dropped in on me, I developed a habit of surfing right up behind the bloke and saying nothing, but just surfing right on their heels. They'd finally look around and there you were, not saying anything, just smiling. It really gave them the shits.'

1981

Peter Crawford

Peter Crawford referred to Dee Why Point as 'The Studio'.
In the same way – as the best kneeboarder in Australia during the 1970s – he'd developed an inside-out relationship with the wave, he was now using his knowledge of Dee Why's ledges and sections, from First Rock to Backdoor to Suck Up, to position himself perfectly to take the last great surf photo of Michael Peterson.

Years later Peter Crawford retold the story of that day in 1981. 'MP had come down to my house and we'd lined up a session at the Point to take some shots. It was early in the morning, 8am. I don't know where he'd slept that night, he just showed up. Michael met me at the house. It was four-to-five foot, clean Dee Why Point. It was overcast so I decided to shoot black and white film. Michael hadn't been out the night before 'cause he was crisp and alert and he was there to do a job. I suited up and swam out to the Point and Michael's paddled out. We'd watched each other's act and he's come flying straight toward me. I wanted to get that cutback. Michael's gone over and come flying straight out of Suck Up and he's just planted the foot on the back and just stopped right in front of me and done this massive cutback. Time stopped. It was up tight and personal. I only shot 15 frames. I felt privileged.' Peter already had the shot of Michael in his mind when he'd swum out that morning. He wanted something that captured the intensity and primal release of a moment in time. Peterson's last hurrah. When the roll was developed, there it was. Michael literally jumped out of the frame, eyes on fire.

The photo was living proof of Michael's session, although the veracity of the next part of the story remains unclear. Separating fact from fiction with the exploits of both

Michael Peterson and Peter Crawford would prove challenging. 'What happened next was extraordinary,' remembered Peter. 'He was extruding self-confidence, it was like he was in a heat with me. Lo and behold Simon Anderson appears on the rock with this new-fangled invention – the thruster. Michael had been surfing for 40 minutes, not that long. So Simon's appeared on the rocks and I've glanced over at Michael and gone, "There's Simon Anderson," and he's just staring at the guy. Simon's got the thruster and he's seen Michael and me ... but as soon as Michael saw Simon on the Point the whole mood changed. Michael paddled in without catching a wave before Simon even jumped off the rock ... I could tell what he was thinking. Michael sensed it was the end of his era then and there. I never saw Michael for another three years.'

Michael, by that time, had been institutionalised in Brisbane and treated for schizophrenia. Peter's name was in the visitor's book at Wooloowin. Michael and Peter had been kindred spirits during the '70s, but at this point they were on divergent paths. While Michael couldn't be found. Peter seemingly was everywhere.

Peter Crawford remained a groundbreaking kneeboarder. He'd won three Aussie titles but, beyond those, his Slab design and his surfing on the Point at Dee Why not only revolutionised kneeboarding, his influence had spilled over into surfing in a way George Greenough's had a decade earlier. Peter surfed more hours out at Dee Why Point than anyone. His dad, Ken, owned a unit in the Beachpoint block looking down on the Point, and Peter and his crew would use the garage downstairs as a hang-out between surfs.

But as the '80s dawned Peter had switched his focus to his photography. His wave knowledge, gleaned on a kneeboard, gave him a unique perspective when shooting from the water and by 1981 he was regarded as one of the world's premier surf photographers. His creative eye and obsessiveness for *the shot* gave his work an edge and while his photographic vision was often quixotic, he had the skills behind the Nikonos and in the water to make it work.

Peter's career timing was perfect as well. Surfing had never been more photogenic. It was a time of big characters and big colour and Peter's work possessed a vibrancy and life force, much of which Peter himself provided. Crawford captured the gaudiness of '80s pro surfing better than anyone. Garrulous and increasingly Gonzo, he'd follow the pro tour and its biggest names and bring the scene to life. He had a knack of entering the lives of surfers at vital points and documenting them. He shot Peterson on the way out. He shot young Occy and Tom Carroll on the way up. Mercurial and a little peculiar himself, those qualities found their way into the images he shot. Crawford had a huge appetite for life ... and a huge appetite for anything that enhanced it. He was effervescent company – talking in riddles, dressing in costume, possessing an impish sense of fun. Peter, by this stage, was father to two young boys, Scott and Justin, and home life for them was often tumultuous. The one constant in their lives would be, as it was for their old man, the waves at Dee Why Point.

Peter had also co-founded *Waves* magazine in 1980, which was being produced by Murray Publishers in Clarence Street, Sydney. The mag tapped the zeitgeist of the flashy big city contests at the time, but also featured pages devoted to windsurfing and kneeboarding. Peter shot and edited the photos and sold the ads. His own magazine described him as 'our lens-carrying paranoid superstar'. Peter shot for his own magazine but he also played the field and was always open to a stray commission. His images that year still appeared in opposition magazines *Tracks* and *Surfer*.

With pages of *Waves* to be filled – he shot the whole magazine – he'd hit the road and follow the 1981 pro tour across Australia. While the Stubbies at Burleigh got skunked, and the Coke at Narrabeen did only marginally better, it was Bells that would really give Peter something to shoot. Saturday, 19 April 1981 would be remembered as 'Big Saturday'. A huge, clean Roaring Forties swell wrapped down the Victorian southern coast. It was sunny, offshore and blue – a photographer's dream. However, Peter's dream didn't involve standing on the cliffs with everyone else. The guys in the contest were having trouble paddling out; swimming out with a camera was an impossibility. Peter, ever resourceful, commandeered a chopper to drop him out the back. The chopper was soon retrieving him as he was quickly washed down the coast past Winkipop.

The tour headed to Bali soon after for the '81 OM Bali Pro at Uluwatu. Peter was a regular visitor to Bali, tapping the ambient spirituality of the joint, and in following years would disappear deep into the Indonesian archipelago on extended missions of discovery. As the chain opened up, Peter would often be in the advance party to shoot and sample it; magazine buyouts from one trip funding the next. Cronulla surfer Jim Banks would win the OM Bali event in 1981, and he and PC would team up for many of these trips, including early runs through Sumbawa, Timor, remote Java and Desert Point on Lombok. It was on one of those trips to Deserts that PC claimed to have scored a 36-second barrel on his kneeboard. The experience, he later recounted, had been so transcendental that he gave up surfing for three months afterward. Peter was out there on the surfing frontier … and increasingly also on the cosmic frontier.

1982

Damien Hardman

In 1977, Damien Hardman entered the first Pro Junior at North Narrabeen as an 11-year-old. He rode his pushbike down the hill from the Hardmans' place on Sydney Road, Warriewood, to get there. That year he wouldn't quite ice the field of Australia's best junior surfers. That was a few years off. 'Nah,' Damien remembers, 'I'd only gone in it that year because you got a free carton of Pepsi. Then I was the last heat of the day and they ran out of Pepsi before my heat! I was devastated.'

In 1982, as a 16-year-old, he'd been favoured to do well on his home beach but bombed. The Pro Junior that year was won by a wild, hairy Queensland kid. 'I'd never seen Kong surf up till that point,' recalls Damien, 'and he came down and made the final with Chappy. It was good four-to-six foot Narrabeen and I remember it was the best backhand surfing I'd ever seen in my life. How is anyone ever going to beat that guy?'

Damien saw a lot of good surfing. 'It was like a who's who of world surfing at the time,' Damien recalls. 'Simon Anderson, Mark Warren, Col Smith, Terry Fitzgerald and they were just the big names. There were dozens of guys who all ripped and the standard in the lineup was amazing. This was the era when Narrabeen got its reputation.' Narrabeen was renowned for good surfing, and with that came a reputation as one of the gnarliest lineups – and car parks – in the country. 'It was a school of hard knocks and the pecking order was real. Depending where you were in that pecking order dictated how you were treated. I was a bottom feeder back then, but I was safe because I was starting to surf okay by this stage. I was in the North Narrabeen team for club contests, so I escaped the Grommet Pole and all of that. But it was a ruthless place to grow up.'

Despite bombing out at the Pro Junior, Damien finished third in the Aussie Titles later in the year at Newport, behind Bryce Ellis and South Australian Bill Sedunary. While Damien didn't have the same profile as rising stars like Kong and Occy, he did have a nickname – 'Dooma' – and he also had a gnarly competitive streak, which you needed if you paddled out at Narrabeen intending to catch a wave.

'I was handicapped though,' Dooma remembers. 'I was riding Geoff McCoy's boards at the time and he wouldn't make me a thruster.' Narrabeen's Simon Anderson had popularised the design the previous year after winning the Bells and Coke events, and within a year Narrabeen was full of them. The top guys had all switched over or were in the process of switching. Dooma, meanwhile, 'rode Lazor Zaps and I suppose in retrospect they actually went pretty good for single-fins. They had narrower noses and turned more easily, but I was the last of the up-and-coming kids to change over and surf thrusters, which I suppose was funny considering the guy who invented it came from my beach. I remember going to contests and every kid had a thruster except for me.'

Dooma was attending Christian Brothers school in Manly [now St Paul's], although attending was a loose description. 'There was a running joke ... because I didn't have a full week at school that whole year.' It didn't help that the school bus drove past North Narrabeen every morning giving a clear view of the waves but Damien was also starting to travel more. 'I was surfing out Northy and Greg Anderson paddled over to me and said, "Do you want to go to Bells for Easter?" A big group of Narrabeen guys went down every year. It was a bit of a ritual. I said, "I'll have to ask my dad." Dad said I could go for a week. I remember we drove all the way from Sydney with Al Hunt, stopping at every McDonald's between Sydney and Bells. We got there and somehow Fatty Al had found out the rest of the Narrabeen crew who were down there had driven to Johanna that morning to go surfing, so we got to Torquay and just kept on driving for another two hours. We got to Johanna that afternoon and it was perfect.

'We finally all got back to the place we were renting in Torquay at dusk, totally stuffed, and Fatty Al and Simon and all those guys have bailed inside, while me and Greg got our boards and wetties out of the car and hung them out to dry. We walked back in and they all just go – "Grommet, I'll have a New", "I'll have a VB" – so we had to fetch them their beers. Then they said, "And after you do that you can get our towels and wetties out of the car and hang them out." We ended up being grommet slaves for two weeks. We had this big house in old Torquay with a tennis court, and the Narrabeen guys were all staying downstairs – guys like Col Smith and Brian Witty,

Mike Newling was there, Maurie Fleming, Fatty Al and Simon Anderson – it was an all-star cast. Upstairs were the South Africans – Shaun Tomson, Pottz and Marc Price. The shit that went on over the two weeks in that house you could write a book on. It was a bizarre experience.'

Dooma only went down for a week, but the waves were so good he stayed for two. 'I couldn't get back! I was a prisoner! The waves were pumping and none of them wanted to come home so we were stuck there anyway. They were the best waves we've ever had at Bells over Easter. It was after that big '81 year, but that was just one big day. In '82 it pumped for two weeks straight. Everywhere was good, every single surf. We had good Johanna, we had good Cathedral Rock, we had good Bells and Winki. And there was a place, I forget the name of it – just before Cathedral when you go around all those bends – and I've never seen it break since, but it looked like a Queensland pointbreak. We were driving past it and went, "Have a go at this!" And we looked down and recognised Phil Byrne out there. There was a car at the bottom of the cliff that had been rolled off and no one had ever bothered to pull it back up. We ended up surfing but we had no idea what it was called, so Simon ended up calling it "Crumpet Rock" because there was a woman down there sunbaking in the nude. The session became pretty legendary with the Narrabeen guys. Every time any Narrabeen guys went to Bells in the years after everyone would ask, "Did you surf Crumpet Rock?"'

Dooma also surfed his first heat at Bells. 'I actually surfed a heat in the trials. I hadn't put an entry in so I was first alternate but I got a run. I didn't catch a wave. It was six-to-eight foot Bells, just pumping, but I went out with no idea where to sit and I was totally rattled. It was a humbling experience.' Simon Anderson was the defending Bells champion and the town was still buzzing after the Big Saturday swell of 1981. However, Simon's status inside the house was even loftier. Simon laid down some house rules early on that trip, first and foremost being that the grommets had to refer to Simon at all times as 'Admiral Anderson'.

'Damien, go fetch me a beer.'

'Yes, Admiral Anderson.'

Enforcement of the rule was strict. 'It was a Narrabeen thing,' remembers Simon.

Dooma and Ando slept under the kitchen table, but there wasn't much sleeping done in the house. 'It got too much for Ando,' remembers Dooma, 'he cracked. He told me, "Mate I'm out of here, this is too much." And I thought, "Fuck that, if he goes I'm here by myself! The only grommet in the house! So I grassed him out. I told the older guys he was going to bail and they chased him into the park one night as he was trying to escape and dragged him back. Brian Witty gave him The Claw, grabbed him by the stomach and lifted him off the ground and said, "You can't leave!" I think that was the turning point in Ando's life, when he became Christian.'

If Bells with the Narrabeen guys wasn't adventure enough, Dooma took off soon after on his first overseas trip. 'I had no idea about Bali at all apart from the fact there were lefts. Geoff McCoy, who I was riding for at the time, organised it with a bunch of his mates from the Central Coast and Geoff was meant to look after me and take me under his wing. That's what he told my old man. We got to Bali and I never saw him again! He checked into a different hotel and I didn't see him for two weeks, so it was me and "Tooky" Stefan and a bunch of other Narrabeen guys who happened to be there, guys like Gordon Barnes, so we ended up with a group of six of us hanging together and surfing.

'The first moment I fully realised we weren't in Narrabeen anymore,' offers Dooma, 'was when I saw the guy mowing the lawn at the hotel with a pair of scissors. "That guy's mowing the lawn with scissors!" No one at Narrabeen mowed the lawn with scissors! We'd got there late at night and it stinks and it's weird and different, and we woke up the next morning trying to work out where we were and here's some guy trying to sell us these paintings at the hotel. He told me and Tooky he was the only guy in Bali selling paintings. I've looked at Tooky and gone, "Shit, should we buy a couple now just in case we don't find this bloke again?" Tooky had no cash on him and has come out and he's trying to swap his underpants for the paintings … and the guy was actually inspecting the underpants and thinking about doing it! I looked at the whole scene and just thought, wow, how weird is this place? By lunchtime we'd seen 500 other guys selling the same paintings and we realised what was going on. My old man gave me a hundred bucks and that was my spending money for *bemos* and food. I wasn't drinking then and I reckon I came home with $50 and that was for two weeks.

'The highlight for me was surfing Outside Corner at Uluwatu three days in a row and I was the only guy in the water. There were guys sitting up there on the cliffs but no one would come out. It wasn't big, maybe six foot, but you tell people now that you surfed Outside Corner on your own and they think you're tripping. Then I remember guys coming up to us in the street in Kuta going, "Do you want to surf the best left in the world?" and I'm going, "*Isn't it here*?" I thought they were talking about Uluwatu, but they're going, "No, it's G-Land." They were holding these little polaroids of G-Land just pumping, and they were telling us there was apparently nobody over there at the time.'

Even though Dooma was one of the best juniors in the country – and two years later would become the Junior World Champion – he still wasn't entirely sure a career in surfing was calling him. Even his dad, Brian, who would soon be the ASP tour's media director, wasn't sure. 'Yes and no,' recalls Dooma about how serious he was about making a career out of surfing. 'I knew I wanted to travel the world and surf good waves and get paid for it, but I didn't think it was a serious career option at that point. I was sponsored by Mango, Rip Curl and McCoy so that was going well, but I still wasn't sure I was going to be a pro surfer. I was actually going to be a pastrycook at that point. I did work experience at a pie shop in The Corso in Manly. The idea with being a pastrycook was that you can work in the early morning and surf all day. But I just hated it. My job was putting the lids on the pies. The guy filling the pies was French with a little moustache and he had a ladle and was scooping from this big vat of sloppy meat and gravy. I remember he smoked the whole time and the ash would fall into the pies as he went. I'm like, "Mate, should that be happening?" I didn't eat the pies.'

Dooma chose surfing, his dream of owning a pie shop put on hold for another 15 years.

1982

Kong

'Enter the next figurehead of Australian junior surfing.
175lbs of beef ricocheted around the pro circuit pinball machine this year always out on the edge of full-tilt. The Kong projectile lit up all the right specials during inspired games at North Narrabeen, Burleigh Heads Cove and Victoria's Winkipop, anybody who watched would have to be impressed, the Kong style embodies a polished maturity spiced with out-there on-edge full-blown power. We'd had a few tastes of his surfing in 1981, enough to realise the raw potential, but the marvels of modern transport didn't bring us the full dose till this year. What more can you say? This new animal blew everyone away.'

This was how *Surfing World* magazine heralded the arrival on the scene of 17-year-old Sunshine Coaster Gary Elkerton, who by this stage had ceased answering to that name. In primary school he'd been 'uncommonly large and uncommonly hairy' and when one of the girls yelled, 'Show us your hairy balls King Kong!' he was typecast for life. In 1982, Australian surfing had found its new spirit animal. *Kong*.

Kong was living with his parents at 22 Tombarra Street, Alexandra Headland, but he spent most of his days either in the surf or out on his father's prawn trawler. He worked as a deckie for 'The Bullfrog' – dad, Keith – as they did runs between North Stradbroke and the southern reaches of the Great Barrier Reef. Kong took a board with him and jumped overboard to surf all sorts of reef passes and empty beaches, surfing alone in waters stalked by tiger sharks. It was a hard life, and one in stark contrast to the other life that was now calling him. 'I want to stay with the prawn

trawler,' he told *Surfing World* at the time, 'then go all out to be a pro surfer. I'd never give it up because there's so many things you can learn from the sea and being on a boat is a great way to learn them.'

Kong would fish by night and surf by day, checking the waves as the *Miss Bernadette* motored back through the heads at first light. He burned daylight. Along with surfing and fishing, Kong also rode motorbikes, played tennis and did karate, although, 'I only do karate in wintertime because in summer I surf till about a quarter to seven and karate starts at six.' When asked if he lived at a fast pace he replied, 'Faster than anyone else.'

Kong went hard, and by this stage had already broken both legs, a collarbone and a wrist. 'I was going surfing down at Alex and there's a hill that's about half a mile down at 45 degrees. I was flying down it on my pushbike with my board under one arm when this wasp happened to get underneath my shirt. It started stinging me so I threw my board toward the grass on the side of the road, but next minute it hit the telegraph pole and breaks in half. After the wasp had stung me seven times in the one spot I fell off and my left leg caught in the pushbike and I went down the hill face first. It took skin off my elbows, my stomach, my legs, my face. I broke my leg in two places. So I got back up to the top of the hill rode my bike home and waited two hours in agony for the doctors to open.'

At 17, Kong surfed like a man. He had the weight to throw around and having grown up at sea was supremely comfortable in most anything it threw at him. He surfed with raw power… and partied with raw power. He might have still been in his teens but he had all the adult vices already down. He was a regular at the pub, drank longnecks and smoked pot, and as his surfing notoriety spread he just went harder. 'It's been a bit radical,' he said at the time, 'too many fights and I'm not into fighting. I like to have a rage, go home, have sex and go to sleep.' It seemed like youthful boasting for the surf magazines who were lapping it up, but Kong lived up to his own billing. The big, boofy Queensland kid in the red and white star trunks was fast becoming a cult hero to every hard-living Aussie surfer.

By 1982 he was spending more time on the Gold Coast, tearing through junior contests and presentation parties with boundless reserves of energy. He'd met Rabbit Bartholomew, who took him under his wing. He then met a skinny kid named James Jennings – 'Chappy' – who'd moved to the Gold Coast from South Australia and who soon became Kong's cartoon sidekick, the pair inseparable.

Kong landed a deal with Hot Stuff surfboards. He loved their airbrushed designs and Rabbit's Bugs Bunny logo, and before long he had his own Kong logo, a giant ape on the rampage through the city. The logo turned out to be prophetic, and Kong did his best to stay in character as he travelled the circuit. 'I'm probably going to have to do something about it in the end,' he said of his raging, pondering for just a second, 'but it's not holding me back at the moment, so I'm not worrying about it.'

The first big contest of 1982 was the Coca-Cola Pro Junior at Narrabeen; the biggest junior event in the land. Kong and Chappy travelled to Sydney, set up a tent in Mark Warren's Narrabeen backyard and immediately set about getting on it, their party program only interrupted by the occasional heat. Surfing on just two hours sleep, Kong and Chappy made the final and had to surf against each other. Chappy thought the final was 20 minutes. Kong knew it was half an hour. Kong won using his trademark layback tube stance and was handed a thousand-dollar winner's cheque and trophy. 'I remember Mark Warren's cat, and to this day I still want to kill that fucking thing,' offers Kong. 'I had my trophy sitting on top of Mark's fridge with a pair of Mickey Mouse ears sitting on top of it, and the cat has jumped up there and I'm watching it in slow motion as it's knocked the thing off the fridge and it's just smashed into a thousand pieces and I'm like … "That fucking cat!" And I'm off after it trying to kill it.'

The pair partied that night and were woken the following morning by Hugh McLeod and Bruce Channon from *Surfing World*, who spirited them south on a magazine road trip. 'We got blind that night after the final,' recalls Kong, 'went into the Cross, and were that hungover the next morning when Hugh and Bruce come around really early. They just threw us in the Saab. We passed straight out and next thing we wake up and we're like, "Shit, we're in Victoria!"'

It was on that trip that Kong was introduced to Quiksilver founder Alan Green down in Torquay. Greeny, with a wild streak himself, took a shine to the kid who he was now paying $750 a month in "expenses". Kong technically couldn't be paid on contract, as he had his heart set on winning the World amateur title later in the year. He'd turn pro after that. With Quiksilver taking off, Greeny saw the marketing potential of the kid named Kong. It was while they were on that trip that Kong, in a throwaway line while walking into the Apollo Bay pub, said, 'If you can't rock 'n' roll don't fucken come!' It would become the title of the *Surfing World* story and later, the slogan for one of the most famous surf industry campaigns ever run.

Kong was Australia's answer to the clean-cut competitive vibe coming out of America, being led by Tom Curren, who was favourite to win the World Amateurs due to be held on the Gold Coast later in the year. Curren and Kong were already subject to breathless hype on their respective sides of the Pacific, but the match-up on the Gold Coast never happened. Warming up for the Aussie titles in Sydney, Kong speared himself in the leg with the nose of his board which took him out of both the Aussie and the World Titles. Unable to sort the Americans out in the water, he instead did it in print, labelling the new crop of young American surfers 'a bunch of soft cocks' in a *Tracks* interview which went halfway to causing a major diplomatic incident.

Kong and Chappy flew to Bali in the middle of the year, planning to stay and surf at Uluwatu but they were met by Made Kasim at the airport who informed them they were heading straight over to Grajagan on the first boat. Kong and Chappy stayed in the jungle at G-Land for a month with just a handful of crew in the camp, the waves barely dropping below eight feet the whole time. On one of the smaller days Kong ventured up to the top section of the reef at G-Land which at that point hadn't been surfed. The wave today bears his name. While they were there, one of the supply boats from Grajagan village overturned on the reef and a local man drowned, throwing some bad magic over the camp. Kong and Chappy were woken later that night by camp staff shouting in the dark. The local man's body, which had been stored under one of the losmens in preparation to be shipped back to the village the following morning, was being dragged into the jungle by a tiger.

Hawaii was next, and while Kong couldn't wait, those around him were worried. Born wild and with no operational filter, Kong was at short odds to end up in some kind of trouble over there with the Hawaiians. Rabbit, still scarred from the trouble he'd found himself in over there a few years earlier, could see it brewing and kept his distance. 'This is what happened,' recalls Kong. 'When we first got to Hawaii we went down the beach at Pipe to meet Rabbit, and at the time there was such a big thing about me coming to Hawaii, and Rab goes, "That's great, I'm surfing out here ... *but you're surfing down there*!" And we walked down and surfed Log Cabins! He sent me all the way down there! But he was freaked out at the time obviously. We ended up getting on all right with the Hawaiians ... just not as well as Chappy.'

To cut off any trouble at the pass, Alan Green had slipped Hawaiian Mickey Neilsen some money to keep an eye on the young Aussies. Mickey was sponsored by Quiksilver, and the Hawaii Kai guys took Kong and Chappy under their wing. The crew got along famously. They showed Kong and Chappy the ropes out at Sunset and Pipe, and they'd head into Honolulu together where they frequented a nightclub called Three Ds. The young Aussies were cut some slack. Driving home one night from town, the car they'd borrowed from Mickey took a detour into the canefields.

The car eventually rolled back to the North Shore on its rims the following morning, banged up and missing some hubcaps. The Aussies rendezvoused with Mickey at Banzai Bowls to return his car. Mickey took one look at the car and goes, 'Brah, that's not my car. That's one of Eddie's!'

Kong may have been welcomed by the Hawaiians but Chappy was fully adopted by them. Bugs was still in limbo, but all was good. The trio were even invited by the Black Shorts to have beers with them on New Year's Eve. The only trouble they ended up in was with the security out at the Kuilima resort. With Hurricane Iwa bearing down on the islands, Kong, Chappy and Rabbit embarked on an extended Long Island Iced Tea session. They emerged as the hurricane hit, and Chappy was caught in a gust of wind and blown down the road and into the night. He returned a minute later, surfing on the bonnet of a hotel guest's car. Hotel security came after them in golf carts and they did a runner onto the golf course. Kong shimmied up a tree, Chappy made it back to the apartment and hid out in a room with Rabbit's wife, while Rabbit himself was the only one apprehended.

In the surf, Kong took an immediate shine to Sunset. Chappy meanwhile took to Pipeline fearlessly. One famous wave, captured by photographer Don King, would make Chappy a cult hero. Gerry Lopez saw the wave and later said to Kong, 'I saw this little runt flying past me, and all I could say was, "God bless him."' Kong and Chappy would stay in Hawaii for four months, surfing themselves into the ground and learning how the North Shore worked. Hawaii, in time, would become a second home for Kong and the setting for his biggest victories.

Once back home in Queensland, Kong won the Jesus Pro-Am stoned out of his mind. He can't remember what he said in his acceptance speech to the assembled group of Christian Surfers, but it didn't go down well. The trophy, in the shape of a crucifix, would later end up snapped in two. He returned home to Tombarra Street with the two halves and received a swift clip to the ear from his mother Joan. Kong had survived Hawaii intact, but had been shortened up by his mum.

Kong had met Jack McCoy at G-Land the previous year. McCoy and Dick Hoole had just released *Storm Riders* and Alan Green, seeing a point in time, commissioned Jack to put a short film together starring Kong, Rabbit and Chappy. Jack met the trio at the Surf Air Hotel on the Sunshine Coast and discussed the project. As they talked, Jack watched waves wrap around an offshore island to the south. Mudjimba Island – Old Woman Island – did indeed have waves. The uninhabited island was actually leased at the time to Peter Troy, who lived nearby. Jack's mind started spinning, and Mudjimba Island soon became Kong's Island. Jack exclaimed, 'Get me a fucking boat!' The shooting for the movie only took two weeks, with sequences shot at Mudjimba, Lennox and Spooks Point. It was the comic sequences of Chappy car surfing, Kong's Magic Cream Puff Tree and the tribal chant of 'Koooonnngggg' that made it an instant cult classic.

'Jack was so ahead of his time,' recalls Kong. 'I'd just go along with him but couldn't visualise what he had in mind. But when it come out, geez, *Kong's Island* was huge. We had a premiere down here in Coolangatta at the Jet Club and the whole place erupted when we walked in. The Sunnyboys were playing that night. Chap got called up and was singing *Tunnel of Love* with them. I didn't realise the impact that slapstick little fucking movie would have on the world. But when we were doing it, remember, we had no idea it was going to come out like that. I was just smoking bongs, rooting chicks, surfing my brains out and filming *Kong's Island*. I was in heaven, mate.'

1984

Cheyne Horan

Cheyne Horan woke at 3am on the morning of 26 September 1983 and switched on the television. He was staying with friends in Avoca, on the New South Wales Central Coast, and all up and down the street, house lights and television sets flicked on one by one.

The deciding race of the America's Cup yachting race was being televised live from Newport, Rhode Island. Australia's challenger – *Australia II* – had squared the best-of-seven series 3–3 with the Americans, and Australia was poised to become the first nation to take the trophy from the Americans in 132 years. It wasn't so much the gripping sporting contest – nor the potential to stick it to the Seppos – that had Cheyne up in the dark. No, it was more the buzz around the Australian contender's revolutionary winged keel. Watching the TV, Cheyne strained to get glimpses of it under the water from the helicopter shot as the boat tacked. The keel had been kept secret from the Americans and hidden from public view. It was Australia's secret weapon, and as *Australia II* crossed the finish line Cheyne's mind was racing, as it often did. He got up, and unlike the rest of Australia that day went straight to work.

Cheyne was no stranger to revolutionary thinking. When he wasn't away on the world surfing tour, Cheyne lived in Goonengerry, outside of Byron, as part of a commune called The Fourth Way. He ate a macrobiotic diet, consulted I Ching coins for a daily divination, spoke in mantras and travelled with a blender so he could start the day with a fresh juice. 'We all cooked and we got into the yoga and from there we were on this path and suddenly you realise there's a spiritual element there. What the diet does, it purifies

235

the spirit. If you've got no impurities in your body you're thinking purely. Then there's the meditation side that purifies the mind, like wiping a computer clean so your mind can see the colours and smell the air. That broken record in your head, that's killing your spirit.'

The world surfing tour in 1984 was a real spirit killer – 10 months of globetrotting for largely horrible surf – so Cheyne would use his time at home for spiritual recalibration. He tells of a dream he had during his Fourth Way days. 'I was walking with Jesus along a dirt road, nothing around, and suddenly here was a farmer building a house on his own. I've started walking down to help the guy 'cause that's the kind of guy I was. I told Jesus, I'm going down to help the guy build this house. Come on, Jesus, let's go!', Well, Jesus tells me the farmer doesn't need any help and he keeps on walking. Now, what do you reckon that means? I took it to mean the farmer will finish the house in his own good time, and I had to stay on my path. So the thing with me, when you talk spirituality, it's about staying true to your own path.'

Cheyne's path, as he saw it, was to take surfing into the future. Collaborating with shaper Geoff McCoy, he'd long ridden *avant garde* surfboards: short, teardrop-shaped surfboards that looked nothing like anything else being ridden on tour. They were also single fins at a time when almost everyone else had crossed over to riding thrusters. Cheyne's boards received plenty of criticism but Cheyne felt 'a sense of duty to being an artist in surfing. I stuck to my guns. They were all riding the same white boards and surfing the same. They couldn't understand what I was trying to do. If I changed and conformed I would have been killing the creativity in my surfing.'

It wasn't just the boards Cheyne was riding, it was where he rode them as well. A year earlier he'd ridden 20-foot Waimea Bay on a 5'8" – a board about half as long as every other board being ridden that day. 'I felt like a dot in the middle of the universe,' Cheyne remembers. 'Everyone was looking at me and it felt like I was paddling out nude. I've made it out the back and all the Waimea boys are going, "Brah, what are you doing? You riding *that*? It's a toy!" I finally got one and surprisingly it wasn't that hard. It capped and it clipped me in and next thing I'm flying down the face of this thing. I'd had this notion in my head that I had to surf this wave like it's a four-foot wave, even though it was 20 foot. It was all perspective. I closed the wave down to these small grids and surfed them like four-foot waves, S-turning and snapping. It felt so loose and free. It was exhilarating.' As strange as it looked at the time, within a decade tow surfing would see surfers – Cheyne included – riding even smaller boards on even bigger waves.

The ASP season in those days was split across calendar years, and the '83/'84 season would end with three events in Australia, finishing at Bells. Cheyne headed into the last three events of the season rated in the top five, although it was debated whether this was because – or in spite of – his surfboards. Cheyne was just getting started with his board designs and with his surfing. He was 24 and considered part of the old guard on tour, but he 'still felt like a kid' and he was looking for ways to extend his shelf life on tour. He needed a secret weapon. Australian surfing's original star child turned to the star fin.

Cheyne knew a lot about surfboard fins, having lived with George Greenough up in the hills behind Broken Head. 'You learn a lot about hydrodynamics living with George, trust me.' Cheyne had lived in a treehouse at Greenough's. 'That was the best room I've ever slept in. It had a Perspex roof so at night you'd look up at the stars and it felt like you were in outer space ... and then when it rained you felt like you were in Atlantis.'

Ben Lexcen was the architect of *Australia II*'s win, the man behind the winged keel. In the euphoric months afterward he'd become a household name in Australia and his services were in demand all over the world. A phone call out of left field however piqued his interest, and he soon found himself on the beach at Dee Why watching a blond guy in a bright red wetsuit walking out to the jump rock carrying a surfboard with a prototype star fin.

'A friend of mine rang Ben Lexcen and told him, "Cheyne Horan would love to talk surf design." He goes, "Sure. No worries." I met up with him in Sydney and was spending time with him right through '84 and '85. He lived near the Spit Bridge but we used to meet at Dee Why and work on designs. That's where PC [Peter Crawford] was and he turned up on one of our testing days on the beachbreak at Dee Why and shot photos that we kept secret. Ben used to watch me surf and watch the board and he'd go, "Do you feel it coming out of the water? Do you feel it pushing up out of the water?" And I'd go, "Mate, I don't know what it's doing, but it's *flying*!" He taught me all this stuff about hydrodynamics. In 1984 everyone had hard edges from the tail to the nose. Ben said, "Take that edge off!" He'd look at my board and go, "If that was a boat, it would crash." That was his saying. It wasn't a wipeout; it was a *crash*. I was working on boards with Terry Fitz at that stage, so we refined a whole bunch of designs using the star fin and it was revolutionary. My board was the fastest board on the planet at the time.'

The star fin made its debut at the Stubbies at Burleigh Heads. Channelling *Australia II*, Cheyne played it right up. He walked down the beach with the fin covered by a towel so nobody could see it. People saw enough to start talking. The initial results didn't match the buzz. Cheyne lost to Martin Potter at Burleigh and then Barton Lynch at the Beaurepaires in Cronulla.

That just left Bells.

'The week before Bells, Claw Warbrick organised a surf trip down the coast with me, Tom Curren, Wayne Lynch and Peter Crawford,' recalls Cheyne. 'We were opening farm gates and walking through paddocks to get to these waves that only Wayne knew about. We had this one session where Curren was going off and I knew he was … *and he knew that I knew*! He was peaking, but I was holding back on purpose. If I got him in the contest I needed another gear to go to. I told myself I need to nail him at the event – not today. I even let him beat me at pool at Lorne pub. Peter Crawford came up to me later and said, "You'll really need to lift your game if you want to beat him at Bells." I told him what I was up to. That was the good thing about Peter; he was on my level. He was on my wavelength totally.'

However, Cheyne's star fin wasn't the star of Bells. The annual Easter contest that year was co-sponsored by rock band Australian Crawl. Coming from the Mornington Peninsula some of the guys in the band surfed and hatched the idea of bringing together the worlds of surf and rock over the Easter weekend. Aussie Crawl were huge in '84. They'd just had a number one hit with *Reckless*, and had just returned from Europe where they'd supported Duran Duran. They rolled into town and on Good Friday played a gig at Torquay Hotel, shooting a live clip for their song *The Boys Light Up*. As it turned out the boys did indeed light up. The crowd spilled out onto Rudd Avenue and a huge fight broke out between punters, security and the cops. The guy shooting the clip couldn't believe his luck and kept rolling.

Once the contest got started Cheyne worked his way through the draw and eventually, sure enough, drew Curren. 'It was a classic,' recalls Cheyne. 'I gave him everything. On the beach an hour beforehand I start staring him down. He's looking around fidgeting and he looks over and I'm looking straight at him. Then I look away for just one second and I look back and he's gone! He's playing this game as much as I am! He's disappeared. We paddle out and I'm totally in rhythm with the sets and Tom's struggling. I'm hassling him and I'd had three bombs and this one wave … I'll never forget this moment. I go into this huge cutback, the board is flying and here he is paddling *right in front of me*. I cut back into the tube at a hundred miles an hour and I snap *inside* the tube and come out flying right in front of him! It crushes him and I know I have him crushed at this point. He paddles away over to Rincon and I go, I've got him.'

Tom Carroll was the world champion elect, and Cheyne met him in the final at small Rincon. 'I played a mean game with him too,' recalls Cheyne. Rincon – which broke under the cliff at Bells – was the perfect racetrack for the star fin, and Cheyne shot down the line in a blue, pink and yellow slick skin wetsuit. Cheyne won the best-of-three final 2–0 and took the $6800 first prize. Claw Warbrick handed him the Bells trophy and Australian Crawl played the after party that night.

Despite the win, the star fin never really caught on. Cheyne and Ben stuck with it for a couple of years, put it into limited production, but like every other fin design and configuration it was wiped out by the thruster. The star fin would be remembered as a point in time and a surf culture kink. Cheyne, on the back of his Bells win, finished the '83/'84 season in third. He finished the following season fifth, and was so buoyed by his success he started work on a *cinema verité* film that followed both his spiritual quest and his fortunes on the pro tour. Cheyne's season tanked, but the movie – *Scream In Blue* – became a cult classic, a candid portrayal of one of surfing's freest thinkers.

Cheyne was far from done as a surfer, and it was in Hawaii, in late 1984, that he found his new calling. 'I was doing the tour and it felt humdrum for me until I got to Hawaii that year,' recalls Cheyne. 'This was the day when I realised I had to dedicate myself to big waves. I remember I was out on a big day at Waimea on a 9'2", which was too small. It was giant that day and kept getting bigger with every set. The Bay was starting to close out. There were only nine of us in the water. Anyway, I'm charging these waves. I was in the guts of it. I was paddling for waves while others were paddling for the horizon. This guy hanging off the side of me, his name was Ace Cool, and Ace and I were paddling for the biggest ones. I've got no idea what I'm doing mind you. I'm just charging.

'I paddled for a bunch of waves without catching them. I'm looking at these waves thinking they're going to break, but every time I'd paddle for them they'd back off and I'd miss it. So this huge set rolls through and I've turned and I'm paddling like a madman. My mind is going, you're crazy! I started screaming like an Indian running into battle so my conscious mind couldn't stop me. I'm head down paddling for this wave and I just see the lip of the wave fold over me in slow motion. I'm going down. I'm getting monstered. This thing nails me. I pop up and I'm in shock, hardly able to breathe, swimming toward the beach when I hear this voice – "Hey Cheyne! Hey Cheyne" – I look and it's Ace Cool riding the next one, which lands on my legs. I come up and now I'm losing it. My mind is telling me I've gone too far. My breathing was panicked but my body was fit, so I started swimming toward the beach.

'Now, there's this rule at Waimea that if you're in line with the lifeguard tower and you're not on the beach you need to swim back out to sea and try again. I don't know that rule. I find out a year later that if you keep trying to swim in you get smashed into the rocks at the end of the bay. Now I'm in the shorebreak down past the lifeguard tower, headed toward the rocks in the corner. I'm looking at it and it's 25 feet down there and I'm thinking, you're dead. You've gone too far. I've got no idea what to do, then out of nowhere this 15-foot wave came through in between the sets and I launch myself into it, thinking if I can get washed up on the beach they can at least revive me. I launch into it and it throws me up onto the beach.

'I wake up and I've got stars everywhere. I'm seeing stars and I try and walk and I feel my legs going … but I draw a breath and suddenly everything is clear. Clearer than clear. I'm feeling strong … I'm feeling like a lion! I walked up the beach at Waimea that day and I knew that was my true path.'

1984

Mark Occhilupo

The Top Shop at Wanda was Occy's hang-out.

The Occhilupo family home was over the dunes in Captain Cook Drive, Kurnell, but young Mark would spend most of his waking, surfing hours gravitating around the beach at Cronulla. 'We'd leave our boards around the corner at Michael Jackson's place. Not *the* Michael Jackson,' Occy clarifies, 'this guy was a shaper at Emerald Surfboards. But from the Top Shop we could see from Voodoo all the way down to Cronulla Point, and we'd sit out the front between surfs and eat hot chips and drink cans of Coke and tune chicks and just write each other off. It was like I was playing my role in *Puberty Blues* all over again.'

Occy was 17 and Australian surfing's latest teen star. His three older sisters had imprinted on their baby brother a flamboyance that was there for all to see whenever he rode a wave, but would also manifest during any public gathering or in the presence of a camera. Three years earlier he'd had a cameo in the seminal Aussie film *Puberty Blues*, which had been filmed in Cronulla. Occy's only line, delivered in his trademark high-pitched squawk, was 'Chicks don't surf!' The line was total improv but for the purposes of the film couldn't have been scripted more perfectly.

Occy had heard a similar line before, only directed at him. 'In Cronulla I used to have guys yelling out all the time, "Wogs don't surf!"' Occy's father, Luciano, had emigrated from Italy to Australia to build high-tension electricity towers before meeting Occ's mum – Pam, a Kiwi – and settling in Kurnell. As it turns out, wogs could actually surf pretty good – well, Occy could, anyway – but young Mark hardly looked like your typical swarthy Mediterranean native. The kid's face was an improbable assemblage with a blond

sweep of hair, suncracked lips, Tic Tac teeth and the formative outline of surfing's most distinctive underbite. It seemed every component of his face had been designed independently, and in years to come, late at night, in clubs, they would indeed operate independently of each other. But, for now, this was a face waiting to be the face of something.

Occy's arrival on the surf scene couldn't have been better timed. They were dark days in The Shire, with a heavy drug scene and many of its best surfers packing up and shipping out, a great Cronulla diaspora fleeing up and down the coast. Suddenly though, here was Occy, and even in his early teens there was a feeling that despite walking around the place like a dog in socks, this blond kid with the strange name was destined to be the Golden Child. But it wasn't just in Cronulla. It can't be understated just how much buzz Occy's arrival was generating, in Cronulla, around Australia, and in 1984 ... right around the world.

Billabong was still a garage enterprise at that point, but future surfwear mogul Gordon Merchant had signed Occy the previous year for $40,000, beginning a partnership that would launch both Occy and Billabong. The timing was impeccable. The surf industry was moving out of garages and into factories, and the pro tour was moving onto big city beaches, in front of big crowds and TV cameras. The whole scene was awash with Day-Glo and hummed with youthful energy. You couldn't have built a better stage for Occy, who increasingly looked and acted like the lead singer of a new wave band.

With Billabong's contract money Occy had done half of the ASP World Tour in 1983. He was just 16. In his rookie year Occy had met Tom Curren, attended Curren's wedding in Cronulla, beat Curren, called the Americans 'Seppo Wankers' in a magazine article and surfed Jeffreys Bay, became ideologically confused by what Apartheid even *was*, found a magic Rusty surfboard, surfed Hawaii for the first time and made the final of the Beaurepaires on his home beach of Cronulla. It was quite a year, and by the end of it he'd scraped into the elite Top 16.

As the 1984 season rolled around, the world was ready for Occy, even if Occy wasn't entirely ready for the world. On this front, Merchant hired Derek Hynd to be Occ's travelling coach. The role itself was a groundbreaking idea for the time, and it would pit Hynd's singular obsessiveness against Occy's openness to the world.

Hynd had lost his eye on the pro tour in 1980 when speared by the nose of his board during a heat in Durban, and like Ahab he was now scanning the horizon with his good eye for his White Whale – Occy winning the 1984 world title. Hynd's philosophy with Occ was simple – 'You don't tamper with pure genius' – and he knew Occ was special. Hynd's challenge was that Occ had a tendency to wander in the direction of anything shiny, and in 1984 *everything* on tour was shiny. The pair were a sight; Occ dressed head-to-toe in rainbow pastel, Derek dressed like a Jackson Pollock painting that had climbed down off the wall, and crowned himself with Hunter S Thompson's pith helmet. For six months in 1984 this odd couple threatened to turn pro surfing on its head.

Hynd also had burn-after-reading orders. As much as he was there to coach, he was there to also keep Occ out of trouble. Hynd was well aware that Occ was an ephemeral talent, a Ming vase that if dropped could not simply be put back together with crazy glue. Derek famously had a no-tolerance policy with drugs that was so puritanical he'd later start a group on tour called On The NOD (Not On Drugs). You had to be clean for two years to qualify, but this was the '80s. 'Globally it had eight members,' offers Hynd, dryly. 'It went nowhere. You've got to remember the tour was only 10 years old and there were no checks in place. It was open season.'

The 1984 ASP World Tour was pro surfing Pangaea, a time when giants walked the earth, stalking an alien landscape – Neptune Beach, Fistral, Trigg, Wrightsville – and the tour was populated by characters so large they bordered on self-parody. They were guys who believed the whole point of pro surfing was to make the other guy disappear in your shadow. Ego and rating were tethered. They could all see pro surfing was set to boom and they all wanted to be front and centre when it did.

The class of '84 was full of future legends. There were the old guard; Rabbit, Shaun and Cheyne, hanging on grimly into the geriatric twilight of their late 20s. There were the new generation; Carroll, Curren, Potter, Hardman, Barton, Gerlach and Kong. But this was not their year. No, it felt destined to belong to the kid from Cronulla. Nineteen-eighty-four was Occy's perfect point in time.

The tour began in May, in Japan. Occ surfed all the way to the final, losing to Martin Potter in tiny surf. It would be in Jeffreys Bay, South Africa, that Occ would announce himself. The Country Feeling Classic was a lowly C-rated event despite Jeffreys being the best wave on tour. Country Feeling was owned by local surfwear baroness, Cheron Kraak, who would soon take the Billabong licence in South Africa, and, with it, adopt Occy like a son. 'I'd never heard of this kid before. He was just this little blond kid with the squeaky voice who turned up and stayed. I needed to remind him to brush his teeth, but when he paddled out there he just blazed. He was light years ahead of everyone.'

Occy's surfing at J-Bay in July 1984 tore through time. He flew down the line at J-Bay like a re-entering spacecraft, the whole thing just threatening to blow apart at any second, only for Occ to load up all those G-forces and train them into searing chicanes at the top of the wave, then do it again, and again, disappearing down into the bay. 'In my exercise book,' recalls Hynd, 'I had to invent new codes for what he was doing.' By the time he'd beaten Hans Hedemann in the final on a dropping swell, Occ came in complaining that his board felt funny. He flipped it over to discover that his inside fin had broken loose and was flapping in the breeze. More than three decades later Occy's surfing at Jeffreys Bay during that event is still held as the gold standard.

The fruitiness of the Tutti Frutti Pro in France, the next event on tour, was matched only by Occy's pink and blue springsuit with the yellow gussets that became his uniform for the '84 season. In waist-high fizzing lefts Occy, surfing without a leash, zipped down the bank before finishing up in the shorebreak amongst the holidaying Parisians, some of whom were even clothed. Occ took down Tom Curren again before winning the final against Tom Carroll. Occy, 17, was now number one in the world. Interviewed immediately after the win, Occ looked down the barrel of the camera and without blinking laid his teenage ambition bare.

Reporter: 'So, Occy, do you consider yourself a serious contender to be the world champion?' Occy: 'Well, yes. Yes I do.'

It wasn't a precocious, youthful boast; most guys on tour assumed it was going to happen. He had Curren on a 4–0 run. America's *Surfing* magazine put him on the cover of the next issue trumpeting, 'He's young, he's hot, he's number #1!' Occy's time had come. It was 12 August.

On 29 August he showed up at Huntington Beach, California, for the OP Pro looking, according to Derek Hynd, 'Rake thin, a different person, a ghost.' Hynd had lost him in the celebrations after Lacanau, and Occ had found his own way to England before heading on to California. 'I'm meant to be taking care of the guy and here I am making calls piecing together where he was.' Occ had vanished and the trail got wafer thin. On the beach at Huntington Occ walked straight past Derek for his round-three heat with Wes Laine, a heat that considering Occ's form should have been no contest. Instead Occ lost convincingly … and would continue to do so for the rest of the season.

'Watching him walk up the beach that day is still one of the saddest moments of my life,' recalls Hynd. 'I knew he was done. I didn't see it coming because Occy was

hiding what he was doing under the carpet. I should have. He was still leading the world title race by a long way but he was finished. He was psychologically in the clutches of a really dangerous scene.'

The tour's growing professionalism was being counterweighted by a Bacchanalian party culture. For a fragile teenage talent it was enough to knock him off axis. The kid was also homesick and, after only one season, his biorhythms clearly were having trouble dealing with the rhythm of tour life. In the years ahead it would take two breakdowns before an official diagnosis of bipolar disorder and some time away from the tour finally allowed Occ to successfully deal with it.

For now though, he returned home to Kurnell 'spun out'. By season's end both Tom Carroll and Tom Curren overtook him in the ratings, and Occy finished the season in third. Occ still sees 1984 as a triumph and in many ways it was, third in the world at 17. 'I was happy with third. Tom and Tom were really good. That year was a blur. I was still a kid. It was epic, so much fun, but it went by so quickly.'

And with that Occy's world title moment was lost, not to reappear again for another 15 years. It would, however, be worth the wait.

1984

Wendy Botha

Getting on that plane was a remarkable leap of faith for
Wendy Botha. At just 16, she'd boarded South African Airways flight SA280 from Joburg to Sydney with no idea what – or *who* – was waiting for her at the other end. Regardless, she knew she had to go.

As the South African junior champion, Wendy was starting to outgrow her home break of Nahoon Reef, outside of East London. Nahoon was starting to feel a long way from anywhere. As a kid the place had been good to her. Her dad was a rock fisherman, but neither her dad nor her mum could swim. Wendy found her own way into the ocean. 'I used to live eight kays from the beach, so if mum or dad couldn't take me I just ran down after school. There was a tree that was past the last turnoff, so anyone who drove past the tree had to be going to the beach. I'd wait under the tree, but we'd surf when it was howling onshore and rubbish so most of the time no cars came anyway so I'd have to run.' Wendy did the last three kays barefoot on a dirt road, Zola Budd style, board under her arm.

The Nahoon crew was small, but welcoming. 'I had a different experience to a lot of the Aussie girls who had a hard time out in the water getting abused and hassled. I was more treated like a princess,' she laughs. 'But I was such a little shit to them. They soon accepted that and the old guys were actually quite sweet to me.'

South Africa at the time was not only isolated geographically, it was politically isolated as well. The country's apartheid racial policy was facing huge international opposition. Surfing was one of the few global sports that still toured South Africa, but it was under

increasing scrutiny. Tom Carroll, the world champ at the time, would famously boycott the South African events the following year.

For a young surfer with stars in her eyes, the world of pro surfing felt like it existed in another dimension. 'We had magazines. We had *Zig Zag* and *Surfer* and *Surfing*. My dad wouldn't buy them and I couldn't afford them, so I'd go to surf shops and flick through them till we got chased out. Then this guy, Dave, had a pub and a room out the back where he'd screen surf movies and we'd all be in there hooting. It was mainly movies of the guys, but I also remember watching Margo [Oberg] and Rell [Sunn] surf. But that's all I had to look at.' But what Wendy did have was Shaun Tomson, world champion, South African and by then possibly also the world's coolest surfer. 'I'd never met Shaun but I'd watched him in 1978 when they had the amateur world titles at Nahoon Reef. I remember Chapstick was a sponsor and to this day if I smell the original Chapstick I think of that day. They were free and I was a typical grommet with 20 of them stuffed in each pocket. I even had the T-shirt from the contest.'

By age 15, Wendy was South African junior champ, but she was running short of competition. 'I actually surfed an open men's event at J-Bay that year,' she recalls. 'I came dead last in my first heat but I surfed against Shaun and against Michael Ho and all those guys. Man, I was so young.' But what happened back on the beach later would open a door for her. Australian contest promoter Bill Bolman was in South Africa at the time and watched Wendy's heat. Bolman ran the Stubbies event at Burleigh and watching Wendy surf gave him an idea. There'd been no South African women surfing at the Stubbies. Wendy could really surf, and the press would love the cosmopolitan angle.

'He came up to me and said, "You should come to Australia and surf against Pam [Burridge] and Jodie [Cooper] and these girls." Well, that set me off. The seed was planted. I'd just won my first SA Champs, so I started begging and pleading with my dad but he said, "Sorry, I just don't have the money."'

Wendy wasn't taking no for an answer. 'I was so strong-willed. I was a good kid, I didn't do anything radical, but I was so strong-willed I think they just threw their hands in the air. I look back and I'm like, what were they thinking? Here are these people who couldn't swim and they've got this kid who wants to go and surf on the other side of the world.' Wendy was sponsored by Graham Smith at Town and Country Surfboards, who she spoke with about the trip. A family friend lent her the money. It was only the second time she'd ever flown. At 16 she was off to Australia on her own.

'I was sitting on the plane next to this Aussie lady and I'm telling her how it was my first time to Australia and how I was going there to surf and how excited I was. She got my whole story over 24 hours in the air. Her name was Donna. We landed in Sydney and I'm thinking, okay, here we go. I'm going to walk out and someone from the contest is going to be holding up a sign with my name on it.' Wendy navigated immigration, collected her boards and walked into the arrivals hall ready to start her life as a pro surfer. 'I'm looking around and there's no one there. Nobody. I just stood there and waited for a few minutes and just burst into tears. The lady from the plane hung with me for a bit but had to eventually leave. I sat there and got more and more upset. I was just sitting there with my boards and a bag just in tears. I'm 16. I was distraught. I had no phone numbers to call and only had $200 on me. I was beside myself. I'd cried myself into a tizz.'

An hour later Donna doubled back. 'She comes back in a taxi and walks over and says, "Come on, I'll take you home." She lived in Hurstville, in the suburbs with her mum, an elderly lady. We got there and I'm jet lagged and I just cried myself to sleep. I woke up 17 hours later and she knew I was about to lose my shit again and she went, "Look, it's all good." She'd found my phone book. "I've rung your dad and told him you're okay." She'd also asked him, "Where is she supposed to be?" He's rung around and got a hold of Graham who said, "Sydney? No, she's supposed to be on the Gold Coast!" How that happened still to this day I have no idea. This lady has then called Bill Bolman and told him she was putting me on a bus the following day.'

Wendy stepped off the bus into the white Queensland sun and when she saw the contest site at Burleigh, 'My head exploded.' Her situation improved dramatically. 'Bill put me in an apartment at Burleigh with Pam Burridge and Jodie Cooper. I couldn't believe it. And then we had all these vouchers and I went to Maccas for the first time in my life. I'd never even seen a McDonald's before. Jodie came with me and watched me eat six burgers. I just went, this is the best!'

As the only South African woman in the contest – and just 16 – Wendy was the centre of attention. 'It was mind-blowing. Rabbit was making a fuss of me, and I had a photo with him in the newspaper eating an ice cream. I'm hanging out with Larry Bertlemann who's making a fuss of me because I'm riding for the same surfboard company as him. These are people I've only seen in surf mags and in movies.' The press also swooned. 'Nev Hyman took me to meet Joh Bjelke-Petersen. I was wearing these pink shorts and thongs and standing there with all these politicians in suits. I had no idea who they were or why I was even there. No idea. I was just standing there thinking, who is this old dude?'

The tabloid papers also worked the apartheid angle. 'I met Ketut Menda from Bali who was surfing in the event, and the press made a big deal out of it because he was dark and I was white from South Africa.' The press cared more about it than anyone at the contest. 'To tell you the truth it was amazing how little I knew about what was happening at home myself. But on that first trip no one really mentioned it … my first trip to America the next year, though, was a doozy. I got smashed. It was really bad, because I was South African and the South African Prime Minister at the time was named PW Botha. They thought we were related and a few Americans gave it to me.'

But while Wendy was the only South African woman on tour, she wasn't the only South African. Her Australian trip was about to go to another level. 'I got my arse kicked in the contest, I didn't do any good, and Bill asked me where I was going next after Burleigh and I shrugged my shoulders and said, "I've got no idea." Next minute here's Martin Potter and Shaun Tomson going to me, "Okay, you can come with us." I couldn't believe it. Here I am on a road trip with the two most famous South African surfers. I'd met Pottz once before but didn't really know him. Pottz was only my age but he seemed so much wiser and more mature. He'd really travelled. He'd been on tour since he was 14. Pottz had won a HiAce van the previous year in the contest so I jumped in with him while Shaun and Willy Morris drove behind us.' Pottz didn't have a drivers licence, but off they drove, south.

'From there we went to Angourie and the surf was six-to-eight foot and incredible. I was pretty ballsy coming from Nahoon Reef, but I was terrified. I was watching the boys pull into these huge barrels, watching Willy snap a board. I remember these huge manta rays with 10-foot wingspans jumping out of the water. Man, my eyes were as big as saucers. From there we picked up Stuart D'Arcy in Sydney and drove to Bells. I stayed with those guys down there. They were so good to me. They were so sweet. That same trip MR and his wife, Jenny, actually took me on a road trip down the Great Ocean Road. The Ash Wednesday bushfires had just gone through and [they] showed me where all the fires had burned. But what sweet people. Everyone went out of their way to help me.'

Wendy lost early in both Stubbies and Bells events', 'got my arse kicked', but remembers 'my surfing improved in leaps and bounds. I was improving daily on that trip. I wanted to surf like a guy. Tom Curren was always my favourite surfer, along with Pottz and Shaun, and I watched those guys surf and I tried whatever they did. I was also blown away that I was surfing Burleigh and Kirra and Bells and all these places I'd only seen in the movies and in magazines. If I didn't come to Australia I would never have improved the way I did.'

When Wendy finally made it back to South Africa a month later her world had changed. She let everyone know about it. 'Of course I got home and I was out of control. "Yeah, I've been hanging with Shaun and Pottz and Pam Burridge." I must have been such a punish. I was shy around people I didn't know, but at home was another matter. I went home and even though I'd got my arse kicked all I could think of was, I don't care what happens, *I'm going back*.'

Wendy left school immediately. 'I went to them, "I'm so out of here you're not going to see me for dead."' She took jobs lifeguarding and working in a burger restaurant on the beachfront. She saved. She handed out a thousand letters asking for sponsorship and a few rand to fund her travels. She returned to Australia the following year and 'had it totally sussed this time. Trust me.' She had it more than sussed. Wendy won the 1985 Stubbies. She then won the BHP Steel contest in Newcastle.

She felt the pull of Australia. 'Straight away I went, this is where I want to live. I wanted to live in Australia. The Aussies were so into their surfing, while back home in South Africa no one really cared. There are contests in Australia, there are sponsors. The first guy to sponsor me was actually Rod Brooks at Piping Hot wetsuits. He was so good to me. I went in there to the factory and got to pick out wetsuits; grabbed all the fluoro colours naturally. I also went through a white wetsuit phase, because I had a crush on Cheyne [Horan] at the time.'

Wendy moved to Australia, settled on the northern beaches in Sydney and by 1987 had won her first world title, still as a South African. She won her second title in 1989 as an Australian. She laughs now. 'The grounds I eventually got let in as a citizen was basically, "This kid can surf and she might win another world title." I was pretty homesick the first few years, but after three years it had turned around and Australia felt like home and South Africa felt like a holiday. It was tough. I love home and that never goes away, but to do what I wanted to do I had to be here in Australia.'

1988

Barton Lynch

Barton Lynch had a ritual. The morning after he flew home from a gruelling leg of the world tour, he'd wake up, check the surf on Manly Beach, then walk down and eat breakfast. Hiding in plain sight Barton would sit down at his favourite coffee shop and order a flat white and the full English fry-up – bacon and eggs, sausage, mushroom, baked beans. 'I'd just sit there, eat the lot, read the paper, watch the world go by.' Barton Lynch thought a lot about surfing. Some argued maybe too much. But for a brief hour 'the thinking man's pro surfer' would allow himself to think about anything *but* pro surfing.

The world tour in 1987 was all consuming. It comprised 21 events, often back-to-back, always intense. The tour was a time-lapsed loop of high-stake heats, two-star hotels, after parties and airports. Away for most of the year, when Barton got back home to Manly he'd take his foot off the gas. His car – a 1984 Holden Astra he'd won at a contest three years earlier – sat rusting in the salt air. 'When I got back from the tour the last thing I wanted to do was go anywhere. I just hated the idea of leaving home again. Why would I want to leave Manly?'

Barton had everything he needed within walking distance. Manly Beach, lined with Norfolk Island pines and wedged between the headlands of Queenscliff and Fairy Bower was a self-contained, surf-themed diorama. Barton however was never in any hurry to surf. 'I had all day to myself so I never really surfed early,' he remembers. 'I'd surf at Gentleman's Hour after everyone had gone to work. I'd surf the North Steyne left mainly. Occasionally Queenscliff. The Bower and Winki when they broke. I hardly ever

Barton Lynch $14,000

Fourteen thousand and no/100 DOLLARS

Richest Surf Contest Ever 1st Place

MEMO

BILLABONG PRO

got in the car to go up the coast. I *might* go and surf Narrabeen if everything else stopped breaking but that was pretty rare.' The pro tour at that point was largely held in junk surf, so surfing exclusively at Manly wasn't without its benefits. 'Manly being Manly it was the perfect training ground for every shitty beach break we'd get dragged to all around the world.'

Barton lived on Pittwater Road, a couple of blocks back from the beach. In the '80s Manly still had its dark corners. 'I was living between the Sunshine Surf shop and a drug referral centre,' remembers Barton. 'We always used to hang in the front yard and see all the junkies coming and going, which was one of those reasons why I took such a strong anti-drugs stance.' Barton lived with his mate, Mick Mock, who was busy assembling what would become in time Australia's largest collection of surfing miscellanea. Mick collected surfboards, surf magazines, surf posters, surf curios and surf kitsch. Mick also moonlighted as the Event Director of the Coke Classic. In April 1988 the Coke would be the final event of the '87/'88 tour, held on Manly Beach just two blocks from Barton and Mick's front door.

Both Barton and Mick had been outsiders when they'd turned up to Manly Beach as kids. Mick was Chinese–Australian and lived in Sydney's inner west. Barton was from the old money suburb of Mosman, having moved there from Whale Beach at 11 after the death of his father. Manly at the time was rough and uninviting. 'Mick was from Strathfield and I was from Mosman and there were only certain areas of Manly Beach where us Westies could hang, we couldn't hang with the Manly guys so we hung at the end of Carlton Street. The guys from Strathfield were a few years older and got cars before us, so the two groups kind of hung out and eventually became Wind 'N' Sewerage Boardriders Club.'

The Wind 'N' Sewerage name was a piss-take of the old Windansea Boardriders, but in Manly during the '80s it couldn't have described the place better. The North Head sewerage outfall was chundering millions of litres of barely treated effluent into the ocean on a daily basis; a strong sou' easter pushing a brown tide back onto Manly Beach. A few years later Barton would be a leading voice as surfers protested against it, the Water Board eventually extending the outfall pipe and moving the problem four kilometres out to sea. For now, though, he took a deep breath and paddled out.

Barton had also been recently nominated as the Surfers' Rep on the ASP Board. Sharp and unafraid of speaking up on matters of principle, Barton was the man for the job. The boys made the call. The timing however was tough. There was a raging debate happening about whether the world tour should end in Australia or Hawaii, and Barton soon found himself in the middle of it. 'Rabbit dumped me into the hot seat,' laughs BL. 'He'd had his troubles over there in the past and wanted nothing to do with taking the end of the tour away from Hawaii. He said, "Look mate, I'm stepping off the Board and you're the obvious person to take over – the only one." It was that first meeting where I had to go and vote against Pipeline finishing the tour and vote for Manly instead.'

Barton was torn. Commercially, and for the profile of the sport, Manly made sense. Pipeline however was … well, *Pipeline*. It communed the sport with the ancients. Barton surfed it religiously every year. 'But I went to the meeting and voted for Manly; voted against my personal feelings just to do the job.' The tour would end at Manly in April '88 at the Coke Classic, but after a backlash would return and finish at Pipeline the following season. For Barton, those two events would bookend a wild oscillation in fortune.

Barton was rebounding from a disappointing '86/'87 season. He'd finished 12th. It was disappointing because the year before he'd finished second and had challenged for the world title, going head-to-head with Tom Curren. In a bold move Barton had employed a coach that season … the only man consumed more by pro surfing than Barton. 'It was 1985 when I worked with Peter Drouyn,' recalls Barton. 'I thought the guy who invented the game must have some good ideas on how to play it and thing is, it worked. I got second in the world that year.' Drouyn was brilliant, but his advice was often so esoteric that the only one man capable of comprehending it was Drouyn himself. The pair got within a couple of heats of the title, but in the end Barton found himself jammed between Drouyn's eccentricity and Curren's increasingly invincible aura. 'I remember we were in the world title race at the time and I came in from the first set of a best-of-three final at Burleigh and Peter was saying, "Your hands … there's something wrong with the way you are holding your hands!" He's really intense and I'm there thinking … *hands*? I need more than that to beat this guy!" We didn't last much longer after that, but I learned a lot from working with Peter, things I wouldn't fully realise or appreciate till years later.'

In 1987 Barton worked with a local coach from Manly named Marc Atkinson. 'I was bouncing back from a shocking year, and so I was pretty fragile emotionally and just wanted to fix it. I was searching for help and Marc was great.' By this stage Barton was regarded as the tour's master tactician – there wasn't much you could teach him about surfing heats – but up against competitive animals like Kong, Tom Carroll and Damien

Hardman he was looking for a hard mental edge. 'Marc was a deep human,' recalls Barton. 'Marc made me ask a lot of questions of myself, and I needed that.' Amongst the animals, Barton was an altogether more sensitive creature. 'That year for me was all about managing my emotions more than anything else … turns out I wasn't very good at it.'

Halfway through the '87/'88 season Barton felt the world title was his. 'It was definitely my year. It *felt* like my year. I went to the US Open at Huntington and I won that. I beat Curren in the semis. Lacanau in France was next and I won that too, beating Curren again. Halfway through the year I was thousands of points ahead in the ratings and the last event of the year was at Manly, my home beach. I felt like that was my destiny. I felt like my destiny was to win the world title at home in front of my family and friends and it was all heading that way.' Barton's winning orbit however would prove fragile.

Greg Clough had been shaping Barton's surfboards ever since he was a kid hanging out in Carlton Street. But at the start of '87 Barton started riding boards shaped by a young guy named Greg Webber. 'I'd been having trouble getting good boards from Cloughy for a while so Greg Webber shaped me some boards and we just ran Aloha stickers on them. The boards were amazing. They were the foundation of the run that put me into that number one spot.' The boards brought immediate results but tested a long friendship with Greg Clough. 'I'd ridden Cloughy's boards from a young age and he'd been really influential over me and my career. He'd been a father figure for me for a long time and there was this unspoken tension there about me riding someone else's boards.'

That tension broke in France. 'In Lacanau I was celebrating the win with Cloughy and his wife and a few other guys when we had an argument. It had its foundations in some comments about South Africa that I snapped at. In retrospect I'm sure I was an egotistical wanker at the time, leading the ratings, number one in the world, I can only imagine what I was like. I know in myself, my delivery sometimes of things is not the most politically sensitive. I just tend to throw shit out there sometimes, but after the back-to-back wins I suppose I was a little bit cocky and probably said too much.' Barton walked off and went to bed and left it at that.

Cloughy was very much a *feel* shaper and it was the primary reason Barton had started riding Webber's boards. Barton was precision-calibrated, and Cloughy wouldn't measure boards. 'You'd just be getting all sorts of stuff you hadn't asked for,' he recalls. 'We were at dinner in France with some of the Aloha riders – Luke [Egan] and Dooma

[Hardman] and the boys – and they were all like, "Hey you've got to tell him to measure our boards." Everyone was complaining to me and asking me to say something to him, So that night I said to Cloughy, "Mate, the boys want you to measure their boards. We need precise equipment, we need to dial this stuff in." By the time we finished that night it had been resolved. It was appreciated and understood. We left on good terms … or at least I thought we did.'

'At the next event in Hossegor I'm putting my rashie on about to surf a heat against John Shimooka when Cloughy comes up to me on the sand. "Hey, I think it's best I don't shape your boards anymore." He dropped me there on the spot. I was baffled. I thought we were cool. Anyway, I paddled out and lost … and that was the start of the demise.' Barton went on an ice-cold losing streak. He bombed in Brazil and Japan. His confidence tanked. Defeat shadowed him. 'I kind of fell apart from that point. I just didn't have the tools to handle that situation and to handle the pressure of leading.'

The final three events of the '87/'88 tour were at home in Australia. Barton bombed at both Bells and Wollongong, which just left the Coke Classic. By this stage he'd dropped from first to third in the ratings. He'd stopped training. His dream of winning the title at home on Manly Beach had soured, replaced now by a gnawing dread that instead of winning the world title on his home beach in front of his family and friends, he'd *lose* it on his home beach. The Coke Classic was supposed to be a triumph. It now loomed funereally, and he couldn't escape it. In a *Tracks* profile Barton told of how haunted his days in Manly felt. 'There's not a human being I speak to or come in contact with,' he said wearily, 'who doesn't say something about it. It's so hard.' Barton got in the car and fled up to Angourie, but by now the noise was in his head as much as anywhere else. 'I just remember it was a really stressful time. I couldn't escape it.'

Barton still had the longest of long shots to win the title at Manly. There were three other surfers fighting it out – Damien Hardman, Gary Elkerton and Tom Carroll – and Barton needed them all to lose, while he needed to win the contest. The trio were gnarly. 'Dooma and I were arch enemies at that point,' recalls Barton, 'even though we'd ridden together for Aloha.' To make matters worse, BL caught a glimpse of Dooma's board on the way back up the beach after an early round heat. 'You've never seen so many numbers written on the bottom of a board in your life, mate. I remember looking at that board and going, oh well, at least Cloughy listened to me. He's measuring them.'

Liberated from expectation, Barton surfed well at Manly and won through to the quarters where he took out Tom Carroll. For an hour that afternoon he was actually back in the ratings lead, but his destiny was out of his hands. If either Hardman or

Elkerton won their quarter finals he was cooked. Barton walked home and watched *Lethal Weapon* on the VCR. Barton watched Riggs and Murtaugh while Hardman and Elkerton were busy winning their heats. For Barton it was over. Damien Hardman took the world title the following morning, the Narrabeen boys going nuts at North Steyne.

Dooma rubbed salt into the wound and beat Barton in the Coke final. Barton cut a forlorn figure on stage but rode it out with a little gallows humour. He congratulated Dooma, thanked the crowd and walked home through the crowd with a towel over his head.

'I remember that night I ended up in Emergency because I put my fist through a window and cut my hand open. I was in an emotional, angry space. I was heartbroken. That year had all of the good, all of what you want … and then all of the bad, what you dread and what you're trying to avoid. I just didn't have the tools to win, to handle the pressure. Maybe it was just ego that did that, I don't know. I thought that was my chance. That was my destiny and I'd blown it. I questioned myself. I asked myself, where do I go from here? I felt like I'd never get another chance.'

The new season began just a few weeks later and Barton let it all slide. 'There was a massive amount of surrender. I went out that next year not even thinking of the world title. I thought it was done. I thought that was my chance and I missed it. I blew it. So I just detached and surfed.' As he told *Tracks* at year's end, 'It was probably the year that felt least like it should be mine.' Barton made an incredible nine semi-finals that year without winning an event … and was entirely comfortable with that. There was a serenity about Barton and his surfing that lasted right up until the final day of the season.

The 1988 tour reverted back to a calendar year and would end in Hawaii, not Manly. Instead of the world title being decided in waist-high waves at Queenscliff, it would be decided on a bluebird day at Second Reef Pipeline. Barton didn't know it yet, but that day was waiting there for him.

The Billabong Pro was the richest surf contest ever held. Finishing at Pipe it would close out the 1988 season. Going into the final day of the season – 2 January, 1989 – Barton had a mathematical shot at the title. Nobody gave him much of a chance, despite him making the final of the Pipe Masters the year before. Damien Hardman led the ratings, but it was the guy behind them both who was a clear favourite. Tom Carroll was not only a Pipe guy – he was *the* Pipe guy – and when finals day dawned 12-foot, cobalt blue, airbrushed and charging out of the west, the world title seemed Carroll's to lose.

He promptly obliged. It was *so* perfect he tried to catch every wave in his first heat and was pinged on a bizarre interference. Tom drowned in honey. Barton heard the news of Tom's elimination and raised a trademark eyebrow.

For Barton the clouds parted, the sun broke through and here was his chance. The moment however didn't weigh heavily as it had at Manly. 'The waves were so good I could detach and just surf it for what it was … perfect Pipeline. The waves overshadowed the situation I found myself in. And while the previous year everything had been hard, this just felt *easy*. It clearly wasn't, but I wasn't fighting anything, wasn't fighting myself or the situation. I just surfed.'

Barton just needed to keep winning that day, which he duly did. He won the contest and he won the world title and he won them both in legitimate Hawaiian waves. It could not have been more poetic or redemptive. The memories of that day at Manly were washed away. 'I'd swap Pipeline for Manly every single day of the week and I suppose one of the great lessons for me is that acceptance of fate. Recognising that destiny is at play. You know, sometimes life has something waiting for you which you've spent your life energies creating … and you get to watch it unfold.'

1990

Wayne Deane

'The house faces east, and even though we were back in Coolangatta a bit you could still hear the surf from up here. When the swells were up on the beach toward Fingal you heard it really loud.' Colleen Deane is describing the sound of the ocean from the house that her husband, Wayne, had built them. 'When he heard the swell at night Wayne got really wound up. He'd get very, very edgy the night before a swell. His adrenaline started for a swell days before. He'd be feeling it. He'd just know. These swells were a big deal for him. The night before he'd start walking around the house getting ready. Boards out, boards waxed up, put them in the car. When he started to bring out the long leg ropes, that's when you knew he was serious, and he'd always use two leg rope strings – he didn't trust one. He'd leave in the dark the next morning and disappear for the day. Sometimes I'd be terrified, hoping he'd come home okay, but then I'd go, what am I worried about? He's Wayne. He's got it sorted.'

The Deane boys had grown up in Ballow Street, up on the hill in Coolangatta. One street over were the Townends. One street over again were the Petersons. The first board that young Robye Dean and his younger brother Wayne had 'made' – a mate's board they'd cut down in the front driveway – they sold to a young kid named Rabbit. But while all those guys would go on to luminous surfing careers, Wayne Deane went down a more modest path. He stuck with his carpentry, built houses, built surfboards and instead of surfing contests Wayne surfed *swells*. Over the decades he'd be the one guy out on the biggest cyclonic days, on the biggest boards, paddling out through the Tweed River and materialising in the lineup to surf maxing Tweed Bar, Snapper or Kirra. Wayne was the

archetypal blue-collar surfing hero … although there was that one time he chased a world title.

Longboarding was Wayne's competitive outlet. Wayne rode long shortboards and short longboards, so the lines blurred. The 1989 Australian Longboard Titles were due to be held at Middleton, South Australia, and would be a big event for the Deanes. Wayne would surf in the opens, Colleen was surfing in the women's, and Wayne's brother, Robye, was surfing in the over-35s. The Queensland team was booked to fly to Adelaide when news broke of the Ansett pilot's strike. 'There were no planes flying,' recalls Colleen. 'The rest of the Queensland team pulled the pin and stayed at home, but Wayne was stubborn. He really wanted to go. He's got onto his brother Robye and said, "Stuff this, let's drive." So we were the Queensland team,' Colleen says. 'The three of us.'

The Deanes hired a silver Tarago from Coolangatta Airport and started piling it up with gear. 'You can imagine how many boards were on it,' says Colleen. 'The stack of longboards on the roof was bigger than the van itself.' With the car packed, the Deanes started the long drive south – Wayne and Colleen, and Robye, his wife Zell and their son, Luke. 'Wayne liked going back roads wherever he went. He loved them, so he thought this was great. Off we went into the outback. We went through Cobar, Wilcannia, Broken Hill. People were looking at us while we're driving down the main street with all these surfboards on the roof. We'd come to towns and they'd look at us wondering what the hell we were doing out there. You could almost hear them saying, "I think you took a wrong turn."' The Deanes drove for two days, taking four-hour shifts at the wheel. The roads got straighter and the only other vehicles were road trains threatening to rip the boards from the roof as they passed in the other direction.

After two days they arrived. 'We were staying in a little house in Victor Harbor then driving out to the comp of a morning.' On the way to Middleton Wayne spotted a go-kart track. After two days driving, he got straight back behind the wheel. 'Wayne just couldn't resist it,' laughs Colleen. 'We gave that place a bit of a flogging. Wayne drove like a maniac.' The rest of the states had full-strength teams and were pretty happy that the full Queensland team hadn't showed. They weren't happy for long. Wayne won the nine-foot opens. Colleen won the women's. Robye won the over-35s. Queensland almost won the teams' title with just three surfers.

There'd been a reason why Wayne had been so keen to get to South Australia. The winner of the opens at Middleton would go to Japan the following year as part of the Australian team for the amateur World Titles. Wayne was going to Japan. 'That was his plan all along,' says Colleen. 'Win that and go to Japan. It was a bit of a dream for him. He always wanted a world title.'

The biggest challenge for a surfer like Wayne, however, was tiny waves. 'When it got closer to Japan we did some research about Miyazaki at that time of year and knew it would be small and closing out, and the waves at Bilinga were the closest thing we could find at home to train in.' By this stage Colleen had become the first accredited female surf coach in Queensland. 'I said to Wayne, "You want me to run heats for you?" So we'd head down to either Bilinga or North Kirra and run 15-minute heats with beach starts, which is what we'd get in Japan.'

The Deanes had never been to Japan before. 'Japan was a real culture shock for us, starting with the public bath houses. That was a weird experience. I don't know how it was for the blokes but it was weird for the women. You'd strip off, put your clothes in a little pigeonhole, soap up, rinse off, then walk naked into this big warm pool full of strangers. Culturally it was pretty weird. It wasn't the Gold Coast, that's for sure. Wayne came out and said, "Hmm, well that was interesting."' The food however was fine. 'Wayne was eating sea urchins, you name it. Anything from the sea he was good with.'

The Aussie team were in good spirits. 'I'll never forget "Flex" Landers was the guy in charge of the music on the bus,' recalls Colleen, 'and it was all Hunters and Collectors. Everyone was singing 'When the River Runs Dry', that was the team song. Anyway, we get to the opening ceremony and it's this huge production. The Japanese really turned it on. They had these Japanese models in bikinis dancing around, and there were thousands of people there.' Wayne, meanwhile, had a plan. Under the cover of darkness he disappeared and came back soon after with a Japanese flag. 'Wayne stole a flag from the opening ceremony,' remembers Colleen. 'He did the Dawn Fraser and nobody knew. He totally had it planned. He had to shimmy up this huge flagpole, and he had someone at the bottom there helping him, but black or blue he was stealing it, and he totally got away with it.'

When they got to the beach at Miyazaki the waves were pretty much as expected. 'It was tiny,' recalls Colleen, 'and Wayne's main competition was coming from the American guy, who was a real trick surfer.' Wayne was *not* a trick surfer. Wayne threw his longboard around like a shortboard, and opportunities for that were limited at knee-high Miyazaki. Wayne finished second to the American in both early rounds.

At that point, as only the Japanese might do, they airlifted the whole event from Miyazaki to Nijima Island for the last round and the finals. 'They moved the whole contest,' recalls Colleen. 'Every single person. We flew from Osaka to Tokyo, the full airlift of the whole event. Everyone is going, what are they doing? This is crazy. Every country. Every surfer.' From Tokyo airport everyone was bused to the ferry that would take them across to Nijima. 'It was this giant six-level thing. We've got onto this thing and been shown our cabin and it was down below the waterline. Wayne's straight away gone, "Fuck this!" He lost it and has gone, "I'm not sleeping underwater!" He was paranoid about the ferry sinking and being stuck down there. He's dragged all our stuff up on deck to where all the surfboards were stacked outside and we posted up there. It was freezing and we were sleeping in boardbags, but Wayne and some of the other Aussie boys got on the rum to keep warm. The sea was pretty rough and this was in the middle of the night. You'd occasionally hear these huge horns in the dark 'cause we were out in this major shipping lane full of freighters and cargo ships.'

The contest changed dramatically at Nijima. The waves were big. Advantage, Wayne. 'It was full survival,' recalls Colleen. 'The American couldn't do tricks.' Surfing down the beach before his heat Wayne snapped his favourite board and needed to retrieve a back-up for his heat. It worked fine. 'Wayne was falling behind in his heat then, out of nowhere, this monster wave came through and he took off and pulled into it on that huge mal and got fully barrelled. The Aussie crew on the beach went nuts. That was it, the winning wave.' Wayne Deane was the World Longboard champ. He returned home to Coolangatta to find the street covered in streamers and 'World Champ' written across the old rusted Sandman out the front of the house. Wayne was back at work the following day.

In the years ahead he'd go on to win another four Australian longboard titles, and he'd continue to chase big cyclone swells at home. They were sessions that never got much press – you couldn't shoot them, the swells coming with weather and Wayne being too far out to sea – but they would, in time, become part of Coolangatta surfing folklore. Colleen recounts the story of Cyclone Yali: 'I'd taken the kids to school then dropped Wayne off at D-Bah. He'd paddled out through the Tweed River on a 10'2" he'd made himself. From there he paddled around the back of Snapper. I sighted him and went, sweet, there he is. He was right out the back at Snapper. He caught a couple then he caught one out wide near the shark nets and I lost sight of him. I thought, where is he? I went up on the hill near the surf club at Snapper and I couldn't see him. I went back to the truck and I bumped into Johnny the fireman, and he asked, "What's up?" I said, "I'm a bit worried, I've lost sight of Wayne." We've kept looking but couldn't see him. Johnny's gone, "Let's jump in the truck and have a look from

Greenmount." We're looking from Greenmount and we can't see him. Johnny's gone, "Jump in the truck, let's go and look from Kirra Hill." We get there and we still can't see him and he's trying to reassure me, "maybe he's just lost his board". He was trying to calm me down because by now I'm starting to think, what am I gonna tell the kids? That's when Johnny points and goes, "Oi, have a look down there." I've looked down past Big Groyne at Kirra and there he is, walking up the beach swinging a busted leg rope.

'We drove back to Snapper and Wayne's jogged back and he's spotted the truck and come over. "Lost me fucking board." He was spewing. I'm thinking, I'm never going to hear the end of this. I'm glad to see you, mate, but I'm never going to hear the end of this bloody board. Anyway, we're in the car park at Snapper and these young guys in a ute have driven past. Well, Wayne's looked in the back of the ute and spotted his board. He's run over to them and they've gone, "We found this board up off Currumbin, we're trying to find the guy who owns it and see if he's okay." Wayne goes, "Unbelievable. Wait right there." He's jumped in the truck and we've driven straight down to the bottle-o and bought them a carton.'

1990

Layne Beachley

Layne Beachley would skate along the beachfront at Manly like she owned the place. Dressed in teenage boys' surfwear, board under her arm, hat on backwards, she'd weave through the joggers and day-trippers along the Steyne with one eye ahead and one on the waves. She'd skate past groups of guys changing after a surf, getting yelled at, yelling back with interest. As she skated past she'd respond to every 'Hey Gidg!' with a wave and a 'Hey' back. Gidget knew everyone along the Steyne and would stop and talk with any of them who'd listen. She'd surf, then post up at the pie shop on the Corso, sit with the guys and write off the tourists. 'Get back on the ferry ya losers!'

At 17, Layne Beachley was already the unelected mayor of Manly Beach. From Fairy Bower to Queenscliff, Manly was her world – Layne's World – a juicy low-hanging headline that the *Manly Daily* and surf magazines in years ahead couldn't help but run with any story they wrote about Layne and her successes on the world stage. 'At that point I was so content in Manly,' she recalls. 'I had so many friends, I thought life's not gonna get better than this.' In 1990 however Layne's world was about to get much bigger and much better.

Layne had finished school at Mackellar Girls' High the previous year. On 12 January she received her HSC results – 299 from 500 – good, but not university good. She'd planned to study Japanese and tourism at Sydney Uni, but that plan was never *the plan* anyway. Manly at that stage was the centre of pro surfing in Australia. It had the Coke Classic, it had Barton Lynch … and it had Pam Burridge. Layne had grown up in awe of Pam, but Pam was now living up at Newport and off on the world tour most of the year

273

anyway, chasing a long-fated world title that kept eluding her.

The world tour was the plan for Layne. She wanted to travel, she wanted to go to California and Hawaii and surf her way around the world. She wanted to make a career out of surfing, even though there wasn't much of a career in pro surfing for women at the time. In 1990 Layne wanted to travel and try her luck with some tour events. Maybe a couple in Australia. Maybe a couple overseas. She definitely wanted to get to Hawaii.

This all sounded great, the only problem being that Layne was unsponsored and broke. Resourceful even at 17, she would find a way.

Layne got a job working at the Old Manly Boatshed, the windowless dive bar at the ferry end of The Corso. The Boatshed was owned by Manly identity Goughy. If Layne was the Mayor of Manly Beach, Goughy was the Mayor of the Manly Night. Layne had gone to a party at the Boatshed and asked him about a job behind the bar, keeping the fact she was still only 17 to herself. She started soon after. Her first shift began at 6pm and finished at 3am the next morning. She stayed and had beers after work. 'I was a beer drinker back then,' she offers. 'My dad worked in the beer industry and the stuff was always around … and it was Manly. There was always a party going on.' After that first shift at the Boatshed her dad drove down the hill from Fairy Bower and picked her up at 4.30am. She climbed in the car smelling of cigarette smoke. The Boatshed was in a basement below the street and these were the days when you could happily smoke in bars and clubs. Layne went home and was asleep before she walked in the door.

Two hours later she was up again. For the past year Layne had been surfing with Queenscliff Boardriders Club up the northern end of the beach, and this was a time when QBC was the dominant surfing club in the nation. They were stacked with great surfers like Rob Bain and Merrick Davis. The Queenscliff Gumby – the club's large green cartoon mascot – would terrorise the beach while the guys from Queenscliff terrorised the waves. They were the best club in Australia at the time, but more importantly the best on Manly Beach, which had three boardriding clubs.

Growing up, Layne wanted to surf like the guys. Then she wanted to surf *better* than the guys. That didn't always go down so well. 'A lot of guys started giving me shit when I started surfing better than them,' she recalls. 'When I eventually became someone recognisable in the industry they started respecting me, but before that they sort of resented the fact that I overtook them and they never went anywhere.' While Manly might have been Layne's world, surfing in 1990 clearly belonged to the blokes.

The Queenscliff club didn't offer a lot of opportunity for a teenage girl at that point, so teenage Layne did what Layne would continue to do for the rest of her life – when the opportunity wasn't there for her, she'd simply create her own. Layne took off from QBC and started her own boardriders club down the beach. Manly Pipe Riders set up next to the stormwater pipe out front of the Manly Pacific Hotel, and Layne turned up for the first club round on two hours sleep and still smelling of cigarette smoke. 'I was the entirety of the club's female membership,' she recalls. She was also, however, elected as its founding president. Twenty guys turned up that first day, including Six Pack, Legs and Bear Man. Layne made the final and finished third behind Andy and Bryce, but in front of Loverboy. The irony wasn't lost on Layne. 'A club full of guys and I still couldn't get a boyfriend! They used to call me "Frigid Gidget".'

'The club felt different though,' she remembers. 'I wanted to create something where I at least felt welcome, and that wasn't easy on Manly Beach.' Her surfing and lifeguard friends would occasionally throw her off the wall down onto the beach, a 10-foot drop onto the sand, but at the time in Manly that was considered a gesture of endearment. This was another time, pre-dating five-dollar coffees, multi-million-dollar real estate and the gentrification of the beachside suburb. Manly was tough. It was tough being a young guy surfing on Manly Beach, let alone a teenage girl. Layne rolled with it, gave as good as she got, and in time those years on Manly Beach would be perfect conditioning for the world tour, which, she'd discover, was also stacked against the women.

Layne's closest friend in Manly at the time was Jodi Holmes, and when the pair weren't surfing they'd hang at Jodi's mum's dress shop on the beachfront, playing backgammon and cards in the change rooms out back. While Layne worked at the Boatshed at night she pulled double duty during the day, also working in the surf shop at Australian Surfer HQ. She submitted photos to a modelling agency but never heard back. She only took it half-personally. She was saving and scrimping enough to get to the first events of the women's tour – Burleigh and Newcastle respectively. Bells, she couldn't afford.

On 1 April that year Layne, Jodi, and a young kid from Dee Why named Shane Herring jumped on the bus for the 12-hour journey north to Burleigh Heads. The daunting prospect of having to surf through the trials for a shot at surfing against the world's best wasn't helped when the bus driver tried to grope her during a stop. 'Scared the shit out of me,' Layne remembers of the incident. The Burleigh trip wasn't quite the introduction to the tour she'd been dreaming of. She lost the first heat and was soon on the bus home to Manly.

Layne took the train to Newcastle. 'Dad was away for work and I hadn't even thought about how I was going to get there,' she remembers. Layne arrived in Newcastle with nowhere to stay and ended up sleeping on the floor at the Smiths' place at Bar Beach. Warren Smith was the promoter of the Newcastle event, and would open his home to competitors from around the world who needed a bed. Newcastle was Layne's big break. She made it through the trials and drew world champion Wendy Botha in the first round of the main event. To Layne's great shock she won, and then watched on as Wendy hobbled out of the water in tears, limping. Wendy's knee injury would end her season. Layne looked on not knowing what to think. Wendy was her idol. Barton Lynch pulled Layne aside and had a word in her ear, reminded her how gnarly the tour really was and while she could feel sorry for Wendy, she couldn't feel sorry for winning. Back home in Manly, Barton had been one of the few guys to offer her advice in navigating this strange new world of pro surfing, and in years ahead, all around the world he'd continue to offer sage advice. The talk worked. Layne made the semis at Newcastle, a huge result.

Layne's world really opened up when she travelled to California in July for the OP Pro. 'I said to my dad, "I'm going to California and I'm staying with this bloke." Dad was like, "Hmm, no worries. Have fun," and kept watching the telly. Dad and his girlfriend were expecting a kid at the time, so I was given a lot of freedom to do my own thing.'

Layne had a contact in Huntington, a South African guy who ran one of the local surf shops and he'd offered to put her up in his apartment on the corner of Orange and Sixth streets. 'He picked me up but I hadn't read the fine print that staying with him also meant sleeping with him. I freaked out when he put it on me. I told him no and ended up sleeping on the couch while he smoked bongs and watched TV. He was so pissed off I wouldn't put out.' Layne again made the main event, shooting the pier at Huntington on her way to finishing ninth.

That just left Hawaii. 'I flew to Hawaii with Neridah Falconer in November. Neither of us had any money and neither of us had organised anything. Back then the flights from Sydney used to land at 1am so we slept in the terminal and Neridah went into Honolulu the next morning and hired a car while I sat with our boards. We then drove the wrong way around the island, around the east side which took forever, especially after we somehow ended up stuck in the middle of a funeral procession. Driving on the wrong side of the road was new to both of us!'

They got to the North Shore with nowhere to stay, eventually finding a caravan up a dirt road at the back of Pipeline with no running water and just one bed. The upside was that it only cost $10 a night. They had to return the car so Layne borrowed a pushbike. Riding down Ke Nui Road to check the surf she heard a car slowing behind her. As she rode past a huge puddle the car accelerated straight through it. Layne's first Hawaiian barrel was courtesy of Todd Holland and Barry Van Der Meulen, who drove off laughing. It was a wet winter, and every morning Layne and Neridah would trudge through the red mud with their boards, hitch a ride to Sunset, and paddle out.

'Sunset I just loved,' Layne recalls. 'I just fell in love with the wave. I remember being so mesmerised by it paddling out for the first time, just overwhelmed by the power of the ocean. I was in awe and I remember sitting in the channel for an hour before I went in and caught a few.' Sunset was the final event of the women's tour that year, and Layne made the semis. She finished the year rated 17th despite only surfing half the tour. She'd officially arrived. Her connection to that wave, to Sunset and to waves of consequence, was there from the start. She'd eventually live a few houses down from Sunset with a view straight into the Inside Bowl.

On the finals day at Sunset, Layne also watched on from the channel as Pam Burridge, her childhood idol from back home on Manly Beach, finally claimed her world title after more than a decade. Layne watched on and while ecstatic for Pam – who she'd travel with on tour the following year – her own ambitions were crystallising. Layne had worked her last shift at the Boatshed.

1993

Pauline Menczer

Bondi was home for Pauline Menczer but at the same time never quite felt like it. 'There were so many locals in Bondi that I didn't know most people's names, apart from the original crew I grew up with. I knew people, but I didn't. I surfed with ITN for a while (Bondi's infamous In The Nude boardriders club). It's so funny, hey, I didn't put two and two together until four years ago who David Gyngell actually was. I thought he was just this bloke at boardriders. I never knew he was this big TV executive. I'd never have picked it.'

Bondi 1993; the last days of Scum Valley. This was before the money came in and before the hardcore surf crew priced out. Bondi was still rough. The beachfront was all concrete and graffiti and police patrols. The vibe in the water was urban-heavy. Pauline was cut no slack. She was 5'2", surfed better than most of the guys on the beach, and possessed an overdeveloped personality with no accompanying filter. Pauline told it like it was. Even as a kid she was outspoken, which if you knew her made her hilarious company but, if you didn't, it often made her a target. 'It was hard. It was really hard,' she recalls. 'There were a few really nice guys but some total arseholes as well.' Pauline was kicked in the ribs by another local surfer. The police encouraged her to press charges. She declined. 'If I was the one who sent him to jail he'd be after me so I said nothing to the cops. I knew when to be quiet.'

Pauline had got into surfing at a time in the mid-'80s when Bondi still hosted pro tour events, often in ocean polluted by the Malabar sewerage outfall. 'I remember them asking me over the PA, over and over, "Can that girl surfing in the area please move!"

279

I remember thinking, this is my beach! I just remember being at Bondi and getting better and better at surfing and then there was this pro event, the first time I'd ever seen pro surfing. I saw some of the women surfing and I thought, you know, I'm as good as them. I should be in this event! Why can't I be there? At the same time I got these cards in a Weet-Bix packet and there was a collection of pro surfers – Occy, Lynne Boyer surfing in Hawaii, and I wanted to be like her and to surf those big waves. In Bondi, Kathy Anderson was the one who got me into surfing big waves. When Bondi was huge and there was no one around at all, she'd make us jump off the rocks at South Bondi and paddle across and surf in. You'd only get one wave and that was it.'

City life had been hard on Pauline. She was just five years old when she lost both her grandfather and father within the space of four months. Her grandfather was killed in a hit and run. Her father was killed when his taxi crashed in a back street near Centennial Park. Both deaths were suspicious and family lore link them to Sydney's underworld. Pauline's mum raised four kids on her own. 'When I was seven years old, there were four of us kids and she was looking after us all and you can imagine how messy the house was. So I said to my mum, "I'm going to start saving for my own house." I started saving at age seven.'

By 1993 Pauline had outgrown Bondi. By this stage she was 22 and had been on the pro tour for four years, finished runner-up to a world title, travelled extensively and realised there was a lot more out there. She wanted to escape Bondi. Her coach, Steve Foreman, was living on the north coast outside of Byron, and Pauline was up there often. This was back when Byron was still Byron, before Byron turned into Bondi. Living was easy. The waves were empty, the coast was green not grey, and you could still buy a house for under seven figures.

Pauline hatched the plan. 'We were in Ocean Street in Bondi, and the neighbour on one side had built a two-storey house, then the neighbour on the other side did the same, so we suddenly had views of brick walls. Mum was miserable in Sydney so I talked her into moving up the coast. I took my mum up there and showed her all the beaches and I spoiled her rotten. She and my grandmother moved up together with half the family. Mum bought at Nimbin, my grandmother bought in Newrybar. I lived in my van.'

Steve Foreman was living in Brunswick Heads, down by the river, and Pauline, when she was home, would either stay at his place or sleep in her van. 'Brunswick was the opposite of Bondi and the opposite of the tour in every way. I surfed around Brunswick and Byron, but a lot of the time I just went fishing. I was a mad fisherwoman. I was so crazy about it. I'd fish off the Brunswick River breakwall. I loved the peacefulness of it.' Pauline had developed chronic arthritis throughout her body as a teenager and managing the condition would be a lifelong challenge. 'I always had to deal with my arthritis, so there wasn't a lot of physical things I could do but fishing was one of them. Fishing was really calming and relaxing for me and I was so crazy about it that I travelled around the world with fishing rods and pool cues there for a while. I put them in with my boards and took them on tour with me.'

Pauline was away on tour most of the year, but between events would live in her van which she parked in friends' driveways. Her life at home began to mirror her life on the road. 'I was with a French girl then, Nadege – who was officially my "coach" on tour – and we'd just pull the van up at friends' houses and stay there. And I loved that life. We'd work for it – I loved gardening so I'd do the gardening to pay the rent. It was such a good life and it was *free*. My mum lived in Nimbin and she was a bit of a hoarder, so we'd fill up the van and go to the Lismore car boot sale and sell all her shit. Mum would let me keep the money and that would pay for our fuel and food. I've never ever, ever in my whole life, actually rented. I lived in the family house in Bondi, my van, and eventually I owned my own house.'

Pauline's attitude to money – or more particularly the lack of money – would shape her time on tour. To her the money didn't matter, which was the perfect attitude to have on the women's tour where there was *no* money. 'I learned the value of money early. I remember clearly my mum giving my brother 60 cents and me and my twin brother 20 cents because we were younger. We had to do chores for it. My house fund I had as a kid was the same house fund I had when I did the tour. I had this account that didn't "exist". I kept it secret from myself. While I was on tour I kept putting money into it, so by the time I was 21 I had $90,000 saved and the house in Brunswick was $137,000. As soon as I won an event I went straight to the bank. I paid the house off in five years.'

In 1993 Pauline was doing the tour off her own dime. Apart from free boardbags and shoes she wasn't sponsored. 'Nope. Nothing. Reebok sponsored me at one stage, but it was only free shoes. They got the shits with me for saying in interviews I wasn't sponsored, and I replied to them, "What am I supposed to do, eat my shoes?" I said, "Thanks, but I'm one of the best in the world, if you think I'm happy just with product you're wrong." Of course I lost that sponsorship. I started wearing the same clothes and wetsuits around as a joke. I wore them till they fell apart and had massive holes in them to see how long it was before someone noticed. I wore a Piping Hot wetsuit till the arse fell out of it and I *still* didn't get sponsored. They don't want to sponsor me? I'll do it myself. I never really went looking for it though. I just thought the companies came and asked you if you wanted to be sponsored, that's how I thought it worked. I never approached them.'

The 1993 season cost Pauline, she calculates, about 25 grand. She earned 30 grand in prizemoney and was not only paying her own way around the world, but Nadege's as well. This was in the days when around-the-world air tickets cost eight grand. The budget was always tight. 'I was a nervous traveller,' she remembers, 'but my biggest fear wasn't the flying, it was being charged excess baggage! Seriously. A couple of times in Paris I had to leave stuff behind. At the check-in counter I had my foot under the boardbag but the woman knew all the tricks, so in the end I started grabbing pillows and sleeping bags and throwing them out. She wanted three hundred francs and I could replace all that stuff for five.'

Pauline was a wheeler and dealer, an art she'd mastered selling second-hand clothes and bric-a-brac at the markets back at home, and she soon discovered ways of making money on the road. 'When I was on tour I was always buying and selling stuff. I bought a bike in America for $400 and sold it for $1200 in France. Then I brought a whole heap of Levi's jeans in America and sold them in France to pay the rent. That's how I survived. I did it to survive and I loved it.' Pauline did it tough, but it created a deep appreciation of what she *did* have. It also kept her hungry. Her results improved when she had no money. 'Not having it was a great motivator for success.'

'I remember Serena Brooke in Japan one time going to me, "Look Pauline, look what I found!" She was holding up a wooden spoon and she goes, "You can fucken sell anything? Try and sell this!" So I got back to the hotel we were staying in and I said to the owner, "I'll swap you this for breakfast." And they did! That's how I survived. That's why I enjoyed it. I loved my life. In Europe I used to live off baguettes and cheese for lunch. It was cheap but I was so happy.' So whenever anyone else would start bitching about life on tour Pauline was onto them. She'd point out the fact they were in France. She'd point out the local gothic architecture. She'd point out the patisseries. She'd point out they were on a beach. 'And you're whingeing about this?' 'Naughty Pauls' was the life of the party on the women's tour – the first to turn up and the last to leave, the first in fancy dress and the first to strip off and jump in the pool.

Halfway through the 1993 season, before the European leg of the tour, Pauline took off on a holiday. When you travel the world for a living, finding somewhere that qualifies as a holiday takes some imagination. Nadege had worked at a resort in a remote corner of French-speaking Gabon, on Africa's west coast.

Apparently it had waves. Pauline was in.

'It was in the middle of nowhere on the coast outside of Libreville. It apparently had a nice left about a mile up the beach and there were no surfers at all. It was so untouched that monkeys and elephants were all over the place. The gorillas were a bit further inland. But it was pretty wild, and there was all this crazy voodoo going on with the locals. Once we got there we heard about how the locals would kill each other. It was about tribal kings and queens and magic and power … and we'd walked into the middle of it.

'The first thing that happened was Nadege's dog went missing. Five hours later we found its body. It had been decapitated. At the same time the resort crew were looking for some local guy who'd gone missing. We found out later that the local queen had just died, and they'd killed both the guy and the dog to bury with her. Then this *other* guy comes out of the jungle and he looks terrible. We took him in and fed him and the story we got out of him was that he'd escaped when he found out he was due to be sacrificed by having his heart cut out. By this time clearly we were starting to freak out.

'Then we had a white film crew turn up who'd been given permission to film a tribal ceremony in the jungle, and they asked if we wanted to tag along with them. It was the first time this ceremony had ever been seen by white people apparently so we said, "Sure." What could happen? Well, we drove through the jungle for three hours and arrived and there's these tiny pygmy houses and I saw all these huge pots, like the ones cannibals cook people in in the movies. I'm thinking, are we being set up here? I said to Nadege, "Hey, I'm worried." They made us shower next and we can hear them giggling outside and I'm thinking, are they making us wash before they chuck us in the pot? It fully felt like we were the guests of honour.

'Then they had this huge feast for us, all this food and we had no idea what this stuff even was. It was bush food and some of it was so disgusting. I do remember the sweet potatoes were okay, they had about 20 different types, but I'm thinking everything else was bush meat or monkey or something. I was grossed out. By the time we finished it was midnight and they said okay, now we're doing this ceremony. They had this plant called *iboga*, which was a psychedelic. They put it in your hand and you lick this stuff and it was like taking a hundred aspirins. What it did, it enhanced whatever emotion you were experiencing … unless you took heaps of it, in which case you lost your shit.'

'Anyway, the village crew painted their faces white, some of them were in these straw costumes head to toe, and then they got the *iboga* out and started dancing. I kept looking at the chief's eyes; he must have taken a ton of that shit. He was off his head and doing this flame dance wearing this huge headdress. Anyway he's come over to me and is dancing all around me and I'm thinking, shit, he's going to set me on fire here. Then he put my hand out and pulled me in and came up face-to-face with me and his eyes were spinning. He was fully possessed. Then Nadege was next and he went crazy holding the flame in front of her and we're both kind of freaking out. I remember the whole time I was busting to do a wee but there was no way I was walking into the bush on my own.

'Anyway, things have wound down by six in the morning and as a gift the chief was going to tell our fortunes. He knew nothing about us, and through a translator from local African to French to English he told me my dad was a motorbike rider, which I found out later was kind of true. Then he told me that I do a dangerous sport and that I was going to be number one in the world. To do that though, he said, "You have to give back to the land." He told me wherever I was I had to find the biggest tree nearby and "give back to it" – whatever I was eating or drinking I had to share it with the tree and I'd be number one. I remember driving back the next day just laughing. We couldn't believe that had just happened, but that last thing the chief had said stuck with me.'

The 1993 season had opened brightly for Pauline with a win at Bells, but it was during the second half of the year – after the African trip – where she caught fire. She won the Lacanau event in France, followed by Hebara in Japan and found herself at number one. The wins came at a cost though. Pauline was so rundown by the end of the year that her arthritis flared up. 'I was so unwell and skinny. It started in France with a flu that I couldn't shake, then I had really bad diarrhoea in Japan and the arthritis just followed.' Pauline had battled the condition for years now and knew its rhythms. "If I'm under stress it'd flare up, or if I was emotionally really happy or really sad. If I had a break-up or a new relationship it'd flare. I had to keep my life on a level … which wasn't easy for me.'

The World Cup at Sunset Beach was the final event of the season, but Pauline could hardly get out of bed in the month leading up to it. Back at home in Australia she worked with a local naturopath who had her on a radical alkaline diet of mainly raw vegetables, but even with regular massage treatments she was still locked up. She couldn't walk and couldn't even sit in a bath, let alone surf. The days until Hawaii

Vanessa Aust
Osborne

Layne Aust
Beachley

Jayde Haw
Wright

Pauline Aust
Menczer

Aust

Aust

h Aust

r

Aus

Aus

COORS
LIGHT

ticked down with no sign of any improvement. 'I remember once I got to Hawaii my arthritis was so bad I couldn't surf at all. I was so weak. I remember going to the pool at Turtle Bay every day and I'd tie my leg rope to a pole and just paddle in the pool because I physically couldn't surf.'

Pauline went to the local medical clinic in Haleiwa to get a cortisone shot in her hip. When she explained she was going for the world title the nurse looked her over, and asked, 'Shouldn't you be in school?' The cortisone needle missed the spot, and Pauline could barely walk out of the clinic, and worse, 'It cost $34 and didn't even work! It was so inflamed it still felt like a knife was being jabbed in there. I couldn't straighten myself out. I was desperate.'

Hawaiian Rochelle Ballard told her to go see this healer over on Kauai who might be able to help. 'He was this hippy guy, and he'd placed one finger on my hip and one on my shoulder and told me to breathe. It was all pressure points and timing. The pulses in my body he said were out of phase. And it *worked*.' Pauline arrived back to Oahu still unable to surf … but there was one thing she could do.

'I remember the surf was flat and they said they were going to wait till the last day of the waiting period to run the contest. Anyway, I always remembered the thing the chief had told me in Africa. I also had this little "mummy water statue" they called it, so I took the statue, found a tree in the yard where we were staying down at Laniakea, and I gave the tree a drink … and then I stripped off and ran around it three times naked to make it extra powerful.'

The next day the surf at Sunset was eight foot and perfect. The contest was running, but Pauline still hadn't surfed. 'I was in pain and hobbled down to the water's edge … and paddled out and surfed like there was nothing wrong with me. That's the adrenaline. That will to win. I surfed like there was nothing wrong. I was surfing this 7'6" that wasn't even mine, but I instantly felt comfortable out there.' Sunset was a solid eight feet. Pauline had always shone in big surf. Three years earlier she'd taken what was regarded as the heaviest wipeout the women's tour had ever seen at 15-foot Margaret River. Pauline's first wave that day was a re-enactment. Wearing a white surf helmet, she went down hard but popped straight up and paddled back out.

There were four other women in with a shot at the title that day, and one by one they dropped until it was just Pauline and Neridah Falconer left. Pauline was already into the final, and Neridah needed to make the final to keep her chances alive. Pauline watched on nervously with good mate Jodie Cooper. In her semi, Neridah was left chasing a 3.67 that she never found. That was it. Pauline Menczer was world champion. 'I just burst into tears. I'd been in so much pain that day but I wasn't feeling anything. I remember calling home to tell my mum and my brother answered. I go, "I just won the world title, is Mum there?" And he said, "That's okay, I'll just tell her later." I went, "Fucken hell mate, don't get too excited!"'

Pauline flew her mum and Steve Foreman over for the world title presentation a week later. Pauline was handed her world title trophy at the ASP banquet at Turtle Bay. 'Someone put a lei around my neck and the smell of those flowers, the frangipanis … I can still remember the smell of them today. Then I got absolutely shitfaced. I can't even tell you how many times at the banquets I've ended up in the garden at Turtle Bay. That night I got put into a golf cart with the trophy and a security guard drove me back to my room.'

1995

Rod Brooks

Rod Brooks and Bruce Raymond sat there, staring spellbound into the sun as it dropped into Plengkung Bay, watching waves spin down the reef at G-Land. They both clutched a glass of gin and tonic, the glasses perspiring in the tropical heat. They'd run out of tonic water the day before and instead had crushed up quinine tablets, which they had on hand as a malaria preventative. It was one of those moments where you don't need to say much, and neither Rod nor Bruce did, but Bruce broke the silence by saying, 'Can you imagine holding a surf contest here?' This was late winter, 1994.

Rod and Bruce had been in Bali running the annual Quiksilver Grommet Titles. Their ritual was to stay an extra week once the contest finished and bail immediately over to G-Land to surf the fabled left. Rod had worn many surfing hats by this stage. He was a five-time Victorian champion, had been contest director at Bells between '76 and '81, been the president of the ASA, was the current chairman of the ISA and had been a key surf industry player with Piping Hot. He now had a roaming role with Quiksilver, who were expanding their global footprint. Rod had been around a thousand surf contests in his life up till this point … but he'd never experienced a contest like the one he was about to run.

Quiksilver and the whole surf industry was, at that point, intoxicated with the idea of tropical surf travel. The Mentawai Islands in the north had broken open a couple of years earlier, a gold rush of unimaginably perfect surf. The magazines and movies were full of the Mentawais. Surf travel boomed. The surf brands, themselves on the cusp of their own commercial gold rush, saw the opportunity to sell the dream and climbed aboard.

The pro tour, meanwhile, was badly bogged. Most of the events were being held on city beaches in grey, shitty surf, and the whole thing was hardly capturing the imagination of surf fans. Back in September 1992 the Quiksilver event in Biarritz had to be cancelled after the North Atlantic went spectacularly flat. That event became a running joke within the company, and it had stuck with Bruce in particular. Quiksilver, despite having the current world champions in Kelly Slater and Lisa Andersen, were questioning their investment in the pro tour. They were sending their stars up to the islands on Martin Daly's *Indies Trader* and coming back with more images and footage than they'd get from a whole year on the tour.

Bruce was a dreamer, Rod was a doer, and the pair were about to change the paradigm of pro surfing. After he and Rod left G-Land, Bruce went home and pulled together a pitch to make their G&T conversation a reality. 'Bruce had to go to meetings overseas and convince the international bosses at Quiksilver to stump up the money for an event at G-Land,' recalls Rod. Bruce sold the vision. 'In mid-December I was in Hawaii and Bruce rang me and said, "We're going to do G-Land." I said, "Fantastic." Bruce said, "Can you get on a plane and go to Bali and set it up?"' Rod, thinking Bruce meant after Christmas, replied, 'No worries.' Rod was on a plane to Bali the next day.

As it turns out, Rod needed every spare day to get this thing organised. He'd have to wade through dozens of layers of Indonesian officialdom all around the island nation. Rod brought together his own high-level surf delegation. He had Doctor Rizani, head of the Indonesian Surfing Association. He had Ketut Kasih and Steve Palmer from Quiksilver. And, of course, he had Bobby Radiasa, who'd been a grommet when Mike Boyum had opened the G-Land camp in the '70s, and now had his name on it. Then the fun began. There were meetings, dinners, golf games. Rod went from Bali to Jakarta to Surabaya to Banyuwangi to Grajagan, and met with governors, ministers, marketing managers and village elders. Rod shook thousands of hands, brokered hundreds of deals, and solved dozens of '*bik prrroblems*' with an avuncular manner and a ready stash of rupiah, all of which while barely being able to speak a word of Bahasa.

The other key meeting was with the ASP, the governing body of the sport. He had to convince them not only of the event, but of the whole concept. What they were pitching was essentially part tour contest, part surf trip. For starters, he needed to extend the usual seven-day waiting period to 12. 'We weren't coming all the way out there to leave a week later. The camp was booked in week blocks, so we'd book the whole camp for two weeks, with a day to bump in and a day to bump out.' The ASP agreed. It was the first time a 12-day window had been granted, and soon the 12-day window would become standard, giving contests a better chance of scoring waves. The contest was signed off and the date was set. The Quiksilver G-Land Pro would start on 31 May 1995.

Then there was the G-Land camp itself. A few days before Christmas and with the camp closed for the wet season, Rod and Bobby boated across to G-Land to walk it out. Bobby's Camp would host the surfers, the Chinaman's Camp down the beach toward Speedies would host the international media. While it was perfect for a surf trip, to run an international surf contest it needed a little extra hardware.

Rod did a deal with New Zealand Telecom to install a satellite dish on the beach. When it went live everyone present was amazed as it began to transmit an email from the edge of the jungle … even if the email took 10 minutes to go through. There was also the trifling matter of having to build a judging tower out on the reef, which required all Rod's resourcefulness. 'I'd done a building course before I moved to Torquay,' he recalls, 'so I knew enough to put a tower together. At least I thought I did.' Rod had two strokes of good fortune. Firstly, after realising his building course might have met its match in the two-storey reef tower, he called in his brother, Alan, who was a builder back at home who specialised in pole homes. The second stroke of luck was that the city of Surabaya had recently replaced all their hardwood telephone poles with steel ones, and Bobby, who'd had to rebuild large parts of the camp after the recent tsunami, had bought a shipping container full of them. Alan and Rod got to work and the tower slowly rose from the reef.

When the contest arrived, the first thing the surfers saw on the horizon as they boated across from Grajagan village was the tower … followed by the lines of swell running down the reef. The official opening ceremony in the village – as these things tend to do in Indonesia – had dragged on with a conga line of dignitaries, and the surfers were getting twitchy. By the time the boats finally pulled in behind the lineup they were howling like jungle apes. Several pulled boards out, left their gear in the boat, and jumped overboard and paddled into the lineup. The pro tour had waited a couple of decades for an event like this, and they weren't waiting another minute to go surfing.

Once the contest got started there was still work to do. While the remoteness of G-Land created a certain primal detachment, Bruce had promised Quiksilver he'd get the event out to the world through the media. They had one of the world's first digital cameras on site, which meant they could upload a digital photo every hour or so through the satellite transmitter. Footage was another matter. 'We had a clip cut every afternoon,' recalls Rod. 'That tape went by boat to Grajagan village, where a guy on a motorbike would take it by ferry to Bali airport where it was flown to Hong Kong [China] where Reuters uploaded it by satellite. That happened every day. We called it the Pony Express.'

For any contest director the biggest problem is always waves… but Rod had no problems on that front. *Tidak apa apa.* G-Land was a dream. 'I'd get up every morning, have a coffee, paddle out for a surf up at Kongs, come in and wait for the trades to kick in at 11am and then off we'd go. That year every heat was at Money Trees and even though we didn't get Speedies that year, it was like nothing the tour had ever seen.' The judges hadn't seen anything like it either, handing out 18 perfect tens.

For the surfers the lines blurred. It felt like a surf trip. There were no crowds; just them and a menagerie of jungle critters like monkeys, monitor lizards and the occasional late-night drunken tiger sighting. Guys would surf their brains out in perfect waves and celebrate their good fortune with beers each afternoon. Some would have a few more. Robbie Bain, celebrating a perfect 10, slept a night in the jungle with the mosquitos. But the rhythms of being on tour were still there. 'I said to Bobby, "We'll need to have boats ready to take them out of here. When they lose, they'll leave." Bobby looked at me confused and said, "No one leaves G-Land." I go, "I'm telling you, they will leave as soon as they lose. You need to have boats ready." Bobby couldn't believe that would ever happen. I remember Sunny Garcia came up and said, "I want a boat ready after my heat," and I said, "But you haven't lost yet." He goes, "I've got Tom Carroll in my heat." I organised the boat, but it turned out Sunny won, and Tom took Sunny's boat out of there that afternoon.'

Kelly Slater would win the contest and the effusive coverage of perfect surf with a palm tree backdrop made news all over the world. G-Land made waves. 'G-Land became something else altogether,' offers Rod. 'It fully changed the game.' Rod would spend the back end of the year in Indonesia preparing for the return to G-Land in 1996, where they'd get even better surf. And 1997? Even better again. Rod didn't know it at the time, but he'd just created himself a specialised role for the next two decades – part cultural attaché, part pro tour sapper, part surf contest director – as the tour moved to other exotic corners of the globe.

As the camp cleared out in the days following Kelly's win and the tower started coming down piece by piece, Rod relaxed. He surfed twice a day, tied up some loose ends, and on the final afternoon in camp he, Bruce and Martin Daly sat down on the beach where he and Bruce had hatched the idea a year earlier. 'Tony Wales came over from Kuta and bought a big cigar over for me,' recalls Rod. 'I didn't smoke but I lit the cigar anyway and had a beer. Fair to say we were pretty chuffed.'

2011

Steph Gilmore

It's a Tuesday morning out in the Indian Ocean, two degrees south of the equator. Steph Gilmore climbs a rope ladder and boards the *Mangalui*, an 84-foot timber sloop anchored off a palm-walled shore. She's bleeding from a deep set of scratches across her back, her right shoulder and right hip. She's just been dragged across the reef at Lance's Right on the wave of the morning. She's still jazzed, the adrenaline hasn't quite worn off yet and she theatrically re-enacts the wave for the crew on deck – the late drop, the bottom turn, the weightless pump inside the tube. She's playing it right up. She tries to look over her shoulder and inspect the damage to her back and spins in a circle like a cat chasing its tail.

Before paddling out she'd reminded herself not to do anything stupid. This was the first morning of a two-week trip in the remote Mentawai Islands. Lance's was solid. Double overhead, ice blue, equatorial Doldrum winds. Steph had been sitting deep on the peak, the only woman jostling amongst a pack of sun-drunk Indophiles. She'd surfed Lance's before but never this big. She was circumspect. She kept looking down at the limestone and coral reef below and reminding herself to play it cool. *Don't hit the reef*. Of course she soon found herself alone on the peak as the biggest wave of the morning rolled through. The wave drained the water off the reef below and Steph could see every detail as she hovered above it. At the last second she lost her nerve and shouted 'go' to the guy beside her. She paddled over the wave half relieved, half in regret and there it was … the next one, even bigger. She could feel all the eyes in the lineup on her. *Ahhh, fuck it*. She spun around and took off. It was a boss move. It was cinematic but ultimately doomed.

The wave put her up on the reef.

Steph stops clowning around when Darren Handley – her surfboard shaper of 10 years – daubs *Tieh Ta Yao Gin* on the bleeding tiger stripes running down her back. The black liquid electrocutes on contact and Steph springs to her feet in shock, voodoo dancing and speaking in tongues. Her right boob drops out of her top, and through the pain she apologises to the all-male audience for the show. Once the pain retreats a little she reasons her new scars will be 'a little story to tell'. She adds, 'You know, it was funny, before I went out this morning I remember saying how reef scars don't look so good on girls in bikinis'.

'There's something when I'm on trips with guys,' Steph later said of that wave, 'it's about impressing them and sitting out the back and waiting for a big one like you guys. I'm not trying to *challenge* you, I just want to do it as well. I want to show you that as a young, feminine girl, I can do that as well. That was the zone I was in. Well, I got a bomb and just ate it and ended up scraping my back off,' she laughs before adding, 'and yeah, part of my leg too.'

Also aboard the *Mangalui* is Simon Anderson, who'd been far too sensible that morning to end up on the reef. With Steph's back cleaned up and the pain levelling off, Steph and Simon discuss how the dynamic in the water changes when a girl like Steph – who before hitting the reef had outsurfed most of the guys in the water – paddles out. Simon ponders this for a second. 'I'm comfortable with you being better than me, Steph … just as long as I don't get beaten out there by a 50-year-old woman.'

The *Mangalui* was deep in the Mentawai Islands and Steph was lapping up time off the grid. Twenty-eleven had been a year that was dark and crazy in equal measure and it was nice to escape it for a little while. Up until that year Steph Gilmore had only known winning. She'd won the world title in her rookie season at just 19, and by now had won four, almost effortlessly. It had been almost *too* good. 'It had been all rainbows and no rain,' she'd reflect later. At just 22, you got a sense she was restless and the surfing tour was beginning to feel a little one-dimensional. After watching her surf a heat in Portugal in October the previous year I'd laid a lazy 10-buck bet with a friend that she'd walk away from the tour at the end of the year. Steph looked disenchanted, and there was a sense she was starting to outgrow the whole scene.

Back home after claiming that fourth title, the rain arrived the day after Boxing Day. Steph had driven home to her Coolangatta unit that night after visiting friends, parked under her building and walked toward the stairs. She sensed she wasn't alone. From the shadows a figure ran at her and struck her with what turned out to be a metal bar. She turned as he swung again, blocking the next strike with her left arm. She screamed and the guy took off on a pushbike. The attacker would turn out to be a homeless guy, a schizophrenic who'd never met Steph before. It was completely random. He didn't even know Steph was *Steph*. It was shitty luck sent from the wider cosmos. The attack broke her wrist but the real damage proved more psychological.

Six months later on the *Mangalui*, no one on board was sure exactly how Steph was coping. Nobody broached the subject of 'the night'. She offered the story after dinner one evening, unprompted. She recounted the details slowly, deliberately. She asked questions of the night, questions of the days after, questions to herself. It was clearly still lurking there and she was obviously still processing large parts of it. For someone of Steph's sunny disposition and good fortune, these were uncharted waters.

It was only June but Steph was already out of contention for the world title. She'd lost heats that would normally win themselves. 'In the past whenever I needed a six in a heat I *knew* a six would come. I *knew* it,' she said that night on the boat. 'This year, for the first time in my life, they haven't.' More than that, 'the night' triggered a wholesale loss of faith in other parts of her life as well.

As Steph worked through it in front of the crew over beers on deck, it was also clear that she was not going to let 'the night' define her. And beyond that, maybe it could precipitate change in her life that had been brewing long beforehand. Already the space it had created – the islands she was currently sailing through for instance – was a silver lining. It was the room to grow she'd been craving.

Much of her 2011 wasn't pretty, but in time she'd see it as 'the most important year of my life'. She'd later characterise the year after the attack in a magazine interview in Montauk, New York, by saying, 'I learned so much about myself, about the way I compete, about the world. It was a real defining moment and time in my life. I wanted to figure things out. For some reason I was able to do that early, even if I was emotional about it. When I look back to it, I surprise myself how quickly I was able to heal.' The initial insecurity was soon replaced with a sense of independence. She developed, as she put it, a 'fierceness' about her.

Steph wouldn't win the world title in 2011 but with that resignation came a certain unburdened freedom she'd never experienced. 'I think not being in the world title race is disappointing and I'm hanging onto that disappointment a little bit,' she offered on the boat, 'but to come here and kick off the rest of my year with that liberating feeling is cool. It's something I've never experienced since I've been on tour. To look on the bright side, it's a chance to stop and think about everything that's happened.'

The change in Steph was already stirring long before that night in Coolangatta. At 23, Steph was growing up. She was seeing a lot of the world and becoming more bohemian with every mile. Her travel schedule broke free from the surfing tour and Steph became a habitué of New York and Paris. She learned jazz licks on the guitar. She wore designer labels. She defined herself *away* from the tour. She moved easily through other worlds.

Back on the *Mangalui* Steph showed photos from her year. There were shots of Catalina Island in California and Christ The Redeemer in Rio. There were photos of her on the red carpet in a red dress standing next to Rafael Nadal in Abu Dhabi. Coolangatta would always be home, but the rest of the world was calling.

On 6 January 2011 – 10 days after the attack – Steph announced she was leaving longtime sponsor Rip Curl and joining rival Quiksilver. The deal, which had been in motion for months, would see her become the face of their new Quiksilver Women's label. The jump hadn't been easy but Steph was craving room to grow and Quiksilver offered her a more sophisticated role. She would be joining Lisa Andersen, who'd transcended *her* four world titles and settled comfortably into a position as a surfing 'icon', a label which drew in elements of surfing style, personal style and deeper character. Steph was already on her way to icon status. She certainly knew how to play to the moment. Late one night on the *Mangalui* she surfed Macaronis under a full moon, her midnight session only cut short when a full lunar eclipse cut the lights. She then picked up her guitar and sat on the bow and broke into a note-perfect rendition of Neil Young's *Harvest Moon*.

In the water, Steph's growth was most noticeable by a penchant for funkier surfboards and bewitching flow on a wave. Her surfing was evolving and having a year where her focus wasn't on the tour, when she was able to travel to find good surf, had hastened the process. Steph's tiger stripes were still bleeding as she headed over to the board rack and picked up a modern-outlined single-fin and paddled straight back out at Lance's. 'Steph brings a lot of femininity to the way a single-fin can be ridden,' said Simon, watching her session from the boat. 'It's interesting to watch her interpretation on a single-fin. It's interesting to watch her approach transform from the hardcore ripper on a high-performance thruster to something more classical.'

Steph, meanwhile, was becoming more self-aware of her own aesthetic on a wave, but to watch her surf nothing seemed more natural and uncontrived. The Gold Coast

points at home had already imprinted her surfing with an easy way about it, but in the years ahead, as she explored and refined it, she'd be regarded in some quarters as surfing's premier stylist, man or woman.

Steph mused aboard the *Mangalui*, 'I think for me, the best female surfer is someone who goes out in the lineup and is powerful and pulls into big barrels and gets scraped on the reef, but then turns around and is graceful and stylish and rides a beautiful board in beautiful waves the most feminine way possible. That's what I'm always trying to achieve. Sure, we're trying to be assertive but we're also trying to be feminine and beautiful and I think it's just a different style of surfing. I love it. The contrast is put together so perfectly. We've got the girls who are charging hard and the girls who are throwing their fins out and then there's the beautiful longboarders, and I suppose I can put myself in the middle, riding the single fin trying to get all groovy. I love that we can do both, and I think female surfers can get away with it more.'

Late in the trip Steph's luck finally turned. The crew on the *Mangalui* were racing hermit crabs on a tiny sand cay and Steph had found herself a sprinter. Watching on with a beer in hand, she saw the crab scuttle home with daylight second. Steph raised her beer, took a sip and toasted her first win of the year.

2012

Joel Parkinson

You felt that by now Joel Parkinson might've been well past caring.
He had everything else in life. He had a beautiful young family, a house on the Tweed
River and a fishing boat moored out back. He'd lived through a golden era for the surf
industry and had done well for himself, with a garage full of toys and even a slice of the
local football team. He could drive down to Snapper Rocks and take whatever wave he
wanted from the crowd behind the rock, and then later head upstairs for a beer at the
Rainbow Bay Surf Club, where he led the footy tipping comp. He often had to remind
himself of his own outrageous fortune. He got paid to go surfing, a fact that was never
lost on him.

But Joel's surfing was a gift; watching him surf was like watching a campfire slowly
burn. Purists and pros alike revered his languid grace on a wave, honed on Queensland's
pointbreaks but equally hypnotic on the walls of Jeffreys Bay or Sunset Beach. Joel
made surfing look easy and in many ways he made life look easy. He just flowed with
it. Monica Parkinson used to joke her husband was the 'no worries' guy. That was his
stock response to anything thrown at him. 'Just the classic laidback Queenslander,' is how
Rabbit Bartholomew described him. So, no, he certainly wasn't letting it consume him in
the way it once had, but in his quiet moments, between sets at Snapper or watching the
tip of his fishing rod in a meditative state, he also knew that if he didn't win a world title
at some point soon, he would be, as he put it, 'going to be really hard to live with when I
get older'.

World titles had always been the metric of surfing success in Coolangatta, and by this
point Joel had finished runner-up to the world title four times. The most heartbreaking

of those losses had been three years earlier, when he'd led the tour by a mile, only to injure his ankle and be run down by childhood friend Mick Fanning in the last event of the season, the Pipe Masters. The loss ate away at Joel and was compounded the following year by a gruesome foot injury and the death of good friend, Andy Irons. Joel spent time at home and thought way too much about everything, the world title included. At 30, that window wasn't going to stay open forever.

In the end he applied some circular, Gold Coast logic to his predicament. He reasoned the only way he'd ever win a world title was to stop thinking about it, and the only way he could stop thinking about it was to just go surfing. That's what he did in 2012. Joel Parkinson went surfing. He surfed new waves. He surfed bigger waves. He threw himself into the dark art. He surfed pure and true and let the tour worry about itself.

And it worked. He started the season building, making the quarters at Snapper, semis at Bells, and a surprise final in Brazil. He was flying high, figuratively. His only problem was that at Santiago airport, en route home from Brazil, he'd made the fateful decision to choose the chicken empanadas at the buffet and what followed he described as the 'worst 24 hours of my life'. He was violently ill on the plane and spent most of the flight slumped in the toilet, the empanada evacuating itself in whatever way it could. He lost six kilos on the flight and landed in Brisbane realising he still had to catch the express train back to the Gold Coast. A wan shadow, he boarded the train. Ten minutes later, his stomach let out an ominous gurgle, he looked around and realised the train had no toilet.

With a break in the tour (and time to recover) it was then onto Indonesia in May. Joel was on a photo trip for Billabong aboard the *Indies Trader IV*, the biggest, most opulent surf charter boat in the islands. It had three levels, its own jet skis, a bottomless beer cooler and a helipad on the roof. The only thing the trip didn't have was waves. Joel was fine with this. Couple of surfs. Couple of beers. Keep nice and hydrated.

Joel and Taj Burrow had to leave the trip early to make the Fiji contest, and the only way they could get to the airport in time to make their connection was by helicopter … the same helicopter that had been sitting on the boat's helipad for three days, broken down. Joel had a phobia of helicopters – an acute phobia for Indonesian helicopters – and when he saw the little red bird his worried reaction was, 'Is that it?' The chopper was Vietnam War surplus. The pilot looked like he was also Vietnam War surplus.

The day came for them to leave and Joel was already white and clammy. The Indonesian crew began jamming boardbags into the tiny chopper, loading it to the gills, and Joel and Taj said their goodbyes and climbed in. The little red chopper huffed and wheezed as it inched free of the boat. It was clear immediately the helicopter was struggling. The Indonesian pilot hit the gas and began to panic. 'Too heavy! Too heavy!' The chopper rolled off the boat and dropped toward the ocean. Everyone on the boat looked on in horror and ducked for cover. The chopper sat inches above the ocean as the engines screamed and after 30 awful seconds finally gained some altitude, spun around, and took off in the general direction of Padang. The last vision of Joel those on the ship saw was a ghostly face pressed against the glass, silently screaming.

The Fijian event, the next stop on tour, had never felt like a tour event for Joel. It felt more like a holiday. The following year he'd actually miss his heat when he went deepsea fishing and didn't make it back in time. In 2012, though, the contest took a back seat to a huge swell that had stormed up from the Tasman.

The swell built during the day on 8 June. Joel sat on Namotu Island eating a fish and chip lunch when he looked across and saw a wave almost close out the channel between Namotu and the reef at Wilkes, which he knew was a hundred foot deep. 'It was monstrous. We were looking across at Wilkes and there were 12, 15-foot perfect right barrels with not a soul out. No one else was interested, so I went, "Fuck it, I'm over there." I just grabbed Tom, the Fijian boatman, threw my 6'10" in the boat and drove over there. I got one big one straight away and rode it pretty far and flicked out in the channel. I was lucky. The one behind me must have been 15 feet, maybe bigger, and if I hadn't caught the first one it would have just destroyed me. I climbed straight back in the boat with Tom and he got on the radio to Scotty out in the channel at Cloudbreak asking, "What's going on out there?" He said the contest had been called off, but I needed to get out there with his biggest board. He said, "You need to see this."'

At 12.57pm, while Joel had been out surfing Wilkes, the first real set of the swell had hit Cloudbreak. It lurched up out of the South Pacific and steamrolled down the reef. There were no takers. The guys were either stunned by the majesty of it, or paddling for their lives. With the contest called off, a bunch of guys on 10-foot boards paddled out to challenge it. Joel didn't have a 10-foot board but, 'I had to go out. This was a once in a lifetime chance.'

He paddled out on the same 6'10" he'd surfed Wilkes on, and ducked and weaved between the sets. By late afternoon it was getting *big*. 'I took off on a wave and I just couldn't set a rail in the water. I tried a bottom turn and my board just wouldn't hold a rail. Being so small it just wouldn't turn, and at the last minute I tried with all my might to pull it up into the barrel but I fell flat on my face. The lip landed on my legs and just blasted the leg rope off. The board was gone.' He was lucky. There was no next wave. 'I was still swimming though when the next set came, a big one, and I had to hustle and dive through it before it broke. I wasn't in harm's way, but it was starting to feather above me when I dived. That was when I realised how big it really was. It was only a swell, but there was so much water in the wave that it went from chest-deep to 30-foot deep in an instant. My ears started killing, and I had to do 10 big strokes to make it back to the surface. There was another one behind it and I tried to dive a little shallower this time. It just picked me up and you had that horrible weightless feeling. I think that was the moment I realised how much force was in that swell, what we were dealing with, and it wasn't even a broken wave. They were the biggest, most perfect barrelling lefts I'd ever seen; maybe the best waves I've ever seen in my life.' A week later, Joel's missing 6'10" was found by a fisherman, floating between the fringing reef and the mainland, somehow still in one piece.

The Tahiti contest in August saw the South Pacific becalmed. Teahupo'o, the most dangerous wave on tour, was flat for 10 straight days and the contest put on hold. Nothing to do but fish, swim, savour a *poisson cru* lunch on the veranda of his French colonial homestay, before pulling up a chair with a beer and watching the sun drop into the Pacific. The most dangerous moment of the event was Joel stepping on a stonefish while walking a tinnie in the shallows, the thong on his right foot saving him.

The contest finished on the last day of the waiting period when Joel drew – of course – Mick Fanning in the final. The pair had paddled out that morning at first light and surfed perfect Teahupo'o on their own. As the sunlight poured out of the valley behind the village, they couldn't believe their luck. That day perfectly framed the awkward dynamic that shadowed their careers, where they'd surf together either as best mates or fiercest rivals.

In the Tahiti final, the symbolism of 2009 was strong. Joel led the final all the way only to gift Mick the winning wave in the dying seconds. Joel washed off the loss. This year wasn't about wins and losses. A dozen Hinanos later and Joel and Mick were wrestling drunk in Joel's front yard, unable to breathe through laughter.

What happened next might have been the pivotal moment of his year … and it didn't even involve surfing. Joel's long-time trainer was ironman Wes Berg, and the pair hatched a plan early in 2012 to compete together in the Molokai to Oahu paddleboard race. 'Molokai' has real significance to the Hawaiian crew, and Joel figured it might have significance for his year as well … he just wasn't sure how. He and Wes trained for months beforehand, paddling long downwind runs a mile out to sea from Kingscliff to Snapper. By July, Joel had never been fitter. On the day, the 42km channel crossing between the two Hawaiian islands was kind to them – downwind, a long sea – and to their surprise they finished third. Six hours and 18 minutes. Committing to the race would be a masterstroke, if for no other reason than whatever else he did that year would seem like a walk in the park.

Joel now had a month at home, and his days included little else but dropping the kids to school, surfing, fishing, then making it back in time for school pick up at 3.30. The Parkinson family had been on the road since eldest daughter Evie was six months old, and by 2012 they were in a comfortable groove. Dad did the first half of the year on his own; the family tagged along for the back half. The Parkinsons spent three months on the road and they were good at it. Evie was eight by this stage, Macy was six and Mahli two, and they had the travel down to a fine art apart from Joel himself, who'd lost so many passports he was on his last strike with the Department of Foreign Affairs. Monica Parkinson ran a tight ship, and when they got to where they were going she could kick back with the kids and take in the cultural smorgasbord while Joel went surfing. It meant that for the back end of the year, for Joel, home was on the road.

Having his family with him kept things steady for Joel, and his results reflected that. He made another final in Trestles, California. He made the semis in France and made the semis again in Portugal. The highlight of his trip however came during the Portuguese event on a day the contest was called off due to a huge North Atlantic swell. Joel jumped in the car and drove an hour north to the town of Nazaré, Europe's new big wave Mecca. Within an hour of being there he was being towed behind a ski, underneath the centuries-old Nazaré *forteleza*, into waves five times overhead. Joel described it as, 'giant, mongo-sized South Straddie'. Later that afternoon he was sitting down to a late lunch of *polvo á lagareiro* and drinking *vino tinto* at Restaurant Celeste in the old town.

Joel, by this stage, was leading the ratings and the title was becoming hard to ignore. It was October. The other development was that Kelly Slater had won two events in a row and was now breathing down his neck. Kelly, already with 11 world titles, loomed large.

At Santa Cruz, California, during the penultimate event of the season, Joel tempted fate. He was in the water at Steamer Lane and had just won his heat. Kelly was paddling out for the next. Joel caught a wave and saw Kelly down the line. Kelly saw Joel. Kelly, in a gesture to defuse any tension between them, held a hand up as Joel surfed past, waiting for Joel to high five him. Joel instead jammed hard on the tail of his board and spritzed Kelly in the face, laughing. Joel would pay for it.

The Turtle Bay Hotel on the North Shore of Oahu. Gated, manicured, and full of rich mainland folk with golf clubs and swizzle sticks. They'd just announced a 1300-room expansion, which hadn't gone down real well with the locals out that way. The handpainted sign down the road said 'Nuff hotels already.' The hotel was teeming. Just try getting a table at Lei Leis… or even a car park. The Pipeline Masters press conference was being held at Turtle Bay, and Joel was running late. He circled the lot in his silver SUV for 15 minutes looking for a park. He finally spotted one and gunned for it. He swung the wheel, only to be cut off by some bald guy in an even bigger SUV. Joel swore.

Kelly Slater got out of the SUV. Joel swore again. Joel was adamant Kelly, if not the universe, was screwing with him. A few days earlier at a charity golf day in memory of Andy Irons – the world's worst golfer – a longest drive contest was held where everyone had to match Kelly's opening 328-yard three wood. No one, not even seasoned golfers got close until Joel – the world's *second-worst* golfer – stepped up. He struck the ball crisply and it shot like a dimpled white comet down the fairway… exactly 327-and-a half yards. Joel swore again and hoped this wasn't symbolic of what was about to happen at Pipeline.

The Parkinson's Hawaiian rental looked directly over Pipe. It was the same house he'd stayed in when he lost the title to Mick three years earlier and the wall around the side still had holes from where Joel punched it that afternoon. The vibe this time around was a little more upbeat. Joel's house boomed Marley's *Three Little Birds*, his theme song for the Hawaiian winter. He danced around the house like a white guy dances to reggae, his easy style stopping at the tide line. The whole place felt *irie* and righteous. Joel had convinced himself this was his time and that every little thing was going to be all right.

Compared to the guy who'd lost the title three years before, Joel was more assured and more in control of his own destiny. He'd learned hard lessons from 2009, where he was racked with self-doubt. 'There are no two ways about it; it fully consumes you', he said at the time. 'To a point this one has, but only as much as I've let it. In 2009 I was second guessing everything I did. Walking down the beach for a heat and just putting one foot in front of the other didn't feel right. I'd question whether I was even walking the right way.'

Taj Burrow says Joel's monastic calm both reassured and made him nervous. 'There must be all sorts of crazy noise in there. There has to be, because nobody can be *that* relaxed.' Joel seemingly had buried all the doubt, all the ghosts, all the bad juju. He'd buried 2009 and he'd buried the spectre of Kelly. The fear for his fans, friends and family was that at some time during the event they'd all crawl out of the ground to ruin the fairy tale. Joel, meanwhile, seemed oblivious to it all, pushing little Mahli Parkinson around on his skateboard, cracking jokes, shadow boxing and whistling Jahwaiian reggae.

The morning of the Pipeline final and there was a rooster in the yard, a dandy golden bird with a green sheen, ghosting beneath the coconut palms in the hour before the dawn. He'd strut in every morning in the darkness from the farm across the road,

grubbing the lawn of the three-million-dollar beach house. Joel was standing in the dark, alone, holding a cup of macadamia coffee while looking out over Pipeline. He could hear the new swell but couldn't see it. He'd been up since four and was wrapped in a hoodie, squinting into the dark to make out the plumes and white lines of breaking swell. He sees the rooster. The rooster sees him. The bird's head twitches nervously while his eyes stay locked on Joel. Slowly, deliberately, Parko puts the coffee cup down. He looks back out to sea. Then in a heartbeat he pirouettes, drops the clutch, and races off after the rooster, who's squawking in panic as it flees into the shadows.

Finals day was a Friday, and Uncle Bryan Surratt woke up at 4am. Nothing special here, that's every other day of the year for him. Uncle Bryan has been collecting sunrise shells on the beaches of the North Shore for years in the pre-dawn dark, and he walked into Joel's backyard at 6am wearing his lucky sunrise shell necklace. The shells are incredibly rare, but the day before Joel had found one while playing on the beach with Mahli, a tiny one, big as a thumbnail, and he took it as a sign from above. Uncle Bryan also brought around a tray of eggs from his backyard chickens for Joel to 'put some lead in his pencil'. They cooked them up together and talked surf. As the light cascaded over the escarpment there was not a soul in the water. The building west swell was butting heads with a whipping north-east tradewind. It was pissing down and ugly. 'Ah, bullshit weather!' barked Uncle Bryan. It was an ugly duckling morning destined, however, to later become something more majestic.

And so began one of the most intense, emotional and breathtaking days pro surfing had seen. Pipe came to the party. The sun was shining, Backdoor was rifling and the beach was full, the Hawaiian crowd split between Joel and Kelly. With less than a heat between them on the ratings, neither Joel nor Kelly could afford to lose. The title rode on every heat, and a loss for either of them would lose the title as well. It was heavy. For both camps it was excruciating, but for Joel's especially. Kelly had won 11. Joel had lost four. Everyone close to Joel was on edge. Monica Parkinson paced the yard, somewhere between despair, joy and catatonia. Most of Joel's crew couldn't even bear to watch. Joel walked around like nothing was happening. He refused to be knocked from his cloud.

Both Joel's quarter and semi were nail-biters, the latter even more so. To get to the final, Joel had to beat the Hobgood twins in successive heats, CJ in the quarters and Damien in the semis. Joel is close to both of them, but the Hobgoods are just as close with Kelly, a fellow Floridian. Against Damien, Joel looked sunk. Damien picked off a rare left on a day of rights, which sucked the oxygen from the room up in Joel's house. With five minutes to go Joel looked cooked. 'Andy would tell himself, "I'm not losing this heat. There is simply no way I'm losing this heat," and that's what I was telling myself in that heat with Damo,' recalled Joel. 'In the past I'd lose dogfights like that, but I just told myself there was no way I was coming this far and losing this fucking thing.' Two waves in two minutes and Joel was in the final.

Kelly now faced Josh Kerr in the other semi. Kerr had been bounced badly on the reef that morning and had just returned from hospital where he'd had X-rays on a suspected broken neck. Yet here he was. Having grown up in Coolangatta, Kerr felt a sense of duty. If he could somehow beat Kelly the title would be heading back to Coolangatta with Joel. When Josh Kerr stood tall in a Backdoor drainer and was spat into the channel, hopes in the Parko camp were cautiously raised. And then a strange thing happened. *Nothing*. Not a wave. It was a becalming, *Ancient Mariner* style and on a day as dramatic as this it actually supplied its most tense minutes. Kelly and Kerrsy sat and waited. And waited.

Kelly couldn't conjure anything and the clock ticked down.

Earlier that morning Monica Parkinson had lit a candle in their bedroom and said a quick prayer to Andy Irons to look after his old friend. That candle burned all day as Joel won his heats, but with two minutes to go in Kelly's semi, as a world title loomed and Joel paced the room, the candle went out. Joel freaked. He kept repeating, 'Are you fucking kidding me?' over and over. Kelly only needed an eight, and then it would be Joel against Kelly in the Pipe final, winner take all. Joel started delaminating. Kelly always finds a wave. The ocean always delivers for him. Joel had managed to stay calm all year but was threatening to come apart at the vital moment. Joel suddenly felt the ghosts of titles past filling the room. Just then Bruce Irons walked in. Bruce – Andy's younger brother – apologised for not coming around earlier. 'I didn't want to ruin your vibe.' The pair embraced on Joel's balcony, Bruce lifted him off the ground, and reassured him, 'It's all good brah, I did a deal with the devil to get you this!'

With 30 seconds left and no lines on the reef outside, a building chorus of hoots from a backyard full of friends drifted up to the balcony above, a paean on the Hawaiian trades. The countdown started and for Joel it was the sweetest sound. Standing on the royal balcony was the new world champion. Monica hugged him in tears. This was it. The place erupted. Grown men cried. Joel cried. Champagne rained.

The following morning, long after Joel had gone on to win the Pipe Masters, and shortly after the last people had left the party, the world title trophy sat on the floor outside Joel's room. Over it was a shirt a friend had printed up for him, which simply said, 'I finally fucking won'.

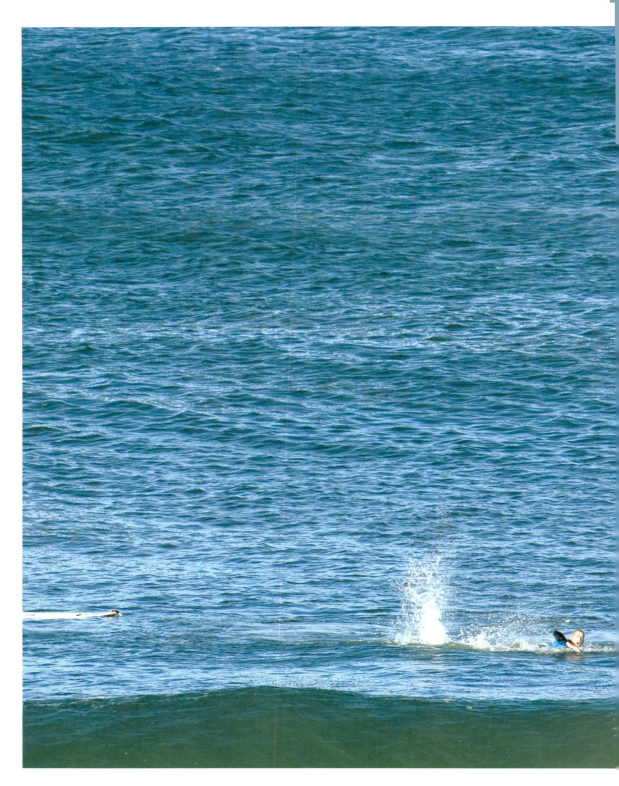

2015

Mick Fanning

In Steven Hall's novel *The Raw Shark Texts*, **the book's central** character is stalked by a 'Ludovician', a giant conceptual shark that swims through his psyche, attacking without warning, devouring great chunks of his memory, leaving him to piece his past life back together while he waits for the beast to strike again.

For most of 2015 Mick Fanning had sharks – both conceptual and very real – swimming through his life. Ever since that fateful encounter with a great white at Jeffreys Bay, Mick's own conceptual shark stalked his quiet moments, swam menacingly through his sleep, followed him into the ocean. The malevolent dream fish then, if you'd believe it, broke free and began taking chunks out of his life – his marriage, his brother, a world title – a lifetime's worth of trouble and tragedy all crammed into a single year, a year that for Mick Fanning took on a feeling of black satire, a year spent walking a gossamer tightrope between his own earthly mortality and a place as one of surfing's immortals.

The most fateful year of Mick Fanning's life began quietly enough. He woke up on the morning of 1 January in Utah, in the snow, with a raging hangover. The -15°C air temp took the edge off it. His snowboarding trip with friends had become an annual decompression. For the past three seasons Mick had gone into the final event of the season – the Pipe Masters – with a shot at the world title, and by the time it was decided one way or the other he was cooked. He found a New Year's snow trip either to the States or Japan allowed him to breathe and reset for the following season, out of the public eye.

By 2015, the three-time world champ was already in a place beyond world titles. They didn't consume his waking hours like they used to, and he'd already shifted his focus away from a one-dimensional pro tour life. Back from Utah he flew south to Tasmania and surfed Shipstern Bluff for the first time. He then scored a week-long cyclone swell at Kirra out front of his house. When the season started with his home event on the Gold Coast, he never really fizzed, losing out to Brazilian, Adriano de Souza. The pair would see plenty of each other in 2015. They would meet again at the next event, at Bells, in the final where the judges couldn't split them. The scores were tied. On a countback it went to Mick. His fourth Bells win forced him, almost reluctantly, to think about world titles again.

De Souza won the following event in Margaret River, and then the next time the pair met was in Fiji ... although the meeting wasn't in the water but at the bar. Mick, approaching career twilight, increasingly relished his role as the social director on tour and with flat days forecast was in the bar handing out Skulldrags – the island's signature cocktail, made with enough shots to euthanise a horse. Adriano, who rarely drank, tried to sneak away in the shadows. *Too late.* '*Souzyyyyy! Get back here!*' Mick spotted him, whistled him back and forced him to skol a Skulldrag. Nobody said no to Mick. Adriano didn't come out of his room for two days and didn't win a heat for two months. Neither did Mick. World titles again seemed a long way away.

Mick took a lot on out of the water as well. His business interests were moving into all sorts of areas. He was branching out from his surf industry sponsorships and investing in his own businesses. He started selling phone chargers. He was working with a group of friends on starting their own brewery (Mick's alter ego, Eugene, the notorious party boy of the early millennium, could barely control his excitement). Mick kept himself busy and was keeping himself busy for a reason.

Privately, Mick was also going through a separation from his wife, Karissa. After seven years the pair had gone their own ways, Karissa living in New York. They were ultimately two very single-minded and driven people, just driving in different directions. Mick was coming home from the tour to an empty house, the palatial whitewashed beachside house they designed and built together. The house was empty with the exception of his dog Harper. It was a quiet and contemplative time for Mick. The peace and privacy wasn't destined to last long.

It still seems impossible to believe. *A great white shark attacked Mick Fanning on live TV in the middle of a tour final.* Just say it again and consider how unlikely that sounds.

The black gravitas of that moment at Jeffreys Bay even shocked commentator Joe Turpel into silence – a sure sign some *really* bad shit was going down – and for a terrible instant as Mick wrestled the shark before disappearing underwater it seemed we were watching something we could never unwatch. Fortunately, we know how it ended. Mick avoided the pointy end of the fish, reset on the ski, did a quick roll call of his limbs, and emerged physically if not psychologically intact.

Whether Mick Fanning was lucky or unlucky at Jeffreys Bay, South Africa, on 19 July 2015 depends on your existential view of the world. Unlucky? Sure he was, in that of all surfers in all the oceans that shark went *him*. We'll never know why. The brain of the white shark is an ancient mystery; two-feet long, shaped like a slingshot and hardwired in ways we'll never understand. As Mick's shark took its leisurely Sunday swim up the coast, the big palooka could've nudged anyone. Instead this shark had a sense of theatre. It swam into J-Bay, waited for the final to start and the cameras to roll, and lined up the champ. The apex predator of the ocean meets the apex predator of the pro tour.

Lucky? Well, Mick was still here, and he knew better than anyone there was no luckier soul on God's green earth. To be served up as hot lunch to a one-ton fish yet escape without a scratch, well, you can draw no other conclusion than some form of divine intervention, some higher reason why the universe saved Mick Fanning's skinny white arse. That night in J-Bay they held a wake for the living. Julian Wilson, who'd been in the water with Mick when the shark had hit and actually swum *toward* Mick to try to save him, was still pale and shaky. Mick, for his part, held it together. While there was an emotional precipice yet to come, for now, with the adrenaline still coursing through him there were plenty of tears and beers and laughing at his dumb luck. In the group that night was Adriano de Souza, who'd been in the departures lounge at Port Elizabeth airport, about to fly home to Brazil, when he'd watched the shark attack live on his phone. He promptly got up, walked out of the terminal and drove back to Jeffreys Bay.

Something told him he needed to be there with Mick.

The footage of Mick and the shark – surfing's own Zapruder film – perversely became the most watched surfing moment of all time. It was the perfect intersection of food chain and major sporting event, the kind that happens so infrequently in this morbidly curious world. The parallels give some perspective. Can you for a minute contemplate Tiger Woods being mauled by an alligator on the 18th green at Augusta? The whole notion of being attacked by a wild animal during the final of a major sporting event captivated a ghoulish public, and signalled, for the foreseeable future, the end of anything resembling a private life for Mick Fanning. He was now the shark attack guy.

The world around him went mad.

At home, Australia was already in the grip of shark hysteria after a spike of attacks clustered around Margaret River in the west and Ballina – Mick's old hometown – in the east. To give you an idea of the level of public paranoia and the media's enthusiasm to stoke it, a Japanese surfer had earlier in the year been attacked and killed by a great white at Ballina, with the attack captured by an unmanned surfcam mounted on a nearby surf club. The surf forecast site that owned the camera spent the following day politely (and not so politely) declining offers from major media outlets to sell them the footage.

The real sharks it turns out had two legs, and Mick flew home to a feeding frenzy. 'To be totally honest, the actual events that went down in J-Bay and dealing with it and getting home wasn't the worst,' says Mick, 'it was waking up and there were four news vans out the front. There were paparazzi following me everywhere I went, and it just didn't stop.' In the days after he got home Mick hired private security to sit outside his front door. 'It was intense. I didn't leave my house for a week.'

Mick did, however, sneak out one afternoon. Just two weeks before Mick had been hit in South Africa, a bodyboarder named Matt Lee had been attacked by a great white down at Ballina, suffering severe injuries to his legs. Mick snuck out the back door and slipped the film crews to visit Matt in hospital on the Gold Coast. 'There wasn't much I could say but I just wanted to see how he was going. After being so lucky I kind of felt I had to.'

In the months after the attack, Mick went to ground. He knocked back Jimmy Fallon, he knocked back book offers, he stopped answering his phone. 'I was getting asked, "Do you want to do all this media?" and I was like, "No. Why?"' Mick – rightly – felt that running a shark hero line would be mocking the gods of fate who'd saved him. He did however take up the offer of a *60 Minutes* exclusive, and quietly gave his $75,000 appearance fee to Matt Lee. Mick also snuck off and got back in the water. Of all places he chose Ballina, figuring if he was going to confront it, he might as well really confront it. The shark, however, continued to swim through his thoughts. 'Every time I go surfing I think about it. If I'm out the back by myself or I'm in a place where I feel it could happen again I'm very aware of it. I jump at splashes and I jump at shadows. I don't think it's one of those things that will ever leave me.'

Karissa flew home from New York to be with Mick in the days after the attack. A brief reconciliation failed; the pair remained amicable. Once the media vans cleared from out front, chasing some other tragedy in some other postcode, the house was suddenly empty again, just Mick and Harper. It wasn't a good time to be alone, so Mick promptly moved a few recently divorced mates into the place and turned a seven-figure bachelor pad into a group therapy home.

Mick dealt with the shark attack by dealing with everyone else's problems. After the attack, most everybody close to Mick could tell you a story about how he'd gone out of his way to spend time with them, to surf or drink beer, riff about life, Mick's own problems barely rating a mention. It became a coping mechanism for him, reprising the role he'd taken on 17 years earlier when his older brother Sean was killed in a car accident. 'It was also healing for me,' said Mick. 'What I've been through recently, I've had so many people pick me up, so if someone needs help I'll be straight there. It's something back from when Sean passed away I reckon. Back then *everyone* was fucked – I'm talking my mum, my dad, my brothers, my sister and all our friends – and I just felt like I actually blocked out my own feelings at the time because I thought, look, you need to help these people before you help yourself. Fuck, looking back it was really hard and it took me years to come to terms with it, but as I said I wouldn't have talked about those things with anyone back then, not even my mates.'

Mick's best coping mechanism, however, was winning. Mick needed to keep moving forward to get through this, and the best way forward for Mick Fanning was surfing heats. It's what he did.

From the minute he survived the shark attack in July, the notion crystallised perfectly that Mick Fanning would win the world title in the same year. Nothing made more sense. As a stunned world replayed the clip over and over, tens of millions of views, it was already being written in the stars. From the primal jaws of a big, dumb fish to his face reflected in a silver world title trophy, the Karmic dots were being joined. Pro surfing follows narrative, and there was no bigger story that season than Mick Fanning. He was destined to join a reasonably exclusive club of surfers who'd been hit by a great white in a tour final then gone on to win the world title that same year.

If he wasn't the world title favourite heading into the Pipeline Masters, the final event of the season, he certainly was after winning the Sunset contest the week before. The day after Sunset he walked into our North Shore rental and did something I'd never seen him do in 20 years. He went straight for the refrigerator, pulled out a two-litre party bottle of Coca-Cola, unscrewed the lid, and chugged half of it down. He put the bottle back on the shelf, closed the fridge and sat down, staring wordlessly out at Pipeline. I'd seen him drink his bodyweight in beer before, but never the Black Death. It struck me as unusual, but then again it had been a year for Mick Fanning that 'unusual' didn't even come close to covering. I asked him how he was feeling, a

question that considering what he'd been through he could have answered on several levels. His response was laboured. 'Tired.'

The following day Mick was walking down the beach at Pipeline when he saw the look on Taj Burrow's face in a nearby yard. He knew immediately something was wrong. Taj had just seen a surfer – Evan Geiselman, as it turned out – pull into a wave at Pipeline and not resurface after one, two … three waves. Mick sprinted down the beach, arriving just as the lifeguards were dragging the lifeless Floridian to shore. Mick joined in to help get him up the beach. Later that afternoon Mick recalled of the scene, 'Mate, he was gone. Blue as fuck. *Gone*. Then the lifeguards got a breath into him and the saltwater just gushed out.' Two days later Mick was checking on his housemate, Owen Wright, who'd had a bad thrashing out at Pipe that morning and had gone to lie down, feeling lightheaded. Five minutes later Owen was being wheeled into an ambulance in the driveway with what would eventually be diagnosed as a severe brain bleed.

Mick Fanning – Ol' White Lightning – had become a lightning rod for matters of life and death that year. The worst was yet to come.

The knock on his bedroom door came at 5am. It was the morning Mick was due to surf for the world title at Pipeline, and as he kicked off the sheets he knew whoever was getting him out of bed at that hour wasn't bearing good news. It was Mick's mum, Liz, in tears. There was a brief pause while she composed herself and told Mick that his eldest brother, Pete, had died in his sleep back home overnight. To find out your brother had died on this morning of all mornings, with the world title on the line and Pipe falling from the sky? Mick had been here before with the loss of Sean but it'd taken years to turn that tragedy around. This time he had just minutes.

At 9.20am he paddled out against Jamie O'Brien and won. After lunch he beat both Kelly Slater and John John Florence. Mick emerged from his winning wave, palms supine, fingers soft, head to the heavens and eyes closed. The still frame echoed a Renaissance fresco. This day at Pipeline was a microcosm of Mick Fanning's life – seismic adversity in the morning; something grand by lunchtime. Mick was surfing for a world title in the hours after his brother's death, potentially his greatest and his lowest moments playing out together. It was macabre, yet compelling theatre. The emotional quotient shot like hot mercury. The world watched on. A military plane flew overhead carrying President Obama.

A window into the grief the Fanning family was experiencing came soon after, when Liz walked up the beach through the crowd. Supported by friends on each side, here was a woman who had already lived through it all – raised a family as a single mum, lost one son, raised a champion and stood by him through the wildest year of his life – and who was now mourning a second son and hanging on by a thread. In a flowing dress, the sand giving way beneath her feet, the matriarch of the clan kept her dignity as she fought back the tears. She walked off the beach and into our backyard, sat down in the dining room, and let it go. Sobbing, she repeated, 'I just don't know how much more of this I can take.' She left an hour later, a whole box of tissues strewn across the floor.

The following morning Mick surfed a quarter final against Kelly Slater. To win the world title he had to keep winning and stay ahead of the one other surfer in range of him. Adriano de Souza. 'The world title gave me a focal point, but yeah, I was running on emotion. I said when I came off the beach after that quarter against Kelly that I was done. The world title, nothing mattered after that. I could've packed up my boards and walked away right there. I already felt like I'd won.' Mick walked back up to a group of 50 of his oldest friends from home in Coolangatta, who'd all bought tickets and flown overnight to be there with him.

When Mick eventually lost to Gabe Medina in the semis, he ran up the beach through the crowd, grey and drained. He pushed to the very back of the tent his crew were gathered under, knelt down and buried his head into a towel, roaring like a wounded bear. He sobbed loudly as every wall he'd built around his brother's death over the past two days came crumbling down. No one spoke. His mates formed a circle around him as a sea of cameras and phones stared in. He composed himself and walked off the beach as Adriano de Souza surfed to the title. 'I guess it was a blessing in disguise,' says Mick later of missing out. 'I would have just come home and the media would have started all over again. But I really didn't give two thoughts about the world title. My tank was empty and I didn't even have the energy.'

That night, with the house full and the floor shaking, a dozen of Mick's crew grabbed two bottles of tequila and retreated to his room. Sitting in a circle, each person took a swig before taking the floor and saluting their old mate with a few words. Blitzed, few of the tributes made much sense, but the sentiments were clear. These were people who'd known Mick 10, 20, 30 years, friends who'd seen him do some extraordinary things along the way, but nothing as extraordinary or courageous as what they'd just witnessed here over the past two days at Pipeline.

Mick flew home the next morning with a volcanic hangover, buried his brother, then took off to Vegas and Japan and didn't return for a month.

2016

Ross Clarke-Jones

If you've ever spent time in the company of Ross Clarke-Jones, you'll understand how a day can feel like its own year. Ross lives life. Sleep is not his friend. Danger is his business. There are never enough hours in the day for Bacchanalian revelry and/or near-death experiences. For the purposes of this entry Ross chose to catalogue not just one year, but *two*. Ross chose the bookends of 25 Feb 2016 and 25 February 2018, the two-year slice of time starting with Ross falling off a saltwater cliff at Waimea Bay, and ending with him clambering up a limestone cliff at Nazaré in 40-foot surf.

'The Eddie' contest is a big deal in Hawaii. It only runs on days when waves are washing into backyards along Oahu's North Shore. It runs on the biggest days at Waimea and has only run nine times in three decades. In honour of Hawaiian great Eddie Aikau, it's a big deal to be invited and an even bigger deal to win. Ross has grown to understand that in time. He surfed the inaugural Eddie event at Waimea in 1987, fresh off a Vegas red-eye and a weekend bender. The Eddie consumed him for years, and after going close a couple of times he finally won it in 2001.

Few gave Ross a chance when the Eddie was called in 2016. The fact that he was almost 50 years old didn't matter. Ross is ageless. However, a whole new movement dedicated to paddling big waves had sprung up while Ross remained more of a tow-surf guy. Ross wanted to make a point that he could still paddle big waves and was in Hawaii ready to go on 11 February, only for the forecast swell not to show on the day. 'I'd been there for three months and it was the most ready I'd ever been and it got called off,' he remembers. 'So I went home to Australia and copped the worst flu. Fully knocked me out. I'd only been home a week and was sick as a dog when they called and said there was another swell, a bigger one, and I probably should come back. I arrived back straight into it, but I think that worked for me. I was so drained, I had no choice but to stay calm.'

What Ross flew back for was the biggest Eddie swell ever seen. 'Waimea was massive and everyone's freaking out,' he recalls of that morning. 'There's closeout sets and everyone's going, "We're not even going to be able to paddle out!" It was the biggest I'd ever surfed Waimea. It was on par with the day when Donnie Sullivan died, maybe. It was huge. Sure enough, I had the first heat. Over 30 years of Eddies I've always been the guinea pig in the first heat of the day. I was fortunate, though, not to have many closeouts in my heat and I got a couple of good ones. I dropped in on Jamie Mitchell a couple of times. I always try to get the first wave of the event,' Ross says and laughs, 'so I've gone and here's Jamie on my inside. I just smoked him. He was in earlier and deeper but my section was steep. It was the steepest drop I've ever had in my life. We both got hammered at the bottom … and then I dropped in on him again! I remember Jamie blowing up. I said, "This is why I'm here … I can drop in!" Jamie was cool … eventually.'

At the end of a dramatic day, Ross finished second to Hawaiian star John John Florence. 'I was very content,' he remembers. 'That was the best Eddie of all and I got second, 15 years after I'd won. Yeah, you know what? I was happy with the second. In saying that, in the week afterwards it was playing constantly on my mind, all the locals telling me, "Man, you should have won."' Ross may be still simmering on it a little. 'It's a 75 grand difference,' Ross grins, 'but, you know, whatever.' Ross knows the Eddie winner almost feels fated. 'Everyone who wins the Eddie either really needs it, or it just felt like he was meant to win it. It's like Eddie sits up there and picks them out, and everything that happens in that event happens for a reason.'

Ross wound down from the Eddie by heading to California to surf giant Cortez Bank a hundred miles out to sea. He then went and snowboarded Squaw Valley, headed to Nürburgring in Germany to race his Porsche (the 'Black Mamba') before flying back to the bottom of New Zealand to surf huge cold-water waves at Papatowai. All of this was simply a warm-up for possibly the most dangerous mission of the year… Ross's 50th birthday in June. Famously, Ross was born on the 6/6/66, and to complete the symbolism of the occasion, the day of his 50th birthday saw the biggest swell in a generation hit the east coast of Australia. Dubbed the 'Black Nor' Easter' it saw houses washed into the ocean and the Cape Fear event run at Cape Solander. 'Sixth of June, everyone's like, fuck, it's the Devil's Swell!'

Ross missed the Devil's Swell. He was in Las Vegas. His birthday party had stretched out over two weeks. 'We started in Sydney then hopped on a plane the next morning and flew to Vegas, 10 of us. We met up with all the American guys in Vegas and partied for a week.' Staying in the MGM Grand, they started the week poolside with thousands of people at the Wet Republic. 'It was just so tacky, and so over the top … just my style!' The trip was billed as a week in 'Ross Vegas' and by the end of it Ross was seeing tigers in his hotel room.

Ross Vegas returned home to Torquay and the closest thing to normal life he'd experience that year. He scored weeks of winter swell at Bells, did a couple of Hotham snow trips, chased some big swells on the reefs down the coast and did a strike mission to Shipstern Bluff in Tasmania. 'I'm still a resident of Australia,' Ross reminds himself, laughing. 'You have to do 181 days here so you're still Australian. I checked.' Ross, as he does every year, then took off in October to 'fly north for the winter'. This time, however, he wasn't flying to Hawaii, as he'd done for the past 32 northern hemisphere winters.

Throughout his big-wave career Ross has a thing where he just loses himself completely in a new big-wave spot for a couple of years. Puts in back-to-back seasons. Surfs it on every swell. Moves into town and gets tight with the crew who surf it. He's worked his way through a colossal list of big waves. 'I'll do quality time in one place, and try and, you know, *get it*. Places like Mavericks. I went to Mavericks and did that in 2000. I was like, I'll just do the Mavericks scene, tow there, paddle there. Yeah, I did the Jaws thing in the early 2000s. I've still got skis there, and boards! All sitting there at Dave Kalama's house.'

Ross first surfed Portugal's Nazaré in December 2014. A deep-water ocean canyon channels swells around the north side of the Nazaré headland, creating some of the biggest surfable waves anywhere in the world. By 2014 its limits were being tested, and Ross wanted a piece of it. 'Yeah, I got to Nazaré, and I was like, fuck, I need to get an act here. The wave had only just broken and I was in town trying to rent skis and hire drivers. It was a nightmare … and that was before I even saw what the wave could really do. After that last Eddie I knew I had to spend more time in Europe. I was like, I'm going to concentrate on Nazaré; it's the biggest wave in the world and I like towing. Once Nazaré hits 30 feet it's impossible to paddle.'

Ross swapped the North Pacific for the North Atlantic. 'The whole European thing was a shift for me,' recalls Ross. 'I do so much time in Hawaii. For 32 years now every winter I'm in Hawaii, you know? Every winter. Then the last couple I had to keep flying to Nazaré from Hawaii and I thought, you know what, I'm doing this the wrong way around. I'm just going to stay in Europe.' With Nazaré as a springboard it also opened up new territory and new waves for Ross to explore in the North Atlantic. 'I went to Ireland that year and I went to Morocco with Jerome Sahyoun. I rode some of the biggest waves I've ever surfed there. Jerome took me to a secret spot with Axi Muniain. I also started exploring the Galician coast in Spain. We're searching there and we're out there alone. It's exploratory stuff again. It felt old school and dangerous … so naturally I felt right at home.'

Ross returned to Nazaré the following year 2017, with the Portuguese fishing town as his winter base. 'I rented a place in town and just stayed there. It didn't stop breaking. It was 20-foot swells every couple of days, some better than others. At the same time I'd also rented a place in Hawaii but I couldn't even get there. Nazaré just kept pumping.' After months of swell in Portugal, Ross finally flew to Hawaii. 'We flew through New York and then went on to Hawaii, but as soon as I got to Hawaii I looked at the forecast back in Nazaré and realised there was a huge swell brewing. A big one. I was in Hawaii for just 12 hours and flew straight back. It was like a full Eddie-Vegas experience from years ago. I'm like, you idiot. I can't believe I left but you know how those North Atlantic swells just pop up? I just did a U-turn and went straight back.'

Ross flew back to Portugal for one wave. 'It was fucking enormous,' Ross recalls of the swell at Nazaré on 18 January 2018. 'Yeah, it was enormous and I'd teamed up with a French guy named Benjamin Sanchis, who I'd never really hung out with or even *met* before, but I knew he could surf and I had good reports about his ski driving. Turns out we got on like a house on fire. Anyway, the morning of the swell we're out there first and Sancho goes, "We got security? Is there another ski out there?" I'm like, "Fuck security! Let's get out there! There will be other skis, it'll be fine. You'll only get washed ashore."' Ross towed Sancho into a massive left. Sancho towed Ross into a massive right. Both waves were amongst the biggest ever ridden at Nazaré, or anywhere else in the world for that matter.

Ross stayed the whole winter at Nazaré and surfed every swell. By February the days were warming and the season was closing and Ross was surfing the last of it before heading home. It was 25 February. 'It was a smaller day,' he remembers, 'half the size of that previous swell. It was clean, sunny, really nice conditions. It was the last swell of the season, I'd be going home soon and I was totally relaxed. I didn't even do the buckles up on my inflation vest. It was the last day you expected anything heavy to happen. The funny thing was, I hadn't wiped out or pulled a canister on my vest the whole season. I'd never even used it. The season before I pulled all four. I got too complacent, too comfortable. I was like, ah, it's not even that big. They're the ones that get you. That's what happened to me.'

Ross had caught an inside righthander, nothing overly dramatic, and was waiting to be scooped up by the ski when he realised he was being dragged toward the rocks. 'I just jumped off and the rip took me like a conveyor belt straight over to the rocks. I was nowhere near the rocks then suddenly I was right there on top of them. At that point I thought I could actually swim out with the rip and get picked up out the back but I just kept getting washed into the rocks. My ski driver couldn't find me. They didn't know where I was. They were searching somewhere else. There were no walkie-talkies and no spotters. There was one cameraman who filmed it all, Alex Laurel, and he was filming all this happening, wondering whether to help me or film me. I'm down there like, film me! Are you getting this? He was watching in horror because there was nothing he could do anyway.

'The whole episode lasted 15 minutes … 15 minutes of me getting washed in and out of the rocks, just getting pinballed. I'd pulled my inflation vest by this stage and was like a rubber ball just bouncing off the rocks. I started looking for rocks to hide behind. When I was a kid we used to play at Tube Rock at Terrigal Haven; you're sitting behind the rock and the wave washes over the rock and you get tubed. I was doing that except that it was 20 foot. Yeah. I remembered when I was 12 years old doing that. That's what it flashed back to. I'll be fine here, I've just got to fucking hang on.

'When the clip eventually went viral, people from Galicia saw it and thought I was down there collecting shellfish off the rocks. There's these things up there called *percebes*, this barnacle that grows on the rocks that's an expensive delicacy; expensive because some maniac has to go down there and collect them off the rocks. The Galicians were watching the clip and thinking I was down there collecting them. I was this extreme barnacle hunter.

'I eventually got washed in a little closer and realised the only way I was getting out of there was to scale the cliff. I couldn't see the waves coming so I just had to time it as best I could. I got washed further down and behind another rock, and then when the waves dissipated I made a break for it. It was like, run! Then I had to scramble up the cliff, which was mossy and steep. I was wearing a wet wetsuit so I had no traction at all. That was more terrifying than the rocks because I was worried I was going to fall to my death. Once I got to the top of the hill and I was safe I was like, fuck this, I'm done. That's my season over. I'm going to look at castles or something.

'You know the funny thing, though? Later that afternoon I was back up at my place and Axi calls me and goes, "Bro, the waves are pumping, the wind is perfect, let's go surfing." I can see it from my place and he was right. I'm a bit beat up and sore from earlier in the day but I'm looking at it and thinking about it. I'm just about to say, "Let's go," when a bee flies down and stings me on the lip. I'm still on the phone and this thing has just flown down and stung me. It fucking freaked me out. I had a full reaction to it and felt all weird and nearly passed out. I look in the mirror and my lips are all swollen. I look like this plastic surgery disaster. I've had to lie down and I'm there thinking, mate, if ever there was a sign from above, that was it. I survived two years of that place and got dropped by a bee sting.

'I rang Axi back and went, "Mate, I'm not going anywhere."'

2016

Tyler Wright

The day before it happened Owen and Tyler Wright ate a late breakfast at Café Haleiwa. The door of the old Hawaiian diner squeaked on its hinges as Owen filled the doorway, long and tall like a character from a spaghetti western, sporting a bushman's hat and a pair of dusty Crocs. He sat down and explained he'd bought the Crocs in honour of their late Uncle Mark, who was famous for wearing them into the exclusive country club back home in Australia where he held a $90,000 annual membership. Owen had been wearing the plastic shoes for months. It smelt like years. He described them as '100 per cent contraceptive'.

It was December 2015, and Owen was coming off a 'gap year without the gap'. He'd surfed the tour and won Fiji with it raining perfect tens, but the tour had merely interrupted a program of exotic surf trips and good times. He and photographer Corey Wilson had chased eight swells before July and lived just as large once the sun went down. Yet, somehow, at the end of the year Owen was still in with a shot at the world title. The Pipe Masters, which would decide the world championship, was due to start in two days' time.

Owen's little sister, Tyler, meanwhile had finished her season on the women's tour rated a disappointing fifth but had won the French event in September with such verve that she'd promised her uncle, shortly before he died, that next year would be *the year*. She'd come close to winning world titles in the past but admitted being mortified by the prospect, being 'too young to deal with the bullshit'. The wonder siblings were both at interesting points in their lives.

'Owen acts all tough, acts like he doesn't care, but really he's a big cuddly anorexic teddy bear.' That's how Tyler summed up her relationship with her older brother back in 2010, just before the pair took off together on the world tour. At the time the Wright family were all staying under the one roof at Lennox Head, having left the sleepy south coast town of Culburra so the talented brood could chase surfing greatness. It appeared a foregone conclusion; all five Wright kids were phenomenal surfers. The house was always going to produce a world champion, it was just a matter of how many kids and how many titles.

Even though they were still so young – Owen 25 and Tyler just 21 – they'd been hamster wheeling on pro surfing for over a decade, done little else. Tyler won her first championship tour event at just 14 as a wildcard invite, the youngest surfer male or female to ever do it. Think about that for a minute. Think of yourself at 14, then imagine living out all your awkward teenage years in the public eye. Talking to the pair over breakfast, you sensed they were both looking to live more on their own terms. As they ate the pair talked about snowboarding Mammoth and driving a van through Mexico as they devoured plates of *huevos rancheros* and buttermilk pancakes, two country kids hooking into a big country breakfast.

With a mouthful of food Owen joked that his catchphrase all year had been, 'I just feel a little … *different*.' The year, it turns out, wasn't over.

The following morning while surfing Pipeline, Owen was caught underneath a Second Reef set and washed to the beach, dazed. He hadn't hit the reef, merely been shaken up, and it seemed totally innocuous for a guy who'd surfed Pipeline exclusively for seven Hawaiian winters. Owen walked back to the house, ate lunch and slept, but when he tried to get up later that afternoon he couldn't. Those long limbs refused to obey all commands. The room started rocking like it was floating on the North Pacific. Owen felt seasick. He couldn't talk. His sister only had to look into his eyes to know something was gravely wrong behind them.

Tyler remembers it vividly. 'When they were loading Owen into the ambulance I was standing there watching, not outwardly freaking but inside just thinking, "*What the fuck*!"' She pauses as it floods back. 'Looking into my brother's eyes and thinking, "*It looks like he's fucking dying.*" It looks like he's way gone. He's not there.' Mick Fanning – who in a cruel twist would lose his older brother only a couple of days later – hugged Tyler as the ambulance drove off. 'Ty, you've got this,' he reassured her. 'You're going to be okay. *He's* gonna be okay.' Tyler noted the date. It was 'a month and two days' after her uncle had died.

Owen was diagnosed with bleeding on the brain, but exactly how bad his condition was, well, even the doctors couldn't agree. One cleared him to fly home immediately, while a second told him under no circumstances should he set foot on a plane. In the end he wasn't home in Australia until after Christmas, and beyond that nothing was clear. This was a serious brain injury and the beginning of a journey into the unknown. He might be back in weeks … or he might never be the old Owen ever again. Nobody knew.

'I looked at him for so long and I didn't recognise him,' says Tyler of those early days back at home on the south coast where Owen recuperated. 'I'd talk to him and I didn't recognise his voice, and in my head I'm thinking … *"What the fuck*!" I couldn't say that, and I don't talk about the details much, but my heart goes out to anyone who's ever had a brain injury and their families who've been there for them. It's hard.'

Brain injuries are cruel, and Tyler had to face the prospect of her brother never quite being her brother again. There was no clear prognosis, no horizons, no guarantees. 'Processing what had happened to him was a massive trip for me. It was crazy, and there were times there when it trickled in and I started to feel … what I was in denial of at the start.'

Reports on Owen's progress were foggy. He'd tried to get up one day and go surfing, forgetting he was struggling to even walk. He tried to swim a lap of the pool but sank halfway, and when pulled to the surface asked what the problem was. The reality was that there wasn't a lot Tyler or anyone could do to help. The family were just left with time and faith.

The Wrights – along with Owen's musician girlfriend, Kita Alexander – had rallied around him, but in Tyler's mind she saw herself as her big brother's primary carer. Tyler was always going to be there. She'd watched Mick Fanning deal with his personal dramas the year before, watched him take control and she took her cues from it. 'I'd go home and there'd be a full hectic situation happening and I'd have to handle it, but I'd think of Mick and say to myself, okay, stay calm, work through this, this is what you've got to do.' Mick stayed in touch with Tyler all year. 'What I learned from him,' she says, 'was to be steady.'

March – and the 2016 World Surf League (WSL) season starting at Snapper Rocks – rolled around real quick.

Tyler was hardly surfing. She was underdone and overwhelmed. Before the accident Tyler and Owen had been planning to travel together on tour and had enlisted Glen Hall as a coach, who in the limited run-in to Snapper discovered the lack of a workable backhand turn was the least of Tyler's issues. 'I wasn't trying to tell her that all that stuff out of the water didn't matter because clearly it did,' remembers Hall. 'That was real life and that was infinitely more important, and for me it seems counter-intuitive for a coach to tell an athlete to block out real life. Every day we'd walk from our hotel to Snapper and every day we'd talk about Owen and some days she'd be crying and other days she'd be fine.'

Tyler, once she hit the water, was more than fine. She won the contest.

Brothers Tim and Mikey Wright carried her up the beach, into the surfers' area and straight into the arms of Owen, who'd flown up to surprise her. He looked washed out and a little spectral, the crowds and the scene too much for him, but Owen wouldn't have been anywhere else. That embrace crystallised Tyler's year. She'd been torn. The title was there to be won, but Owen was blood. She had a choice. She could stay at home with her brother, put her life on hold to help him get back on his feet, or she could go back on tour, channel her emotions and distill this tragedy into something truly great.

In the end Owen made the choice for her. Owen said, 'Go.'

'I was numb for the first six months of his recovery,' offers Tyler. 'I don't think I processed any of it, what was going on, until halfway through the year when it became clear that it was in Owen's best interests, for his recovery, for me to go and do what I had to do, to go away and leave him. I didn't want to leave but I knew it was the best thing for him and the promise I'd made to him.'

'She got to Brazil and I could see there was a really heavy energy around her,' recalls Steph Gilmore, 'and I could tell her emotions were boiling away and she was channelling it into this … this *fierceness*. She was so headstrong. She was on a mission. It was, like, "Get out of my way."'

After winning two of the first three events, Tyler went to Brazil and dropped like a stone, sick. A doctor was called in the middle of the night and it looked like she wouldn't surf the event. She not only surfed her heat the following day, she won it, and again went on to win the contest. 'Something just clicked with her,' says Gilmore. 'She went, *this is bigger than me, I'm going to do this for my family, I'm going to do this for Owen*, and I really think Tyler needed a bit more than her own goals. It showed her qualities as a person.' At that point it became clear that Owen's injury was no longer the thing that would hold her back from a world title, it would be the thing that would win it for her.

But the promise weighed heavy.

The carefree kid who'd once danced like *Seinfeld's* Elaine Benes before her heats was suddenly shadow boxing, throwing heavy shots. Around the contest there was a cold ruthlessness to her. 'It wasn't until she got to Fiji and lost to Bethany Hamilton that she kind of had this moment where she realised she wasn't invincible,' remembers Steph. 'I thought it was perfect, because it brought balance into her year and I think she needed that.'

Steph then convinced Tyler to hang in Fiji for a week and decompress. 'Tyler would have rushed home and stressed about the result and stressed about everything going on at home, and in the end we had an awesome time. I think it was good for her. I think Tyler really found clarity in Fiji. She was like, *okay, cool, I still need to be myself, be the playful grommet who just loves to surf.*' Steph laughs. 'It's amazing what a few piña coladas can do.'

Like most world title years, there were milestone freesurfing moments that were the bedrock to heat wins. There was her backhand tube in Fiji, a wave she'd never have considered taking except that she 'had these voices in my mind – Mikey, Tim and Owen – just yelling, "You're going!"' The following week back at home Tyler had the *real* Mikey beside her, calling her in during the 'Black Nor-Easter', the biggest east coast swell in years. 'This wave came and I was looking at Mikey and he was looking at me, and I'm like, "Not it, mate!" And he was like, "Fuck off, you're going!"' The wave was a coalmine, a mile long and a mile down, and a disbelieving Tyler came flying out the end of it. It was the best wave anyone, man or woman, rode during that swell. Little brother Mikey described the wave to Tyler as 'okay'.

Mikey kept it real. The youngest of the five Wright kids, sporting a party mullet a year after the party, Mikey was the spirit animal of Tyler's year. Mikey reconnected her back to a simple time when the Wrights were all about surf, a time before it all got so serious. A time before Owen got hurt. If Tyler dared claim during a heat she'd walk back up the beach knowing the message that would be waiting on her phone. 'What the fuck was that claim all about?' Mikey and Tyler messaged photos to each other, flipping the bird at each other for no reason. When she was home, Mikey – out of the water with a knee injury – led dancing flash mobs at Tyler's place, throwing away crutches to dance on one leg.

And then there was Matt Wilkinson, who under the coaching of Glen Hall had led the men's ratings for most of the year. Hall credits Tyler for some of Wilko's success, namely her ability to compartmentalise game day steeliness with lay-day good times. But it was more than that. Wilko was also one of Owen's best friends, had been for years, and having Wilko there for Tyler felt in many ways like having another Wright brother along for the ride. Tyler works best in family environments, and Wilko simply became family.

Tyler wasn't winning on pure sentimentality, however. Her surfing had transformed. 'When we started she wasn't self-aware about what she was doing,' offers Hall. 'She paddled out and surfed and just happened to be good at it, but I think that year opened her eyes, in the water and out. She asked a lot of questions. She wanted to learn.' Tyler had the big turns, the biggest turns, but they often seemed like independent, angular thoughts. As the year went on the space between the notes started to sing, her surfing flowed, and in many ways began to mirror her approach to life on tour. 'It felt smooth for me, very even-keeled in a professional sense. Personally, there was a bit on, but maybe that's why it felt so smooth and easy, because compared to my personal life, which was so hectic, just going surfing and catching two waves felt easy. It wasn't the hardest thing I was dealing with at the time.'

With the tour half a world away from Culburra, with the title looming, with Courtney Conlogue looming, Tyler felt every mile between her and home. She'd spent four days in four months back in Australia and found herself fighting the urge to buy a one-way ticket home. 'There definitely were times I just wanted to go, fuck it, fuck this, and just get on a plane and go home. I'd have moments where I'd just feel like I was having my legs taken out from underneath me. I'd feel weak, and that happened so many times but each time I just had to say, nah, we're doing this, I'm doing this. I need to.'

Tyler wouldn't mention Owen or his condition publicly during interviews that year. She 'kept my private life very private' to protect her elder brother. With concussion injuries being topical there was understandable and well-intentioned interest in how Owen was doing, but there were also elements that interpreted the lack of news as a conspiratorial silence, and that something was being covered up. 'I read articles that have been so insensitive about Owen, and for that to be happening in the public eye makes it so heavy.' Tyler carried on, juggling a tumultuous private life with a very public world title campaign.

Watching her, though, you'd never know. She was, in many ways, indistinguishable from the old Tyler. She never outwardly lost that lovable smart-arse attitude. She did everything her own way. She had dedicated 'fat bitch days', where she'd sit on the lounge in tracksuit pants and a basketball singlet and eat ice cream from the tub, before knuckling down into 'skinny bitch mode' before events. Anytime she'd start a sentence with, 'I don't know about anyone else ... ', you knew you were about to get a truth bomb delivered with just a hint of inappropriateness. 'I don't know about anyone else, but something that doesn't get talked about enough in women's sport is that we have to do all of this, this sporting rollercoaster, and we still get our period. That stuff doesn't stop. We still get them and we have to deal with being this hyper-emotional being while still dealing with surfing heats and dealing with life. I just wanted to point that out.'

But if you knew Tyler well enough, and you watched her closely enough during the year, you'd see it. She'd buried it pretty good, but a call home or an offhand comment might trigger it. 'I've cried more in one year than I've cried in my whole life. I used to be that kid who didn't cry for a whole year, but during that year if I wanted to cry I just would, I wouldn't hold it in anymore. I'd just cry or laugh and then get on with it. I had so much going on I couldn't hold it in anymore. "You know what, Tyler? If you feel like it, you can cry for an hour and a half if you like. No one's around, it's sweet. Just do it." So I went for it.'

After winning her semi-final at Trestles she was asked in passing how Owen and the family were and the dam wall came down. She found a quiet corner of the surfers' area, sat on a lounge, and bawled her eyes out. 'I missed them *sooooo* much that I just started crying.' She got up off the lounge, pulled herself together, paddled out and won the final.

A week later a clip of Owen surfing Aussie Pipeline back at home was posted. He was a bit shaky, but he was back on the horse, and it began to feel like Tyler's world title and Owen's recovery were somehow cosmically tethered. Owen had turned a corner at home, and Tyler was now free to, as Wilko would say, 'Get it *dooone*.'

At this point a lightness came over her. 'After she lost the final in Portugal, we went straight to this little bar on the cliff top at Cascais about lunchtime and had a few drinks,' recalls Glen Hall. 'Tyler had the presentation down on the beach at 6pm, by which stage we'd had a few. She walked straight up on stage and she's being interviewed and we're all thinking, this is going to be good. She got through three questions and then just lost it laughing. She came down off stage, walked straight down to the water, and jumped into the ocean in her jeans and T-shirt.'

The following week she was in France with the world title in range, although no one told her just how close. She walked down the *plage* on finals day 'ready to go to war' only to be crash-tackled by Steph Gilmore, who informed her she'd just won.

After surfing the final in France wearing Owen's number three jersey and riding a wave goofy foot in his honour, Tyler's speech afterward was something grand. You never quite know what you're going to get with a Tyler Wright speech. The inner monologue that accidentally becomes conversation. The off-topic thought bubbles. The moment when she forgets you're actually there. But suddenly here was a woman who'd matured a decade in a calendar year, calmly, eloquently, beautifully laying it all out there. 'I just promised him I'd do it. And that was my thing, my way. Something I knew in a small way could be my gift to them, to him. It won't take away their pain but it was my way to give back.'

Tyler didn't cry. Three nights earlier she had locked herself in her room and just bawled and got it all out. 'A few people have mentioned it to me, and I'm like, "Brah, I've done so much crying this year I don't need to do anymore."' Back at home Owen cracked his first beer in a year to celebrate. Mikey, meanwhile, drank his tenth beer that morning and posted, 'Fuck yeah Tyler! You fucken stuck it to 'em all and now you're the mother fucking world champ, fucken oath big sis!'

'After she won and we were partying that night,' recalls Steph Gilmore, 'she'd had a few strawberry daiquiris by that stage and just kept saying to me, "I can't believe you've won *six*. How? But… *how*?" She was genuinely baffled. Then I had a voicemail from her the other day, "What the fuck! I can't believe you won *six*!" You kind of forget how much goes into one full year, all the emotion and all the experiences and all the living, everything that happens, let alone a year like Tyler just had. I think Tyler finally had a moment where she realised what she'd actually done.'

'Life happened,' was how she would later describe her year. Whether she'd have won the world title without all the hardship at home, whether she'd have been as driven, we'll never know, but she'd have handed the trophy back in a heartbeat to get Owen back exactly as he was.

Tyler got her wish. Six months later Owen not only returned to the men's tour, he won the first contest of the year at Snapper Rocks. It was a miracle of neuroplasticity and sibling love, and you know who was the first person there to hug him, wading out into waist-deep water to do so …

Thanks

Telling the story of just one year from a surfer's life sounded easy in theory. I didn't read the fine print, however, that to write about *one year* of their life, you actually needed to understand their *entire life*, otherwise that one year just didn't make any sense. Then there was the small matter that many of the surfers couldn't remember where they were on 1 January *this year*, let alone 1 January 1978. I quickly realised I needed help to join the dots. Pulling this together, along with dozens of interviews, I've drawn from hundreds of books, bios, magazines, documentaries and personal archives. There's a long list of surf writing brethren whose collective body of work I've consulted to get my ducks in a row here. Rather than list the titles, maybe it's better to simply thank the people who've done the bulk of the historical heavy lifting: Phil Jarratt, Nick Carroll, Tim Baker, Andrew Crockett, Nat Young, Vaughan Blakey, Craig Baird, Michael Gordon, Wayne Murphy and Kirk Wilcox. For the photos, a big *mahalo* particularly to Justin Crawford, John Witzig, Albe Falzon, Bill McCausland, Rusty Miller, Barrie Sutherland, Bruce Channon, Howie Owen, Peter Wilson, John Pennings, Dick Hoole and Corey Wilson. As for compiling the book itself, I need to thank Christa Moffitt (who designed the book in between chats with Albe at Crescent) and of course Vanessa Radnidge for her patience. I'm sure at one point she became nostalgic for the golden days of the book's original deadline, but hung in there without losing her enthusiasm for the project. And finally – and most importantly – I need to thank the surfers themselves for taking the time to shoot the breeze and allowing me to tell their stories.

Photo Credits

Front cover: Newport Plus club championship round. [Peter Crawford]

Front endpaper: Phyllis O'Donell, Manly Beach, 1964. [Ron Perrott]

vi-vii *Top row*: Occy at D-Bah. [Peter Crawford]; Mark Warren, south coast. [Peter Crawford]; Pam Burridge and Eddie Money. [Bill McCausland]; Col Smith, 1977 Aussie Champ. [Bill McCausland]; Nat Young, new boards and setter, Broken Head. [Albe Falzon]

Middle row: Peter Crawford, Dee Why. [Crawford archive]; Freshwater Beach, January 10, 1915. [Isabel Letham archive]; Martin Potter and Wendy Botha, 1985. [Wendy Botha archive]; Occy, Gary Green and Ratso Buchanan, Bells, 1985. [Peter Crawford]

Bottom row: Barton Lynch, Mick Mock, Peter Crawford. [Crawford archive]; Joel Parkinson, world title year boat trip. [Pat Stacy]; Peter Townend, 1972 World Contest board. [Townend archive]; Bob Evans, Phyllis O'Donell, Peter Drouyn, California, 1966. [Gail Couper archive]

viii Isabel Letham, South Curl Curl, 1914. [Isabel Letham archive]

6 Snow McAlister, 1923. [McAlister archive, Surfworld Museum]

10 Barry Bennett, Brookvale. [Bennett Surfboards archive]

16 Bob Evans, filming at Dee Why. [Bob Weeks]

20 Peter Troy, Antigua, 1963. [Rennie Ellis Archive]

26 [Peter Troy archive]

36 Gail Couper and Phyllis O'Donell, Manly. [John Pennings]

42 Midget Farrelly, World Championships, Manly, 1964. [Ron Perrott]

50 Wayne Lynch and Gail Couper, Lorne, 1966. [John Witzig]

56 Bob McTavish, Palm Beach. [John Pennings]

60 Bob McTavish, Honolua Bay, December 1967. [John Witzig]

66 Claw Warbrick. [Barrie Sutherland]

74 Wayne Lynch, 1968. [John Witzig]

78 Wayne Lynch, Lorne Point. [Barrie Sutherland]

84 Albe Falzon, north coast, 1970. [Albe Falzon]

92 Peter Drouyn and Johnnie Walker, Bells, 1970 World Contest. [Rusty Miller]

98 Nat Young, Garth Murphy's house, Fernleigh, 1971. [Rusty Miller]

103 Nat Young and chickens, Broken Head, 1971. [Albe Falzon]

106 Paul Neilsen, 1971 Australian Champion, Bells Beach. [John Witzig]

112 McCoy Surfboards team. Mark Richards (*second from left on top of car*). [Albe Falzon]

118 Peter Townend, Sunset Beach, 1972. [Steve Wilkings]

126 Michael Peterson, 1972. [Howard Owen]

132 [Peterson family archive, Howard Owen]

136 Ted Spencer, Johnson Street, Byron Bay. [Rusty Miller]

144 Midget Farrelly and Stan Couper, Bells. [Dick Hoole]

150 Terry Fitzgerald, Sunset Beach store, 1975. [Steve Wilkings]

154 Terry Fitzgerald, Sunset Beach, 1975. [Steve Wilkings]

159 Ian Cairns, 1975 Duke contest winner. [Steve Wilkings]

162 Ian Cairns, Waimea Bay. [Steve Wilkings]

166 Rabbit Bartholomew, Sunset Beach, 1975. [Steve Wilkings]

172 Rabbit Bartholomew, Off The Wall, 1975. [Steve Wilkings]

176 Mark Warren, Hawaii, 1977. [Steve Wilkings]

182 Col Smith, Narrabeen. [Bill McCausland]

188 Simon Anderson, Coke Surfabout Presentation, 1981. [Bruce Channon]

196 Louie Ferreira and Tom Carroll, 1979. [Bill McCausland]

200 Tom Carroll, Narrabeen Pro Junior, 1978. [Bill McCausland]

206 Pam Burridge, Avalon, 1979. [Bill McCausland]

210 Pam Burridge, North Avalon, 1979. [Bill McCausland]

216 Peter Crawford, Dee Why garage. [Crawford archive]

220 Damien Hardman and Greg Anderson, Narrabeen. [Bruce Channon]

226 Kong and Chappy, Burleigh. [Peter Crawford]

230 Kong, 'If you don't rock'n'roll, don't fucken come' ad shoot, Torquay. [Bruce Channon]

234 Cheyne Horan. [Peter Crawford]

242 Occy, 1984. [Peter Crawford]

246 Occy, D-Bah, Billabong Pro, 1984. [Peter Crawford]

250 Wendy Botha, Newcastle Surfest winner, 1985. [Dick Hoole]

256 Barton Lynch, Billabong Pro winner, 1989. [Joli]

260 Barton Lynch, Pipeline, Billabong Pro. [Dean Wilmot]

266 Wayne Deane, 1990 World Longboard Champ. [Deane archive]

270 Wayne Deane, cyclone swell. [Deane archive]

274 Layne Beachley, 1990. [Beachley archive]

280 Pauline Menczer and Jodie Cooper, 1993 World Champ, Sunset Beach. [Joli]

284 [Pauline Menczer archive]

290 Rod Brooks, Quiksilver Pro, G-Land, 1997. [Joli]

296 Steph Gilmore, Mentawai Islands, 2011. [Dane Peterson]

300 Steph Gilmore, Mentawai Islands, 2011. [Dane Peterson]

304 Joel Parkinson, 2012 world title party. [Steve Sherman]

310 Joel Parkinson, Snapper Rocks, 2012. [Jon Frank]

314 Mick Fanning, Jeffreys Bay, 2015. [Jimmicane]

320 Mick Fanning, 2015 Pipeline Masters. [Corey Wilson]

324 Ross Clarke-Jones, Nazaré, 2017. [Tim Bonython]

332 Tyler Wright, 2016 World Champion, France. [Corey Wilson]

338 Tyler Wright, France, 2016. [Corey Wilson]

Back endpaper: Mick Fanning and Joel Parkinson, Pipeline, 2012. [Pat Stacy]

Back cover: Pam Burridge, North Avalon, 1979. [Bill McCausland]

Published in Australia and New Zealand in 2020
by Hachette Australia
(an imprint of Hachette Australia Pty Limited)
Level 17, 207 Kent Street, Sydney NSW 2000
www.hachette.com.au

A catalogue record for this
book is available from the
National Library of Australia

ISBN: 978 0 7336 3944 9 (hardback)

Cover and internal design by Christabella Designs
Cover image courtesy Peter Crawford, back cover image courtesy Bill McCausland
Typeset in Baskerville Greek 10/16 by Christabella Designs

Printed and bound in China by 1010 Printing International